MULTICULTURAL QUESTIONS

Multicultural Questions

edited by

CHRISTIAN JOPPKE

and

STEVEN LUKES

OXFORD

UNIVERSITY PRESS

OXFORD

UNIVERSITY PRESS

Great Clarendon Street, Oxford OX2 6DP

Oxford University Press is a department of the University of Oxford.
It furthers the University's objective of excellence in research, scholarship,
and education by publishing worldwide in

Oxford New York

Athens Auckland Bangkok Bogotá Buenos Aires Calcutta
Cape Town Chennai Dar es Salaam Delhi Florence Hong Kong Istanbul
Karachi Kuala Lumpur Madrid Melbourne Mexico City Mumbai
Nairobi Paris São Paulo Singapore Taipei Tokyo Toronto Warsaw

and associated companies in Berlin Ibadan

Oxford is a registered trade mark of Oxford University Press
in the UK and certain other countries

Published in the United States
by Oxford University Press Inc., New York

British Library Cataloguing in Publication Data

Data available

Library of Congress Cataloging in Publication Data

Multicultural Questions / edited by Christian Joppke and Steven Lukes.
Includes bibliographical references.
1. Multiculturalism—Philosophy. 2. Social evolution.
I. Joppke, Christian. II. Lukes, Steven.
HM626.M85 1999 305.8′001—dc21 99–24526

ISBN 0-19-829610-X

1 3 5 7 9 10 8 6 4 2

Typeset by Graphicraft Limited, Hong Kong
Printed in Great Britain
on acid-free paper by
Biddles Limited
Guildford and King's Lynn

PREFACE

This book is based on the conference 'Multiculturalism, Minorities and Citizenship', which the editors organized jointly with Tony Judt (New York University) on 18–23 April 1996 at the European University Institute in Florence, within the context of the 1995–6 European Form on Citizenship. We acknowledge generous funding by New York University and the European Commission (DGV).

CONTENTS

IV What Can Europe Learn from North America?

NOTES ON CONTRIBUTORS

RAINER BAUBÖCK, Assistant Professor in Sociology, Justitute for Advanced Studies, Vienna.

SEYLA BENHABIB, Professor of Government, Harvard University, and Senior Research Affiliate, Center for European Studies.

ÉRIC FASSIN, Maître de Conferences, Department of Social Sciences, Ecole Normale Superieure, Paris.

ADRIAN FAVELL, Lecturer in Geography and Migration Studies, University of Sussex.

NATHAN GLAZER, Professor Emeritus in Sociology and Education, Harvard University.

MARTIN HOLLIS was a Professor of Philosophy, University of East Anglia.

CHRISTIAN JOPPKE, Professor of Sociology, European University Institute.

WILL KYMLICKA, Research Director of the Canadian Centre for Philosophy and Public Policy, Department of Philosophy, University of Ottawa.

STEVEN LUKES, Professor of Moral Philosophy, University of Siena, and Professor of Sociology at New York University.

MARTIN SCHAIN, Professor in `Politics and Director of Center for European Studies, New York University.

AYELET SHACHAR, Tutor in Law and Fellow in Legal Ethics, Yale Law School.

JEFF SPINNER-HALEV, Associate Professor, Department of Political Science, University of Nebraska at Lincoln, Nebraska.

YAEL TAMIR, Department of Philosophy, Tel-Aviv University.

1

Introduction: Multicultural Questions

CHRISTIAN JOPPKE AND STEVEN LUKES

A safe way to misunderstand multiculturalism is to take its claims at face value. For multiculturalism is not the oppositional movement its protagonists generally proclaim it to be. Rather, multicultural claims for recognizing ethnic, religious, or sexual difference have been widely accommodated and institutionalized in *fin-de-millennium* liberal states. Reviewing the heated curriculum battles in American colleges and high schools, Nathan Glazer (1997: 4) drily noted that multiculturalism 'has won'. In the name of 'diversity', many North American students are now routinely asked to familiarize themselves with cultural Otherness, particularly of the ethnic, racial, and sexual kinds. Most multicultural commentators have taken the *affaire du foulard*, one of Europe's more notorious multicultural conflicts, as symptomatic for the assimilatory pretensions of the French state. Few have taken notice of its legal outcome: the French Constitutional Court's vindication of the right of Muslim girls to wear a veil in public schools, provided that they do not proselytize. In fact, the courts in liberal states have been widely receptive to multicultural minority claims—exempting Muslim girls from physical coeducation in schools, allowing Islamic mosques to use electronic sound equipment in their public calls for prayer, lately even acknowledging homosexual partnerships as quasi-marital unions. This legal receptiveness is grounded in the public neutrality of liberal states, whose citizens may follow their private demons as they see fit, within the limits prescribed by maintaining the rules of liberal democracy themselves. Not by accident, the best current scholarly defence of multiculturalism draws its particular strength from showing that claims for minority rights are not an abstract imposition on liberal states, but reflective of the very practice of liberal states (Kymlicka, 1995: ch. 4).

Despite its routine acceptance, multiculturalism is still a 'position-taking stance' (Glazer, 1997: 10), and neutrality is not usually the position taken. Multiculturalism has mostly appeared as a polemical attack on key tenets of liberal societies and states—universalism, nationhood and citizenship, and individual rights, provoking no less polemical counter-attacks against the relativism, fragmentation, and illiberalism inherent in some of its more strident versions. This contrast between routine acceptance and polarized debate calls for a sociology of knowledge explanation. Such a sociology of multiculturalism would doubtless show that its protagonists are rarely the oppressed minorities themselves, most of whom do not have their 'own voice' (to introduce a first instance of multicultural discourse), but élites who claim to represent or to speak for these groups.[1] More importantly, the main site of multicultural claims-making is education and cultural institutions, with educators and symbol specialists as the main protagonists. They operate in a lofty world of discourse detached from the constraints of fact, experience, and compromise. From a sociology of knowledge perspective, multiculturalism's favoured cognitive tenet, the social or cultural 'constructedness' of reality (a second instance of multicultural discourse), corresponds to the worldly interests of its protagonists. If the world is built of symbols, the symbol experts attain a central position in the maintainance or—here is a third of multiculturalism's favourite notions—'change' of this world. One could even argue, with Pierre Bourdieu, that the protagonists of multiculturalism (educators and intellectuals) are the dominated faction of the dominant class, and thus prone to anti-institutional stances of radical critique and change.

Because multiculturalism has mostly appeared as a 'questioning' of key tenets of liberal societies and states, it is appropriate to question some of its own key tenets—its epistemological relativism and attack on Enlightenment universalism; its socio-moral elevation of primordial group over society-wide citizenship identities and loyalties; and its legal-political preference for group over individual rights. *Multicultural Questions* seeks to capture the polemical nature of the phenomenon under discussion, where there are no non-controversial answers to the questions raised. The four multicultural questions structuring the volume are deliberately catchy and simplifying, as if drawn from the contents page of *Reader's Digest*. They reflect the polarized public discussion about multiculturalism, and its inclination to give unequivocal 'yes' or 'no' answers to a multiculturalism *taken überhaupt*.

However, the actual answers elicited from our contributors indicate that the debate about multiculturalism has, in the mean time, shifted from a polarized into a more consensual mode. Few liberals today question the legitimacy of multicultural minority claims. Indeed, Will Kymlicka (1995) has argued that liberal defenders of individual rights and citizenship need not fear their being complemented (not replaced) by (well-defined and context-sensitive) group rights and multicultural citizenship. In the same spirit, all our contributors show a resistance to either endorsing or rejecting a hypostasized multiculturalism as such, and a preference for dissecting and differentiating the concrete historical and geographical contexts in which specified versions of multiculturalism make sense, and others in which they do not. This volume thus suggests a Burkean stance towards multiculturalism, in which it is 'circumstances' that render 'every civil and political scheme beneficial or noxious to mankind.'

CULTURE AND CULTURES

As a word or a thing, 'multiculturalism' first appeared in Canada and Australia in the early 1970s. After belatedly abandoning their 'whites only' immigration policies, these young immigrant societies called an official multiculturalism to the rescue in order to juggle the incompatible claims of defeated homeland minorities (both Aboriginal and settler), newly entering Asian and other non-European immigrant groups, and their old European immigrant cores. Interestingly, official multiculturalism was instituted in post-colonial societies that lacked independent nation-founding myths and clear breaks with their colonial past, *à l'Americaine*, thus conceiving of themselves as multiple cultures coexisting under the roof of a neutral state.[2] This could not be so in the United States, the next stage of multiculturalism's *tour de monde*, where a strong sense of political nationhood and centripetal melting-pot ideology could only clash with multiculturalism's ethnicizing and centrifugal thrust. Accordingly, only in the United States did multiculturalism adopt the oppositional, anti-institutional stance that it would retain in its further march towards Western Europe.

As its name indicates, multiculturalism refers to cultures in the plural, not to culture in the singular. Stemming from the Latin word '*colere*', which means to cultivate or till the soil, the notion of culture has always had a double meaning: a specific activity resulting in explicit artefacts, and the way in which society rises above nature, where culture becomes an implicit dimension of social life as such and defines a collectivity as a 'personality writ large' (Benedict, 1934). Explicit culture (as distinct from other social spheres and practices within a collectivity) is culture in the singular. It is the product of symbol specialists in the arts, sciences, and religions, and endowed with context-transcending validity claims. Evoking a similar concept of culture in the singular, Immanuel Kant conceived of culture as the mark of human beings as rational agents directing their lives according to universal moral laws (see Parens, 1994: 169 f.). Post-Kantian nineteenth-century German historicists, chief among them Herder, forged a second notion of cultures (in the plural), which opposed the universalistic pretensions of Anglo-French 'civilization'. For the German bourgeois intellectuals striving for power within a unified nation-state, the particularity of national *Kultur* was a weapon against the rootless cosmopolitanism of the French Enlightenment and the French mannerisms of the Prussian court. If 'civilization', as the mode of French culture, was not pluralizable but conceived of as highest stage in a development to which other parts of the world were expected to aspire, *Kultur*, as the mode of German culture, was inherently plural, because born in confrontation with another culture deemed superior.

The historicist notion of cultures in the plural, capturing the particular life form of a collectivity as against the life forms of other collectivities, was adopted by modern anthropology. As Marshall Sahlins (1995: 12) draws the connection, 'the anthropological concept of culture as a specific form of life ... emerged in a relatively underdeveloped region, and as an expression of that comparative backwardness, ... as against the hegemonic ambitions of Western Europe.' Modern anthropology has drawn the sting of inferiority or superiority from this notion of cultures, celebrating the plurality in which human life has expressed itself. Clifford Geertz (1973: 49) argued influentially against the 'consensus gentium' approach of searching for cultural universals: 'We are ... incomplete or unfinished animals who complete or finish ourselves through culture—and not through culture in general but through highly particular forms of it: Dobuan and Javanese ..., academic and commercial'. In Levi-Strauss's *Tristes Tropiques* the respect for the plurality of human life forms was undergirded by the sad portrait of the uniform West flattening the plural Rest, partly through the very encounter of the anthropologist with his or her subject, which culminated in an impoverished world of cultural entropy and sameness.

Multiculturalism inherited anthropology's relativist, anti-élitist, and comprehensive notion of cultures in the plural. But it also incorporated the preoccupation with pride and shame inherent in the encounter between what were taken to be 'superior' and 'inferior' cultures. Culture as a weapon of the weak received a new lease of life in the post-war anticolonial movements. Marshall Sahlins (1993: 4) has called the ensuing disposition 'culturalism' —'the claim to one's own mode of existence as a superior value and a political right, precisely in opposition to a foreign-imperial presence'. Interestingly, the colonizing powers never conceived of their enterprise as carrying a particular culture, as distinct from other cultures, into the colonies. Rather, as immortalized in Rudyard Kipling's *White Man's Burden*, theirs was a culture-blind, pedagogical project of turning 'sullen peoples, half-devil and half-child' into adults. Only from the perspective of the colonized was this experienced as encounter with a different, foreign culture, incompatible with one's own. Having one's culture ignored and despised in an allegedly culture-blind civilizing process was an immense affront to human dignity, experienced above all by the indigenous élites educated in the centres of the colonizing powers. For W. E. B. Du Bois, the noted nineteenth-century black American intellectual, enslaved and colonized people were plagued by a 'double consciousness': '[T]his sense of always looking at one's self through the eyes of others, of measuring one's soul by the tape of a world that looks on in amused contempt and pity' (in Young, 1990: 60). Accordingly, Frantz Fanon's wildly romantic epos of anticolonial liberation, *The Wretched of the Earth*, was a cultural epos of 'mocking at' and 'vomiting' the values forcibly inculcated by the settlers, depicting the liberation of the colonies as first and foremost a cultural liberation (without being clear, however, which values could replace those of the settlers). As Charles Taylor (1992: 63) correctly sees, multiculturalism inherited from anticolonialism the abhorred 'imposition of some cultures on others, and . . . the assumed superiority that powers this imposition'. The anticolonial impulse favoured various multicultural expressions: a moderate, Herderian plea for respecting and rebuilding the indigenous cultures lost through migrations or colonization, and more radical claims of, for instance, Afrocentrism, according to which not the West but the Rest was the Best. Indeed, one feature of multiculturalism is the bewildering variety of claims gathered under its umbrella.

TROUBLE WITH UNIVERSALISM

To the degree that there is a coherent intellectual doctrine beneath its manifold manifestations, multiculturalism appears as a critique of Western universalism and liberalism, with affinities to post-structuralism and communitarianism. Ontologically, it posits the group over the individual. Not any group, but 'social groups' defined by 'cultural forms, practices, or way of life', which are not the result of choice but of some existential 'thrownness' (Young, 1990: 42–8). Society is composed not of individuals, or systemic spheres, but of groups, each constituted by a particular way of life, or 'culture'. One group has managed the 'universalization of [its] experience and culture, and its establishment as the norm' (ibid. 59), and thus is dominant. The critical, multicultural enterprise is to unmask the false universalism of the dominant group, and to give 'voice' to those groups who have been 'culturally oppressed', that is, 'both marked out by stereotypes and at the same time rendered invisible' (ibid.).

The ontology of social groups is complemented by epistemological relativism and a critique of universalism. Universalism, the claim to the context-transcending foundations and applicability of abstract principles, is exposed as the ethnocentrism of the dominant group, or 'the unwarranted establishing of the specific values of one's own society as universal values' (Todorov, 1993: 1). As Todorov's characterization suggests, one social underpinning of universalism is imperialism and colonialism, the subjugation of the Rest by the West. In this perspective, multiculturalism asserts the West's reduced epistemological status after the confrontation with its rebellious Oriental 'other'. After the end of empire, argues James Clifford (1986: 22), 'there is no longer any place or overview (mountain top) from which to map human ways of life, no Archimedean point from which to represent the world.'

In anthropology, this 'tectonic' change (Clifford, ibid.) has provoked a vivid (some would say narcissistic and self-destructive)[3] discussion about the impossibility of objective knowledge about the 'other', turning the discipline's attention away from the investigated object to the investigating subject. As

Ernest Gellner castigated this turn, the principle of Cartesian doubt has been transformed into the principle of subjectivity, thus 'destabiliz[ing] everything' (Gellner, 1992: 24). In multicultural diction, in cultural studies (perhaps the true domain of multiculturalism) no less than in sociology, the one remaining yardstick of quasi-objectivity is taken to be authenticity. What counts is to be *true to* the subject rather than *true of* the object, to give 'voice' to oppressed races and genders rather than say what is true, probable, or plausible. The cognitive search for objective truth gives way to aesthetics, the authentic expression of a subjective experience. In addition, in order to bridge the gap between investigating subject and the 'other', the notion becomes accepted that women do feminist studies, gays and lesbians do gay and lesbian studies, Latinos or Latinas do Latino/Latina studies, and so on. Various dichotomies are thus put in question: notably those between rhetoric and argument, between power and knowledge, and between politics and science. If, after imperialism, there is no longer an 'Archimedean point' of objective or absolute knowledge (not even as a regulative principle), scholarship can be put to the service of those 'other' points of view that had been marginalized and distorted by ethnocentric universalism. Multicultural scholarship is a bit *Gesamtkunstwerk*, authentic, political, if not necessarily (aspiring to be) 'true' in the presumed absence of such a possibility.

It may be 'as old as the hills', as Thomas Nagel (1997) ironized his 'last word' defence of universalism, but it bears repeating: multiculturalism's epistemological relativism is self-defeating, because a context-transcending, universal claim is made about the reducibility of meaning and truth to their social and cultural contexts (see Benhabib and Hollis in this volume, both of whom set the *tu quoque* trap to relativists).

However, if it only serves their political cause, multicultural advocates sometimes even resort to universalism. Consider the fascinating *cause célèbre* between two renowned anthropologists over the right way to interpret the death of Captain James Cook, some two hundred years ago, at the hands of Hawaiian natives. Marshall Sahlins, no multiculturalist he, suggested a strictly culturalist interpretation of this untoward event: 'different cultures, different rationalities' (Sahlins, 1995: 12). In Sahlins's account, the Hawaiian natives had taken Cook's arrival as the return of the fertility god Lono, which was just being celebrated in their yearly Makahiki ceremony. Cook, arriving in the right manner and from the right direction, appeared to the natives as Lono come to flesh, and he was accordingly celebrated and consecrated in the island temple. After having departed but forced to return to shore because of a sprung mast, Cook was beaten to death by the agitated islanders. According to Sahlins, Cook's unexpected return provoked a 'structural crisis' in the islanders' cosmology, which was remedied by the killing.

The passionate response to Sahlins's account by Gananath Obeyesekere, a Sri Lankan anthropologist teaching at Princeton University, opens up a window into multicultural-style reasoning. Consider his reaction when first encountering the Sahlins thesis: 'I was completely taken aback at his [Sahlins's] assertion that when Cook arrived in Hawaii the natives believed that he was their god Lono and called him Lono. Why so? Naturally my mind went back to my Sri Lankan and South Asian experience' (Obeyesekere, 1992: 8). As Sahlins (1995: 5) retorted, it is not clear why the reference to 'Sri Lankan' experience should shed light on an event in distant Polynesia, unless one assumes that all 'natives' think alike, thus depriving the poor Hawaiians 'of their own voice'. But Obeyesekere's argumentative strategy was indeed to show that the natives disposed of a 'practical rationality' that led them to reject Cook as what he was: a Western explorer and colonialist (Obeyesekere, 1992: 21). Accordingly, the anthropologist siding with the natives turned the tables on his Western colleague: 'I doubted that the natives created their European god, the Europeans created him for them. This "European god" is a myth of conquest, imperialism, and civilization' (ibid. 3). In this account, the European reporters of Cook's brutal death, and not the natives, were in the business of myth-making—'mythos still reigns there (in Europe) under the banner of logos' (ibid. 11). And in an aside to Sahlins: 'The native can make all sorts of subtle discriminations in his field of beliefs; the outsider-anthropologist practising a form of reverse discrimination cannot' (ibid. 22). Here was an opening too obvious for Sahlins to miss. Isn't it 'reverse ethnocentrism' to endow Hawaiians with 'the highest form of Western mentality', while depicting Western scholars as 'slavishly repeat[ing] the irrational beliefs of their ancestors' (Sahlins, 1995: 9)? Moreover, and more importantly, wasn't the Sri Lankan anthropologist's defence of the natives' rationality really 'imperialist hegemony masquerading as subaltern resistance' (ibid. 197), because it endowed the natives with a 'bourgeois rationality', thereby making them the unwitting 'dupes of European ideology'?

Robert Borovsky has noted that this interpretative battle raises such questions as 'To what degree . . . do the present politics of identity demand a rethinking of anthropology's ethnographic effort? Who has the right to speak for whom across the present borderlands of difference?' (Borovsky, 1997: 255). And Clifford Geertz (1995: 6) observed the 'curious reversal' of the frontlines here over the British seaman's death: 'the offended and injured "native subject" as Enlightenment universalist and the removed and ironical "stranger observer" as relativizing historicist.'

Only in brackets, but nevertheless, Geertz claimed victory for Sahlins, whose analysis he found 'markedly the more persuasive', and 'less prey to the confusing noises of the confused present' (ibid.). Borovsky, who offers a detailed and judicious examination of the controversy, plaintively asks whether one can 'make one's preferences central to assessing the evidence' and reports that 'several scholars have told me in private that they prefer Obeyeskere's argument to Sahlins's because it fits better with present-day post-colonial concerns. Even if Obeyesekere lacks the evidence, they suggest, he grasps the big picture; he understands the politics of oppression' (ibid. 279). Sahlins (1995: 193) sees it similarly: Obeyesekere's truth lay more in his political cause than his cognitive case. The preference for politics made him a true soldier of multiculturalism—even if that meant stealing the cognitive clothes of the enemy.

HODGEPODGE OR MOSAIC

As a model for society, multiculturalism comes in two opposite versions. One has been eloquently formulated by Salman Rushdie, in a defence of his *Satanic Verses*: the novel 'celebrates hybridity, impurity, intermingling, the transformation that comes from new and unexpected combinations of human beings, cultures, ideas, politics, movies, songs. It rejoices in mongrelization and fears the absolutism of the Pure. Melange, hotchpodge, a bit of this and a bit of that is how newness enters the world.'[4] A different model of a multicultural society can be found in *L.A. 2000*, a report about the future of Los Angeles commissioned by the city government: 'Think of Los Angeles as a mosaic, with every color distinct, vibrant and essential to the whole . . . More than one hundred cultural and ethnic backgrounds . . . exist together in Los Angeles . . . Each brings its own ethos, arts, ideas and skills to a community that welcomes and encourages diversity and grows stronger by taking the best from it. They respect each other as mutual partners.'[5] 'Hodgepodge' is about the intermingling and fusion of cultures, even within the same individual; 'mosaic' is about the coexistence of distinct cultures held by separate groups.

In the mosaic model, the individual is connected to the larger society and state not directly, as in the classic model of national citizenship, but only through prior membership in his or her cultural group. The flip-side of the mosaic model is thus social fragmentation, and shortly after the publication of *L.A. 2000* the very case of Los Angeles has demonstrated that 'mutual partnership' can quickly give way to something less desirable. One of the standard critiques of multiculturalism is accordingly its 'disuniting' or 'fragmenting' of national societies.[6] If one ignores its notorious hyperbole, this critique is not unfounded. Mosaic multiculturalism is the negation of monoculture, that is, the nation as the locus of an individual's ultimate loyalties. Mosaic multiculturalism replicates at the sub-state level the Modiglianesque demarcation of modern societies into sharply bounded blocs, each couched in its own monochrome national (or cultural) colour. Yet, while redirecting loyalties from the nation to the cultural group, multiculturalism still has to reckon with a world in which states are the main agencies of political organization. Not providing an organizational alternative, multiculturalism behaves like a parasite, feeding upon elements of modern states—such as the universal language of citizenship as prerequisite for equality and recognition claims—while doing nothing to sustain and reproduce these elements. David Miller (1995: 139) has captured this paradox well: 'The radical multiculturalist is relying on an appeal to the majority which makes sense only if a common identity is assumed, while at the same time arguing that minority groups should throw off an identity that is seen as "oppressive" from the standpoint of group difference.'

The strongest scholarly defence of mosaic multiculturalism has been delivered by Will Kymlicka (1995), who develops some criteria for different cultural groups to coexist under the roof of liberal states. As he suggests in the title, *Multicultural Citizenship*, Kymlicka sees a properly understood multiculturalism as supplementary rather than opposite to citizenship. His strongest argument to make multiculturalism compatible with liberalism is this: liberalism has been blind to the fact that its principles are realized only in a world of bounded states, which cannot but prioritize the culture of the majority nation. As he rightly says (ibid. 108), 'the state unavoidably promotes certain cultural identities and thereby disadvantages others.' Individuals, however, need stable cultural identities in order to make meaningful choices; freedom is contingent on the existence of a 'societal culture' that gives people 'access to a range of meaningful options' (ibid. 83). If people can be free only through having access to their 'societal culture', liberalism demands that states must protect these cultures. Kymlicka concludes: '[T]he orthodox liberal view about the right of states to determine who has citizenship rests on the same principles which justify group-differentiated citizenship within states' (ibid. 124).[7]

Kymlicka's defence of multicultural citizenship is, however, limited in its scope and implications. It is based on a narrow definition of 'societal culture', which drastically restricts the universe of multicultural claimants— at least if liberal principles are to be followed. Kymlicka describes societal cultures as covering 'the full range of human activities', and thus to be 'territorially concentrated' and 'based on a shared language' (ibid. 76). In a word, 'societal cultures . . . tend to be national cultures' (ibid. 80). Cultures that lack the requisite institutional completeness are not entitled to special recognition by the state. Women, gays and lesbians, and other non-territorial 'life-style' groups plainly have no place in mosaic multiculturalism *à la* Kymlicka. But nor do immigrants, since they have 'waived' the right to recreate their own culture by migrating (ibid. 83 ff.).[8] The prime candidates of multicultural citizenship are territorial homeland minorities, such as the Quebecois in Canada or the Aborigines in Australia, and innumerable such minorities stranded in the ruins of the former Soviet empire. As the victims of colonization and nation-building, only territorially rooted 'national minorities' are entitled to 'self-government' and 'special representation rights', the prime benefits in Kymlicka's scheme.

Kymlicka's mosaic multiculturalism is evidently much narrower than the one prescribed by Los Angeles's city planners—in fact, his strongest provisions apply to none of the groups in that polyglot immigrant city.[9] If one takes mosaic multiculturalism more generally as the claim that people need homogeneous cultures (or 'communities') to make meaningful and autonomous choices, an obvious objection is that such cultures exist nowhere, neither as minority cultures nor as the majority cultures of nation-states. If states get into the business of protecting such alleged cultures, they can only create inauthentic Disneylands, whose inhabitants evade 'the complex actualities of the world as it is' (Waldron, 1992: 763). Against the mosaic version of multiculturalism, Jeremy Waldron holds the alternative version of Rushdian hodgepodge multiculturalism which he dubs the 'cosmopolitan alternative'. It is based on the empirical observation that we are 'living in a mixed-up world and having a mixed-up self' (ibid. 754), which communitarianism is found guilty of ignoring. Certainly, people need 'culture' and 'community' to make autonomous and meaningful choices. But communitarians (as advocates of mosaic multiculturalism) are systematically inexplicit about the scale and scope of these communities, unjustifiedly extolling the primordial variants. In a global world, it is 'the international communities [of] merchants, clerics, lawyers, agitators, scholars, scientists, writers, and diplomats' (ibid. 778) that individuals most identify with—perhaps even the community of 'frequent flyers'. Withdrawing from the larger structures of complex societies into the cosiness of primordial community is hypocritical, because 'minority communities need larger and international structures to protect and to sustain the cultural goods that they pursue' (ibid. 780).

Waldron–Rushdie's hodgepodge or melange multiculturalism has the advantage of taking culture as it meets the eye: always in flux, impure, and hybrid, and to be kept pure and protected only at the price of creating Toon Towns. While not denying the role of culture in the constitution of agency, Waldron argues against Kymlicka that it need not be one, homogeneous culture that assigns meanings to an individual's options: 'Meaningful options may come to us as items or fragments from a variety of cultural sources' (Waldron, 1992: 783).

Hodgepodge multiculturalism is empirically supported by recent developments in anthropology, which has questioned the 'assumed isormophism of space, place, and culture' (Gupta and Ferguson, 1992: 7). As in the extreme examples of borderlands and border-crossers, urban metropolises, or postcolonial societies, ' "cultures" and "peoples" . . . cease to be plausibly identifiable as spots on the map' (ibid. 10). Identities under such conditions are notoriously 'contested, uncertain, and in flux' (ibid. 19). Cultures are not windowless boxes, each containing a discrete territory. And in any cultural group whatsoever in the modern world, there will be at least the following: identifiers, quasi-identifiers, semi-identifiers, non-identifiers, ex-identifiers, cross-identifiers, and anti-identifiers. A multicultural politics of identity is angled exclusively towards the concerns and interests of the first group.

In short, mosaic multiculturalism, which equates culture with territory, is a wholly inaccurate account of and inappropriate response to this mixed-up world. As Yasemin Soysal (1996: 7) observes, concerning the multicultural immigrant policies of European states, 'the cultural complexity offered by immigrants is beyond the taxonomical capacity of the official.' It is no small irony that, just when so many people have discovered the existence of their culture, recent anthropology has come to deny it.[10] As Renato Rosaldo (1988: 87) sees the contemporary picture,

The view of an authentic culture as an autonomous internally coherent universe no longer seems tenable in a postcolonial world. Neither 'we' nor 'they' are as self-contained and homogeneous as we/they once appeared. All of us inhabit an inter-dependent late twentieth-century world, which is ... marked by borrowing and lending across porous cultural boundaries.[11]

Which raises the further question of whether the view here under attack was ever more than a deceptive appearance.

But there is one drawback to hodgepodge multiculturalism: no political claims can be derived from it. In fact, hodgepodge multiculturalism is, in the first instance, an aesthetic phenomenon, expressed in world music, fashion, literature, and cuisine. It characterizes the life-world of individuals rather than the imperatives of political organization and state policy. These, by contrast, require identifiable groups to be mobilized and represented and identifiable categories of persons to be accorded benefits or rights. This forces multi-culturalism into the mosaic mould, which has the advantage of providing sharply demarcated, clear-cut constituencies. A good example is the recent 'mixed-race' movement in the United States, which demands the introduction of a new 'mixed-race' category into the next national census. The mixed-race phenomenon itself is pure syncretism and hodgepodge *à la* Rushdie, which has the potential to destroy the whole edifice of race-based classifications in the United States—after all, the American citizen who is not the product of some ethnic and racial mixing is exceedingly difficult to find. Politically, however, the mixed-race movement takes shape as a separate claimant, in competition with blacks, Latinos, and other minority groups, as one more piece in the 'mosaic' of ethnic and racial groups.

WHICH GROUPS, WHICH RIGHTS?

When does a 'group' qualify for membership in the multicultural club? This apparently simple question is trickier than it seems.[12] Necessarily, if a multi-cultural group is to be a 'minority', it must be smaller than the majority society. In a democracy, a numerical majority group cannot be a multicultural claimant. But it is not sufficient to be a numerical minority. The losers of the last elections would not qualify for entry into the multicultural club, because they have the chance to become the majority next time round. So a minority must be a 'structural' minority, locked over time into a minority status. But this is also not sufficient: the rich are a structural minority in all societies, but nowhere are they multicultural claimants. Therefore, a third pre-requisite is to be an 'oppressed' structural minority. Yet only a specific kind of oppression qualifies: oppression on the basis of an immutable ascriptive characteristic. In Iris Marion Young's (1990: 123) unappealing words, only those who have experienced the 'epidermalizing of their world' are legitim-ate multicultural claimants, seeking remedies for 'racism, sexism, homophobia, ageism, and ableism' (ibid. 130).

Even this definition of the relevant type of group as an ascriptively oppressed structural minority runs into problems. What counts as oppression? If Chinese Americans have experienced oppression in the context of a racist immigration and citizenship law at the turn of the century, does this still make them an 'oppressed' minority today, especially when the majority of today's Chinese Americans have immigrated exactly after the *removal* of the racist immigration regime in 1965? American civil rights law has said 'yes', including Chinese Americans as 'Asians' into one of its protected classes. But when does a historical legacy of oppression end? This is a legitimate question considering the assimilatory successes of recent Asian immigrants. And when does oppression begin, as one may ask regarding the curious case of (non-native) Indian Americans. Americans from the sub-Indian continent, who are entirely a product of post-1965 immigration, successfully lobbied the Census Bureau to be reclassified from 'white/Caucasian' to 'Asian-Indian' in the 1980 census questionnaire. This has led to the strange result that members of a group whose average educational and occupational attain-ments exceed those of white Americans qualify for affirmative action benefits, such as 'minority set-asides' from the Small Business Administration (LaNoue and Sullivan, 1994: 450–2). Aware of the absence of past discrimina-tion, these Indian Americans have defended their campaign for minority status as a 'prophylactic measure' on behalf of future immigrants arriving under family reunification quotas, who are likely to lack the high professional pro-file of the first generation admitted under occupational quotas. Obviously political savvy, in combination with a confused and spineless state bureaucracy, may help make an oppressed minority.

Once minority status has been granted to a group, there is an inherent like-lihood of proliferation. The recognition of a minority group divides the world into three segments: majority, recognized minorities, and not-yet-minorities. Historically, there are two types of minority: the descendants of black slaves in the settler societies of the New World, who had their crystallizing moment in the American civil rights movement; and homeland minorities, the losers of nation-building, especially in Europe, who were first recognized in inter-national law in the Wilsonian minority schemes after World War I. The crucial moment in the proliferation of minority status was the piracy of minority discourse by immigrants (who could ride on the colonialism ticket because of their predominantly Third-World origins) and by lifestyle groups, such as gays and lesbians (who could claim race-like, ascriptive discrimination). By way of isomorphism and imitation of a strategy once proved successful, the practice of minority-based claims-making has ramified, producing ironically homogenizing effects in the political styles of all sorts of groups, from women to gays and lesbians to the defenders of plant and animal life. In some parts of the world, such 'minorities' have already become numerical majorities—for example in California, where by 1995 over 70 per cent of its residents were either Latino, Asian, black, or female, each thus qualifying as a multicultural group entitled to affirmative action benefits.

One of the practical problems in an era of multiplied minority claims is which to heed and which to reject. What are the criteria for identifying the relevant kinds of oppression and for deciding who is more and who less oppressed? Are these (political and administrative) judgements to be made on the basis of the minorities' (or rather their leaders') claims? What, in practice, counts more: the strength, or the loudness, or the persistence of claims? And as the net widens, the whole process trivializes the legitimate claims of original victims. This has been the fate of blacks in multicultural America.[13] *The Economist*, tongue-in-cheek, recently made the case for 'severely height restricted individuals of the male persuasion' (SHRIMPS) as a minority group, because the empirical evidence abounds that SHRIMPS suffer from 'pervasive', 'systematic', and 'irrational' discrimination on ascriptive grounds. Why not SHRIMPS?[14]

Secondly, which are the rights to be accorded to minority groups? Multicultural claims-making aims prominently at recognition, not only at the redistribution of resources, which distinguishes it from traditional interest politics. To the degree that multicultural claims-making materializes in rights, it is rights attributed to individuals not qua individual, but qua membership in a group. Multicultural group rights come in many forms. A typical group right is *exemption* from certain legal standards and duties. Such exemptions are common practice in liberal states, often on the basis of religious freedom, which is a constitutionally guaranteed right in most liberal states. Bhikhu Parekh (1994: 443 f.) has discussed some of these exemptions in the case of Britain (perhaps exceptionally tolerant towards minority practices): allowing Hindus, in a provision of the Water Act of 1989, to scatter the ashes of their dead in rivers, even to submerge corpses off the coast; allowing the Jewish and Muslim method of not stunning animals before slaughtering them, as required by religion; tolerating the Asian practice of arranged marriages; and, not mentioned by Parekh but most curiously, exempting turban-wearing Sikhs from the legal duty of wearing crash helmets on motorbikes. If they do not touch upon the core values of the majority society, such exemptions are trivial and routinely granted, because no majority society interests are involved.

A second type of group right is *special benefits* granted to individuals *qua* group membership. Examples are bilingual education programmes for the children of immigrants, or refugee resettlement programmes. While more precarious than exemptions, because costing scarce majority society resources, special benefits are uncontroversial if no majority society interest is directly touched. This is not the case if special benefits amount to *privileged treatment* of minority groups. The notorious example is US-style affirmative action, in which the members of minority groups are granted privileged access to education, employment, or the political system. In the case of privileged treatment, members of the majority society equally (perhaps even better) qualified or situated lose out against members of a minority group. Accordingly, privileged treatment, which entails reverse discrimination, is inherently controversial, and requires extraordinary justification. If one leaves aside the example of women, who benefit from positive discrimination in many Western states, no country but the United States has instituted an elaborate programme of privileged treatment for minority groups. Affirmative action is justified by two rationales: past discrimination and diversity. Because the expansion of minority claimants in multicultural America has hollowed out the 'past discrimination' rationale, 'diversity' has increasingly taken its place. The diversity rationale was first expressed in the Supreme Court's *Regents of the University of California* v. *Bakke* case (1978), in which Justice Powell's swing opinion famously held that, in the interest of 'educational diversity', universities could take race into account in their admission practices. However, the diversity argument has a catch: in removing the sting of past discrimination it makes affirmative action less morally compelling. Moreover, whites now figure as just one group among other groups, perhaps even potential victims of discrimination just like other ethnic or racial groups. The diversity argument equalizes all claimants and thus offers an obvious inroad for the current affirmative action backlash in the United States.

A final group right is the right of *self-government*, which figures prominently in Kymlicka's defence of multicultural citizenship. Self-government may be feasible in the case of territorial groups, essentially proto-nations. In fact, in the case of self-government, the line between multiculturalism and nationalism is difficult to draw. Note that French-speaking Quebec has always viewed the official multiculturalism of the Canadian government with suspicion, because this was seen as watering down that restive province's monocultural, nationalist pretensions. While perhaps the strongest claim in the multicultural arsenal, the right of self-government has also been widely recognized. The Charter of the United Nations, for instance, stipulates that 'all peoples have the right to self-determination'—with an eye, of course, on the former European overseas colonies (see Kymlicka, 1995: 27). Kymlicka admits that self-government rights, as the 'most complete case of differentiated citizenship' (ibid. 182), pose a threat to the integrative function of citizenship—albeit one to be waged if liberal values are to prevail. Some recent European experiences (notably in Spain) might calm his nerves, suggesting that 'devolution' can be an effective means to keep divided nation-states together.[15]

If the problem of 'which group' to choose consists in the proliferation of claimants, the problem of 'which rights' to grant consists in the escalation of claims (see Offe, 1998: 131–4). Escalation is due to the lack of a 'clearcut measure as to what kind of rights and how many of them are required for exactly that purpose to be achieved' (ibid. 133). Once a right has been achieved, a vested interest and institutional structure to maintain and expand this right has come into existence too, further fuelled by the 'me too' dynamics of inter-minority competition. A good example is the self-propelling dynamics of the American Voting Rights Act of 1965, first introduced as a temporary measure to enfranchise blacks in the segregated American south, but now a permanent measure to guarantee all minority groups privileged access to the political system. 'As the emergency subsided emergency powers expanded' is how Abigail Thernstrom (1987: 49) summarized the paradox.

Group rights are not without costs, even for minority members themselves. First, there is the opportunity cost of, for instance, learning an indigenous language, which may be useless for educational or occupational advancement. This is increasingly recognized by American Hispanics, a majority of whom have supported the successful 1998 referendum in California to outlaw state-mandated bilingual education in public schools.[16] Secondly, being granted extensive group rights might provoke a backlash by the majority society, which is harmful to minority individuals. This is demonstrated by the recent backlash in California against affirmative action. Thirdly, and perhaps most critically, group rights may entail curtailments of individual rights. In attributing group rights, a state also empowers authorities within a group to restrict individual freedom within the group. A notorious example is Quebec's Law 101 that forbids Francophones and immigrants from sending their children to English-language schools while allowing Canadian Anglophones to do so; another Quebec law outlaws commercial signage in any language other than French. Unlike Charles Taylor, Kymlicka wants to prohibit such 'internal restrictions' within his liberal theory of minority rights, but concedes that 'liberals have no automatic right to impose their views on non-liberal national minorities' (Kymlicka, 1995: 171)—the only hope being the soft power of 'dialogue'. The curtailment of individual rights in the name of group rights is a problem not only in Quebec. In large parts of the United States, Spanish-surname children are automatically enrolled in bilingual/bicultural education programmes, without consideration of their actual English capacities and often against the wishes of their parents, who want their children to succeed in an Anglophone environment first.

Where are the limits of group rights for minorities? Using the example of immigrants, Bhikhu Parekh (1994) has suggested an ideal procedure to determine which rights to grant, and which not. As 'probationary citizens', according to Parekh, immigrants have a 'moral right' to preserve their difference (a distinctly stronger assumption than made by Kymlicka). If the immigrants' way of life offends the 'operative public values' of a society, Parekh envisions a court-like procedure, in which 'spokesmen' of the majority society and of the immigrant group enter into a 'dialogue' about the legitimacy of the disputed practice. If the practice is central to the minority's way of life, it should be allowed; if it violates a core value of the majority society, and is not important to the minority, it is to be abandoned; and, as Parekh realistically concedes, if a practice is dear to the minority but also violates a core value of society, it should be abandoned too. Interestingly, the outcome of Parekh's ideal dialogue exactly corresponds to the British state's actual response to the disputed practices, outlawing only female circumcision and polygamy as in violation of basic individual rights and sex equality. This confirms our claim that, contrary to multiculturalism's oppositional rhetoric, liberal states have been widely receptive to most minority claims.

TRANSATLANTIC COMPARISONS

The message of most contributions to this volume is clear: there is no multiculturalism *tout court*; there are only specific, context-dependent multicultural problematiques; the search for a universal formula, and final judgement, is misguided from the start. This casts doubt on our last multicultural question, 'What can Europe learn from North America?' This question suggests a commensurability of multicultural problematiques on both sides of the Atlantic that perhaps does not exist. The pidgin comparisons abound, in which 'multicultural' America is either celebrated as a model of cultural pluralism and tolerance, or demonized as a late-civilizational Gomorrah of riots and ethnic strife. Such ill-conceived and ill-informed comparisons, especially popular in France, are really monologues about the like or dislike for one's own society's treatment of cultural difference (see Fassin in this volume).

In the first place, the very notion of North America (chosen to avoid the presumptuous 'America' and as logical complement to the regional notion of Europe) swallows the distinction between Canada and the United States, both of which adhere to rather different ideas and practices of multiculturalism. Canada, after adopting official multicultural policies in the early 1970s, even extolled its new-won tolerance for cultural pluralism above and against its allegedly 'assimilationist' southern neighbour—which is ironical, because Canada turned multicultural just when the melting-pot model fell into disrepute in the United States. Canadian multiculturalism is a specific response to the problem of Anglo-French biculturalism. It may have helped immigrants to integrate better, but it has aggravated Canada's original problem, French separatism. A close observer of the Canadian scene noted that

Trudeau's decision to institute multiculturalism as a state policy . . . further activated the radicalization of the independentist sentiment in Quebec, and had an alienating impact among moderate elements within Francophone society, who saw their status lowered from being one of the two 'Founding Nations' to just one cultural community among the many making up what was now hailed as the 'Canadian mosaic'. (Ramirez, 1998: 16 f.)

If there is a Canadian 'lesson' for Europe, it may well be not to water down specific, territorially based minority conflicts with general multicultural policies, but to tackle them directly and in their own terms.

As we learn from Nathan Glazer in this volume, the United States too is a questionable reference point for Europe. In the United States, multiculturalism is race-based, and amounts to remedial action directed towards discriminated insiders of the national community. In Europe, by contrast, multiculturalism is directed at foreigners, most notably at postcolonial and guestworker immigrants. Multiculturalism there aims at a 'civic' redefinition of essentially ethnic nationhood: of nationhood too closely associated with a particular culture. In the United States, by contrast, there is no national culture that immigrants would have to adjust to. Consider why Muslims are considered a 'difficult' immigrant group in Europe, but not in the United States. It is because church and state are (still) insufficiently differentiated in Europe (especially in Britain, site of the infamous Rushdie affair).[17] European nations are Christian in a way the United States, with its strict separation between church and state, is not. In sum, nationhood in Europe has strong cultural connotations that are absent in the United States, conditioning different multicultural problematiques. Because European multiculturalism concerns groups from the outside, towards which there is only a weak sense of historical guilt and indebtedness, it is unlikely to switch from the passive toleration mode (which is commanded by the logic of liberal states) to the active restitution mode of the United States. The multicultural 'lesson' of the United States for Europe is thus also negative, and one already heeded: to avoid the socially divisive *privileged* treatment of expanding categories of minorities.

Secondly, if the notion of North America swallows distinct and incommensurable multiculturalism problematiques in its constituent countries, so does the notion of Europe. Not only does the integration of, say, postcolonial Asian immigrants in multinational Britain proceed along rather different lines from the integration of North African immigrants in self-consciously Republican France (see Favell, 1998*a*) or of Turkish guestworkers in divided Germany (see Joppke, 1996). More importantly, Europe itself is now growing from a regional into a political entity separate from and above its constituent states. The emergent European Union is a *sui generis* supranational, multi-level, non-state polity. Its minority problematique is, therefore, also unique. So far, there has been a notable lack of *internal* European Union policies on ethnic minorities. EU concerns for minorities have arisen only *externally*, in the context of the pending accession to the EU of East-Central European states plagued by long-standing national minority conflicts (see Witte, 1998). Here the EU has held to a strict line of demanding elaborate constitutional protections and remedial policies for national minorities in the applicant states as a prerequisite for EU membership. The resulting charge of 'double standards' in the EU treatment of its internal and external minorities points in two possible future directions. One possibility is the lessening of the focus on ethnic minorities once the new states have acceded, the relegation of the issue to the jurisdiction and discretion of the new member states, and thus a continuation of the EU's traditional internal 'agnosticism' with regard to minorities. A second possibility is the incorporation of elaborate ethnic minority protections and policies within an explicitly 'multicultural' European Union (ibid. 23 f.).

If one follows the political science practice of analysing the European Union as if it were a federal state (e.g. Scharpf, 1988), there are two ways for multiculturalism and ethnic minority issues to arise within the European Union: as recognition claims by the constituent units of the federal system, or as recognition claims within these units. By instituting formal equality of member states (however big and influential they are), it was ruled out from the start that some member states could take on the role of 'minority' claimants. For instance, 'minority' language claims are ruled out by the fact that all national languages of the member states are recognized as official languages of the European Union. Multicultural claims-making in the EU is thus limited to intra-unit claims. Here it was, and is, considered unacceptable for the EU to interfere in member states' dealings with their domestic minorities. To the degree that minority policies deal with culture, education, media, or language, there is simply no authority for the EU to become active on this. Only with regard to immigrant minorities have there been long-standing (but so far inconclusive) attempts to breach this abstinence. However, here the focus is not on recognizing immigrants as minority, but on removing a discrimination against them on the basis of their immigration status. The creation of the internal market without mobility restrictions has created an insidious distinction between 'privileged' and 'ordinary' foreigners, the former being the citizens of member states to whom no mobility restrictions apply, the latter being third-state nationals who are not allowed to take up work and residence in other member states. As some of the EU's own 'progressive' institutions (most notably the European Commission and the European Parliament) claim, the exclusion of third-state immigrants from the European project is arbitrary and indefensible, and much of these institutions' 'multicultural' energies are invested in bringing the excluded third-state nationals in. A first step in accomodating immigrants is the new Article 6a of the Amsterdam Treaty, which gives the European Community (the supranational core of the European Union) the competence to 'combat discrimination based on . . . racial or ethnic origin' (among other ascriptive markers). Looking at a polity that stretches from Sicily to Norway, and from Portugal to (prospectively) the Baltic States, it is clear that the European Union is by nature a multicultural thing, but one that has to invent its own distinctive understanding of multiculturalism and related policies it implies.

Finally, there is a third aspect in which our multicultural question 'What can Europe learn from North America?' is itself questionable. The word 'learn' conveys a sense of 'higher' and 'lower' levels of development, somewhat reminiscent of the modernization theories of the 1960s in which the United States represented the highest stage of modern society that the new states of the Third World were asked to catch up with. Accordingly, some European authors have branded as a 'trick of imperialist reason' the global spread of American conceptual fads, such as 'multiculturalism' or 'underclass', which—if detached from their specific historical context—must lead to a misreading of non-American realities (Bourdieu and Wacquant, 1998). Furthermore, even if one accepts the 'learning' metaphor, why not in the opposite direction, from Europe to North America? Indeed, the leading theoretical contributions in the growing literature on immigration, citizenship, and nationhood have been made by North American authors who—in a sort of Tocquevillianism in reverse—have looked at Europe 'as a looking glass for their own social and political concerns' (Favell, 1998a: 209).

If, after so much doubt, we still stick to our fourth multicultural question, it is for the simple reason that it has guided our authors in writing their chapters. Interestingly, all of them have intuitively questioned the commensurability of multicultural problematiques outside their specific national contexts, and they have understood their task as one of circumscribing distinct national ideas and practices of multiculturalism, before cautiously speculating about their transportability across states or continents.

OVERVIEW

The contributions in this volume revolve around four questions that have been raised by and against multiculturalism. These are questions about the epistemological, normative, and sociological aspects of multiculturalism. They seek to capture some of the main arenas and angles in and from which the debate about multicultural matters have been conducted. Since three of the four are yes/no questions, we were keen to collect opposing answers. This reflects our distaste for definitive answers.

Martin Hollis (in one of his last writings before his untimely death) opens up the first section, *Is Universalism Ethnocentric?*, with a fiery defence of Enlightenment universalism and an attack on the relativist who says 'Liberalism for the liberals; cannibalism for the cannibals.' Focusing especially on universal claims about human nature, civil society, and the best forms of government, Hollis argues for a substantive and not merely procedural liberalism as a 'fighting creed with universalist pretensions' that can justify 'robust and sharp-edged moral declarations'. As Hollis argues, universalism works for minorities too. This is because excluded minorities must show that they have been wrongly excluded; they need a standpoint that is 'not cognitively arbitrary' to exclude racists and sexists. Seyla Benhabib's case for universalism is somewhat more cautious. She approaches the lead question through the negative, by contesting various fashionable versions of cognitive relativism, radical incommensurability and untranslatability. She then shows the untenability of the (mosaic) multicultural version of relativism. Such relativism, Benhabib says, is 'poor man's sociology', relying upon a holistic view of cultures and societies (even evident in the work of Kymlicka) that is at odds with our mixed-up, global world. Just because we live in an interdependent world, a context-transcending 'pluralist universalism' becomes ever more a necessity, but fortunately also a reality.

In his response to our second lead question, *Does Multiculturalism Threaten Citizenship?*, Jeff Spinner-Halev distinguishes between various kinds of multiculturalism in practice. 'Thick' multiculturalism (also dubbed 'cultural pluralism'), which seeks state funds for group separation, is a threat to citizenship. 'Inclusive' multiculturalism, according to Spinner-Halev the mainline brand, enhances citizenship—an example being the turban-wearing Sikh in the Canadian Royal Mountain Police. Discussing the case of Hutterites, Spinner-Halev introduces a third kind of multiculturalism for insular communities that stay away from the society's common life and invoke what he calls 'partial citizenship'. This is a variant of 'thick' multiculturalism, without, however, asking for state funds. If the exit for apostates is guaranteed, partial citizenship poses no threat to citizenship, and is to be tolerated. Spinner-Halev's approach is pragmatic, not principled: if the context allows (say, in ethnically homogeneous Sweden), even thick multiculturalism may be exceptionally tolerated. Ayelet Shachar is a good deal less 'catholic', pointing at the losses in individual rights that multicultural accommodation may entail. She calls a 'paradox of multicultural vulnerability' a situation in which group members may reap some benefits from multicultural accommodation while individuals with 'other' identities (for instance, women) bear disproportionate costs for preserving their group's identity. Discussing religious family law in Israel, she puts her finger on a sore spot in Kymlicka's theory of multicultural citizenship, which prohibits individual rights violations in principle but lets them pass in practice.

The third question, *Do Minorities Require Group Rights?*, has provoked sharply opposite answers. Rainer Bauböck presents four arguments for ethnic group rights, one based on historical boundaries, a second referring to past discrimination, a third and fourth insisting on the intrinsic values of membership and diversity, respectively. Bauböck urges liberals to abandon their hostility to ethnic group rights on grounds of principle, while conceding that such rights are justifiable in some, but not all circumstances. Yael Tamir argues that the notion of collective rights, understood as entitlement bestowed on a group rather than the individuals that make up a group, should be rejected in principle. According to Tamir, the notion of a collective right is meaningless, because groups are not moral agents; it is unnecessary, because most morally relevant interests to be protected by such rights can be protected by individual rights, and those that cannot are better taken care of by contingent policies or institutional arrangements that are not couched in a discourse of rights; and it is dangerous, a threat to the individual rights of members and non-members alike.

Our last question, *What Can Europe Learn from North America?*, has generated mostly sceptical answers. American multiculturalism, Nathan Glazer holds has been 'exceptional', in its benign version reflecting America's positive legacy of multi-ethnic immigrant nation, in its less benign version compounding America's original sin of slavery. Glazer also points to a unique limitation (or, conversely, strength) of American multiculturalism. For all its ethnic pluralism, the United States has held firm to its rejection of foreign enclaves. There is nothing 'multicultural' about its formal citizenship regime yet, which requires a change of identity and loyalty. Martin Schain hammers the last nails into the coffin of hypostasized 'national models' of immigrant integration. His comparison of France and the United States shows that the 'pluralism' attributed to the American model has been of very recent origins, and that the 'Republicanism' attributed to the French model has been hollowed out by the state's practical interest in incorporating (and controlling) its immigrant population, which has entailed *de facto* multicultural policies in allegedly 'assimilationist' France. Eric Fassin tackles the same theme from a sociology of knowledge angle. He shows how the 'rhetoric of America' in France has served the political purposes of French intellectuals, who found in the discourse of culture and ethnicity a welcome replacement for their outworn discourse of class. Fassin thus hints at a sociology of multiculturalism, whose topic is not oppressed groups but intellectuals making claims about them or on their behalf.

NOTES

1. Interesting thoughts about a sociology of multiculturalism can be found in Favell (1997), which discusses the European Union as an emergent political field of multicultural claims-making.

2. One could also see official multiculturalism as a form of nation-building, as Stephen Castles *et al.* (1988: 5) interprets the Australian experience.
3. See Gellner's (1992: 22–72) scathing attack on 'postmodernist' anthropology.
4. *Independent on Sunday*, 4 Feb. 1990.
5. Quoted in Rieff (1991: 135).
6. As an example for many, see Schlesinger's *The Disuniting of America* (1992).
7. Anna Elisabetta Galeotti's (1993) case for the public, rather than just private, recognition of minority group identities is based on a similar argument: '[T]he liberal public sphere has always been open to some particular collective identity, namely, to the white Christian male: to him, the public/private divide does not require him to change his dress, his appearance, his behavior, or his habits about religion and everyday life' (p. 600). The public recognition of group identity rectifies the inevitable cultural bias inherent in the public sphere and the state. For a critique, see Lukes (1997).
8. At best, immigrants are entitled to 'polyethnic rights', such as bilingual education, to smoothen their adaptation to the receiving society.
9. As Kymlicka himself concedes, there is no place for the descendants of black American slaves in this scheme, who are neither an immigrant group nor a national minority.
10. Marshall Sahlins (1995: 13 f.) has made this observation.
11. Consider, for example, the strange story of black African world music hero Fela Kutti, who said of himself to have been 'Africanized' by his black American girlfriend in California (see Hannerz, 1987).
12. In the following, we build on Claus Offe's (1998: 125–31) excellent discussion of 'what is a group.'
13. After the anti-affirmative-action backlash in California, which was fuelled also by the inflation of minority claims, there was only one black student in UC Berkeley's law school class of 1997. The original victims are victimized again.
14. 'Short guys finish last', *The Economist* 23 Dec. 1995: 21–4.
15. 'Devolution can be salvation', *The Economist* 20 Sept. 1997: 37–8.
16. See 'A steady lot, the Californians', *The Economist* 6 June 1998: 27 f.
17. See the recent overview of the Islam in Europe by Vertovec and Peach (1997).

REFERENCES

Benedict, Ruth (1934), *Patterns of Culture* (Boston: Houghton Mifflin).
Borovsky, Robert (1997), 'Cook, Lono, Obeyesekere, and Sahlins' followed by Comments by Herb Kawainui Kane, Gananath Obeyesekere, Marshall Sahlins and a Reply by Robert Borovsky, *Current Anthropology*, 38/2 (1997): 255–82.
Bourdieu, Pierre, and Wacquant, Loic (1998), 'Sur les ruses de la raison imperialiste', *Actes de la recherche en sciences sociales* (March): 109–18.
Castles, Stephen *et al.* (1988), *Mistaken Identity: Multiculturalism and the Demise of Multiculturalism in Australia* (Sydney: Pluto Press).
Clifford, James (1986), 'Introduction: Partial Truths', in J. Clifford and George Marcus (eds.), *Writing Culture* (Berkeley: University of California Press).

Favell, Adrian (1997), *European Citizenship and the Incorporation of Migrants and Minorities in Europe*. Unpublished manuscript.

—— (1998*a*), 'Rediscovering Civic Political Culture in Western Europe,' *Theory and Society*, 27: 209–36.

—— (1998*b*), *Philosophies of Integration. Immigration and the Idea of Citizenship in France and Britain* (London: Macmillan and New York: St Martin's Press).

Galeotti, Anna Elisabetta (1993), 'Citizenship and Equality', *Political Theory* 21/4: 585–605.

Geertz, Clifford (1973), *The Interpretation of Cultures* (New York: Basic Books).

—— (1995), 'Culture War', *New York Review of Books*, 30 Nov.: 4–6.

Gellner, Ernest (1992), *Postmodernism, Reason and Religion* (London: Routledge).

Glazer, Nathan (1997), *We are All Multiculturalists Now* (Cambridge, Mass.: Harvard University Press).

Gupta, Akhil, and Ferguson, James (1992), 'Beyond "Culture": Space, Identity, and the Politics of Difference', *Cultural Anthropology* 7: 6–23.

Hannerz, Ulf (1987), 'The World in Creolisation', *Africa*, 57/4: 546–59.

Joppke, Christian (1996), 'Multiculturalism and Immigration', *Theory and Society*, 25/4: 449–500.

Kymlicka, Will (1995), *Multicultural Citizenship* (Oxford: Oxford University Press).

LaNoue, George, and Sullivan, John (1994), 'Presumptions for Preferences: The Small Business Administration's Decisions on Groups Entitled to Affirmative Action', *Journal of Policy History*, 6/4: 439–67.

Lukes, Steven (1997), 'Toleration and Recognition', *Ratio Juris*, 10/2: 213–22.

Miller, David (1995), *On Nationality* (Oxford: Clarendon Press).

Nagel, Thomas (1997), *The Last Word* (Oxford: Oxford University Press).

Obeyesekere, Gananath (1992), *The Apotheosis of Captain Cook* (Princeton: Princeton University Press).

Offe, Claus (1998), ' "Homogeneity" and Constitutional Democracy: Coping with Identity Conflicts through Group Rights', *Journal of Political Philosophy*, 6/2: 113–41.

Parekh, Bhikhu (1994), 'Cultural Pluralism and the Limits of Diversity', *Alternatives*, 20/3: 431–57.

Parens, Joshua (1994), 'Multiculturalism and the Problem of Particularism', *American Political Science Review*, 88/1: 169–81.

Ramirez, Bruno (1998), *Canadian Multiculturalism: Genesis of a Policy*. Paper presented to the European Forum on International Migrations, European University Institute, Florence, 12 Mar. 1998.

Rieff, David (1991), *Los Angeles: Capital of the Third World* (New York: Simon & Schuster).

Rosaldo, Renato (1988), 'Ideology, Place, and People without Culture', *Cultural Anthropology*, 3: 77–87.

Sahlins, Marshall (1993), 'Goodbye to *Tristes Tropes*: Ethnography in the Context of Modern World History', *Journal of Modern History*, 65: 1–25.

—— (1995), *How 'Natives' Think* (Chicago: University of Chicago Press).

Scharpf, Fritz (1988), 'The Joint-Decision Trap: Lessons From German Federalism and European Integration', *Public Administration*, 66: 239–78.

Schlesinger, Arthur (1992), *The Disuniting of America* (New York: W.W. Norton).

Soysal, Yasemin (1996), *Boundaries and Identity: Immigrants in Europe.* Unpublished manuscript.

Taylor, Charles (1992), *Multiculturalism and 'The Politics of Recognition'* (Princeton: Princeton University Press).

Thernstrom, Abigail (1987), *Whose Votes Count?* (Cambridge, Mass.: Harvard University Press).

Todorov, Tzvetan (1993), *On Human Diversity* (Cambridge, Mass.: Harvard University Press).

Vertovec, Steven, and Peach, Ceri (1997), (eds.), *Islam in Europe* (London: Macmillan).

Waldron, Jeremy (1992), 'Minority Cultures and the Cosmopolitan Alternative', *University of Michigan Journal of Law Reform*, 25/3–4: 751–92.

Witte, Bruno de (1998), *Ethnic Minorities, The European Union and its Enlargement.* Paper presented to the Reflection Group on 'Long-term Implications of EU Enlargement: The Nature of the New Border', European University Institute, Florence, 19 June 1998.

Young, Iris Marion (1990), *Justice and the Politics of Difference* (Princeton: Princeton University Press).

I

Is Universalism Ethnocentric?

2

Is Universalism Ethnocentric?

MARTIN HOLLIS

'I have placed you at the centre of the world so that from that point you might see better what is in the world.' Thus God spoke to Adam in Florence five centuries ago, giving him the freedom 'to determine your own nature, . . . to mould and fashion yourself into that form you yourself shall have chosen.' This divine assurance is given in Pico's *Oration on the Dignity of Man*, the voice of Renaissance humanism and harbinger of modernity. It signposts a trail which has led to the recasting of Reason to serve new sciences of nature and then, with the Enlightenment, of human nature. The resulting social sciences continue to prompt attempts to mould human beings and fashion suitable institutions. But the promised freedom has brought very mixed blessings, even if the benefits include today's return to Florence for further inspiration.

If universal Reason proves suspect, perhaps the centre of the world is an imperfect vantage point for seeing what is in the world. To make a human perspective central is one thing, to achieve a detached and objective point of view another. Besides, even if a single Adam can integrate what he sees on the way to deciding his own nature, are there not in truth many Adams with many angles of vision and many interests? This insidious thought did not much trouble the Enlightenment, when it turned Reason inwards to discover the laws of human nature and human society. Confident that it was applying a universal scientific method to a universal human nature, it could presume that the variety of human cultures, institutions, beliefs, and aspirations was due to identifiable differences in initial conditions. By reconciling perspectives which had an angle on the truth, and correcting those in error, Enlightenment thinkers could offer the prospect of a human race shaped in ever more perfect form as knowledge advanced. The prospect inspired, among other developments, the civilizing mission of Enlightenment colonialism.

But what if there are indeed many Adams and, be it said sooner rather than later, many Eves, or at least as many as there are distinct cultures? Then God's singular invitation takes on another face. Renaissance man is being bidden to think of himself as the whole of humanity and, with the spread of Enlightenment, thereby beguiled into prescribing ways of progress in morals and politics which are ethnocentric beneath their universal, perfectionist surface. If so, a ramifying virus is at work, vitiating an Enlightenment programme based on the proposition that, in Condorcet's words, 'Nature has linked truth, virtue and happiness in an unbreakable chain.'[1] Happiness? Bold social policies bring misery, if the happiness of different people is not commensurable. Virtue? Ethics are plural, if justice is relative to social meanings and the good life varies from China to Peru. Truth? If universalism is ethnocentric, even what is scientific truth on one side of the Pyrenees might be error on the other. In that case any universal chain is one of bondage.

This, I take it, is the broad challenge to the claims of universal reason posed by asking 'Is universalism ethnocentric?' Since it raises more issues than I can tackle here, I shall slant it with an eye to tensions between liberalism and multiculturalism. The chapter has three parts. The first tries to establish what a charge of ethnocentricity needs to prove. It introduces four slippery terms and reflects on the prongs of Edward Said's *Orientalism*. The second puts liberals in the dock, arguing that they are indeed universalists, committed to universal reason in pressing their ideas of a free, just, and equal society on persons or cultures not of liberal persuasion. Even a minimalist version must take a stand. The third asks whether liberal concepts are too thin to motivate political action: perhaps it takes a breath of ethnocentricity to live in the world. But I recommend sticking to Reason through thick and thin, even if that gives trouble with multiculturalism, and end with a brisk answer to the original question.

I

Four terms are central, slippery, and crucially ambivalent. Here is how I shall use them (despite the risk of begged questions). 'Ethnocentricity' I leave for the moment.

Universalism: the thesis that *there are true universal propositions, nomological or normative*. If indeed true, they have a scope and authority which do not depend on who believes what. Some versions require an absolute, Cartesian, point of view, a 'view from nowhere', but, for others, a less ambitious kind of objectivity suffices. In ethics, the thesis is that what anyone should do, everyone so placed should do. But 'so placed' makes for unavoidable complications, since 'No parking on weekdays' or 'No parking, except for disabled drivers' is as universal as 'No parking'. Hence it is unclear whether what anyone should do in China everyone should do in Peru. What is clear, however, is that universal rights and duties do not brook denial on the grounds that they conflict with local practice.

Objectivism: the thesis that *the reality of things and the truth of propositions are independent of what is believed real or true*. It is clearly incompatible with subjectivism but is ambivalent about intersubjectivity. So it might be objectively true in ethics that in China one should do as the Chinese do and in Peru do as the Peruvians do. If so, objectivism is consistent with some versions of relativism.

Relativism: the thesis that *reality or truth is relative to a standpoint.* Versions range from those which merely introduce a notion of perspective and are thus far consistent with objectivism and even universalism, to those which deny that any criterion can have more than local standing. While all relativists think an absolute point of view impossible in science or ethics, not all conclude that everyone is equally entitled to their own. Whether and where an ice-pick can be dug into this slope are matters of fierce debate.

Pluralism: the thesis that *there is no unique source of moral or political authority*, either because there are many or because, finally, there is none. Either way, liberal values can be neither universal nor neutral. Pluralism goes readily with a strong thesis about the incommensurability of conceptual or moral schemes, unless liberals can persuade us otherwise. Hence contradictions threaten to surface in the idea of a plural, multicultural yet liberal society.

With these terms and their ambivalence in mind, let us ask whether universalism is ethnocentric. I shall work out what is at issue thinking about imperialism with the help of Edward Said.

To set the stage, here is Arthur Balfour addressing the House of Commons in 1910 on the problems of governing Egypt and other countries in the East. Some honourable members had doubted that Britain had any such business or moral authority. 'I take up no attitude of superiority,' the former prime minister assured them, as he launched into a contrast between the Western capacity for self-government and the despotism attendant on all periods of Oriental greatness. Since Easterners could not achieve the benefits of self-government for themselves, they had much to gain from being ruled by self-governing Westerners:

Is it a good thing for these great nations—I admit their greatness—that this absolute government should be exercised by us? I think it is a good thing. I think that experience shows that they have got under it far better government than in the whole history of the world they ever had before, and which not only is a benefit to them, but is undoubtedly a benefit to the whole of the civilized West . . . We are in Egypt not merely for the sake of the Egyptians, though we are there for their sake; we are there also for the sake of Europe at large.

Said uses this revealing speech as the curtain raiser to his *Orientalism*.[2] Balfour is so sure that Western institutions are of universal value that he does not hesitate to export and impose them. Imperial rule (not a despotism, presumably, but a kind of vicarious self-government?) makes them available to people who lack the requisite moral character. This justifies imposing ways of administration alien to the oriental mind. Meanwhile sceptics at home can reflect that an imperialism, whose blessings include the flourishing of science, industry, and commerce, benefits the West as well as the fortunate East.

This is ethnocentricity in universalist garb, Said argues, and not just because of its presumption of Western superiority (covertly made, even while overtly denied). Ethnocentricity lurks in the whole underlying contrast between Western and Oriental, a contrast largely constructed by Westerners to suit Western interests. *Orientalism* traces the construction by analysing 'aesthetic, scholarly, economic, sociological, historical and philological texts' from ancient Greece to the present day. Said discloses a long and elaborate history of geopolitics, of power gained and exercised by making the oriental exotic in some ways and childlike in others. Some of it has been the recent work of unabashed imperialists, like Balfour and Lord Cromer, in whose hands 'the Oriental is irrational, depraved (fallen) childlike, "different"; thus the European is rational, virtuous, mature, "normal"' (p. 40). Other contributions are older and less deliberate, for instance those made inadvertently by explorers and ethnographers reporting the strange ways of oriental folk. Yet others have come from critics of Western society, who contrast Western failings with the wise and exotic ways of the East. Nor have orientals themselves always been passive in the construction, when it has suited them to aid and abet it. In sum, the mysterious Orient is the work of many hands and many motives, a fabrication whose consequences are nonetheless real for that.

Said analyses Orientalism as a construct from two contrasting standpoints. One recalls a Marxist theory of ideology, whereas the other relies on a general thesis about the construction of social reality. In the former vein, he gives Orientalism the ideological functions of legitimating imperialism, of shrouding its material workings in a cultural mist, and of consoling exploited orientals with a tale of their good fortune. Here he seems to run a classic two-tier story about base and superstructure, with the universalism in which Western interests are couched seen as a function of those interests. This is certainly one way of arguing that universalism is ethnocentric, at least granted the objectivity of propositions about the base and the functions of the superstructure.

But, overall, he is not a materialist, vulgar or otherwise. He more often treats cultures as social realities, not as distortions of something more basic. They provide meaning for human lives and define the people who live them. Hence universalism is at fault for failing to recognize the autonomy and distinctiveness of the cultures which it deems primitive. This line of attack strikes me as fertile but double-edged. If cultural realities are defined by what those who live them accept, then success in constructing orientals as 'irrational, depraved (fallen) childlike, "different"' might seem to imply that this is therefore what they indeed are. The implication is strengthened, moreover, by Said's remarking that the construction has been aided and abetted by orientals themselves. The obvious riposte is to deny that orientals are as Westerners say.

But this is no longer an appeal to an independent fact of the matter. Presumably it becomes a move in a power struggle for the winning definition.

At any rate, we should take care to separate the two lines of objection to universalism. Both attack a cultural imperialism couched in an Enlightenment language of universal reason, science, and ethics. One is modern and speaks the language of a rival universalism, here functionalism or historical materialism. The other is post-modern and seemingly rejects all claims whatever to universal truth and to a standpoint from which to discern it. They have sharply different implications, as we shall note presently.

Meanwhile, the charge of ethnocentricity needs defining. To take Orientalism as an example may suggest a narrow construal, with race to the forefront. That would be too narrow. Universalist claims are made by many groups of people, for instance by Chinese Marxist-Leninists, Islamic fundamentalists, and patriarchal white males. But Marxist-Leninists are not all Chinese; religious fundamentalists are found in many creeds; and some feminists are as authoritarian as patriarchs. So I suggest taking ethnocentricity to include 'centricities' of class, religion, or gender. On the other hand, if it is construed too broadly, the issue becomes simply one of the truth of relativism. Here, for instance, is Richard Rorty:

To be ethnocentric is to divide the human race into people to whom one must justify one's beliefs and others. The first group—one's *ethnos*—comprises those who share enough of one's beliefs to make fruitful conversation possible. In this sense, everyone is ethnocentric when engaged in actual debate, no matter how much realist rhetoric about objectivity he produces in his study.[3]

Although we may wish to postpone pitting the universal, timeless, and abstract against the particular, historical, and concrete, it is too soon to relativise truth to conversation.

To avoid making ethnocentricity universal from the start, I suggest taking ethnicity as a matter of cultural affiliation and ethnocentricity as ethnic myopia. The charge is that *the accused did unwarrantedly presume the truth of a universal proposition and/or its applicability to persons of contrary opinion, such presumption being of cultural origin.*

This wording calls for four comments. Firstly, it allows universalism to be arraigned in all realms of thought, even though we happen to be most interested in universal claims about human nature, civil society, and the best modes of government. That is partly because science, religion, and other realms are not immune to ethnic bias and more because I am wary of assuming a fact–value distinction. The warrants claimed for universalism in ethics and politics are often metaphysical. Secondly, it makes the truth or justification of universal propositions crucial. This may seem rash, given widespread doubt about the objectivity of reasoning and evidence in ethics and politics, but I shall address the point when we reach liberal neutrality. Thirdly, 'crucial' does not mean decisive, since it may be an offence to force even good medicine down unwilling throats. Fourthly, having caught universalists generalizing from their own case, the prosecution still has to prove that the failing has a cultural explanation. That leaves 'cultural' undefined but does suggest where to look.

Back to Balfour. Were British imperialists ethnocentric by the test proposed? No doubt they included cynics, who did not suppose that imperial rule worked wonders for subject peoples, and patriots too blinkered to enquire. But what of the long line of thoughtful persons who sincerely believed in its civilizing mission and, when the time came to bow out, in the universal virtue of the Westminster institutions bequeathed to the new nations?[4] Whether they were ethnocentrics depends on a complex reckoning. Consider, for instance, the alleged economic benefits. In reckoning whether they were genuine, one must also ask how widely and evenly they were distributed and whether they had non-economic costs and effects, for example in creating new élites at the expense of traditional ways of life. Then there are wider questions of justice and legitimacy. Was imperial rule just in theory and in practice? Was it legitimate to impose it on other cultures? Finally, if imperialists fail this stiff examination, is that because they saw what is in the world through the distorting lens of British imperial culture?

I lay out these questions not in search of answers but to head off snap verdicts. That goes for both of Said's lines of attack. For the first, a functional or Marxian analysis claims its own scientific objectivity. That claim must be established before a demonstration that imperialism, or Orientalism at large, serves Western interests is any proof of ethnocentricity. We might also note that, if it succeeded, then it would show one form of universalism not to be ethnocentric. This does not involve any paradoxical self-reference in an approach which distinguishes science from ideology and claims to be scientific. But any case for pulling the rug from under all versions of universalism whatever would invite a query about the *locus standi* of judge or jury.

The second line does offer such a case. It treats cultures as self-subsistent sets of practices which tell their members who they are and where they belong. Cultures furnish internal criteria for what is real, rational, and right; and there is no external standpoint for assessing these criteria. Admittedly we need not accept this whole package. That cultures are constructs does not entail that whatever they get up to is *eo ipso* always rational and right. Also there is reflexivity to think about, as just noted, when a denial of universalism is premised on universal propositions about the construction of cultural reality. But, for anyone who buys the whole package and does not fret about reflexivity, the second line gives a clear answer to the original question. All universal prescriptions for how one should live or what institutions one should have are ethnocentric. There is nothing but cultural practice to sustain them and hence nothing to warrant their export.

Here, then, are two lines of attack on universalism. They conflict, but either alone is enough to convict cultural imperialists of ethnocentricity.

II

Both lines of attack challenge liberals who fancy that liberalism and liberal forms of government are of universal validity. How shall they respond? Rather than slog it out, they may be inclined to protest that the question of legitimacy undercuts the rest. If no case for thinking that a way of life or form of government is universally good for everyone could possibly yield the conclusion that it should therefore be imposed, then they are spared the rest of the examination. This move may appeal especially to those who agree with J. S. Mill that 'the only freedom which deserves the name is that of pursuing our own good in our own way'.[5] But I shall try to convince them that refusal to discuss the rational justification of normative claims would leave them in a fix at home as well as abroad.

Are liberals universalists? They certainly used to be. Enlightenment liberalism was a fighting creed, armed with a universal account of human nature and of how societies arise and function, universal notions of human interests and human freedom, and universal prescriptions for education and moral progress, all of which could be established from a scientifically objective and universally attainable point of view. This uncompromising universalism, backed by Reason, was out to destroy and replace every rival universalism based on superstition, prejudice, and the maldistribution of power. 'There will be no peace on earth, until the last king is hanged from the entrails of the last priest.'

Seeing how swiftly the Revolution led to the Terror, we can wonder whether a fighting creed so bent on improving the human race and so intolerant of unenlightened practices was truly liberal. Yet *Liberté* was its watchword and many liberals have espoused a positive notion of freedom, a definite, if schematic, view of the sort of life proper for the truly free. Positive liberty goes with a licence for social engineering in the name of *Egalité* and *Fraternité*. Hence we should not automatically contrast liberal societies with those which embody and enforce a substantive view of the good life. Nor should we assume that, since faith endorses commitment, reason favours scepticism. We can certainly contrast a Puritan community, based on faith and, in its public concern for the welfare of souls, stigmatizing adultery, with a liberal association, based on reason and maritally permissive. But, just because since religions prescribe substantive values grounded in an interpretation of experience, the order of things and our place in it, there is no reason for liberals to eschew all such underpinnings.

That depends on whether they hold a positive or negative notion of liberty. The difference shows most clearly in attitudes to toleration. Positive liberty is not outraged by the very idea of forcing people to be free. Its reasons for refraining are typically ignorance and belief in autonomy. Thus Condorcet had no inhibitions in principle about social engineering aimed at strengthening nature's links between truth, virtue, and happiness, so as to hasten the time 'when the sun will shine only on free men who know no other master than their reason.' But, with this time far in the future and the social sciences still in their infancy, he was content to preach toleration in the interim. Mill tolerated, indeed encouraged, experiments in living partly as a source of lessons in human potential, to be embodied in social policies designed to cultivate a morally concerned individuality. Since his idea of individuality required autonomy, he could not force people to be free. But he was all for a cultivated public opinion to drive couch potatoes from the couch and give them suitable aspirations.

In other moods Mill has a negative notion of liberty: 'there is a circle round every individual human being which no government . . . ought to be permitted to overstep.'[6] Individuals singly, and, by mutual consent, collectively, have a realm where they may do as they please. Fighting liberals who do not like what goes on there can lump it. They can post leaflets through the letter box but they have a duty not to interfere, and to ensure that no one else does.

With these differences threatening disunity, there seems everything to be said for the familiar distinction between procedural and substantive values, as a way of separating the right from the good which all can unite upon. Government can then be a limited exercise in upholding procedural values, while leaving everyone, liberals included, to their own substantive ideas of the good life (short of doing harm to others). Hence the question about the legitimacy of imposing a way of life does indeed undercut the rest. Or does it?

The distinction between substantive and procedural values sounds like one between a morality and a *modus vivendi*. Substantive values are unmistakably moral values and, if unleashed, issue in morally sanctioned norms for both public and private conduct. Procedural values, by contrast, seem morally neutral, prescribing rules only for public business and for the protection of the private realm. If they have any 'moral' authority, it is only that of an overlapping consensus about the proper rules. Moreover, consensus on a *modus vivendi* avoids having to come to terms with a fact–value distinction which might prevent any rational justification for substantive values—a further contrast between substantive and procedural. We thus arrive at a familiar contemporary liberalism, one seemingly consistent with pluralism and so with multiculturalism.

Is it ethnocentric? At first sight the answer is 'of course'. A consensual solution to problems of political obligation and public order for modern, especially Western, political democracies in the historical aftermath of wars of religion, has no universalist pretensions. But this cannot be the right answer. The consensus is not unanimous and, being (more or less) liberal, forbids illiberal practices by dissenting groups and subcultures within its ambit. It outlaws sundry forms of discrimination against women, ethnic minorities, atheists, gays, and others denied recognition as first-class citizens in various circles. What warrants this imposition of liberal values exactly? A soft answer might be that illiberal practices are in breach of procedural values, namely those enshrined in the consensus itself. But this soft answer cannot suffice.

The idea of an overlapping consensus has sound-bite appeal but is misleading if it suggests neutrality between existing patterns of power and practice or equal friendliness to emerging one. It is more like an election slogan for a coalition of parties, each with its own manifesto. If their combined manifesto contained only what everyone has in their own, I suspect that it does not give liberals enough. For instance, they are not content with a lowest common denominator for religious education which says vaguely that every child should get a bit of it. But every way of including some of what most, but not all, parties favour sets problems of arbitration and consistency. To extract a consensus on equal rights for women, gays, and ethnic minorities out of component reservations, liberals need to work sheer magic in the name of reflective equilibrium. The liberality of the overlapping consensus is an artifice, in short, rather than a distillation.

That may seem too political an image of consensus-making. In theory, an appeal to the neutrality of procedural values provides a rationale. But there is trouble over both 'procedural' and 'neutrality'. Take Rawls's procedural definition of a just society as 'a fair system of cooperation between free and equal persons'.[7] Does it truly entail a difference principle, which prescribes distributions of goods favouring the worst off and equal opportunity of access to social positions? If so, this can emerge only after seeing off internal critics, ranging from libertarians, whose idea of 'procedural' excludes all whiff of social justice, to social democrats, whose idea of social justice flirts with communitarian notions of the self. The internal need to defend on both flanks does not impugn Rawls's definition but, to my mind, does show that what counts as procedural is itself a substantive question.

Hence neutrality is tricky also. G. K. Chesterton ridicules the man of universal goodwill as the man who says, 'Whatever we may think of the merits of torturing children for pleasure, and no doubt there is much to be said on both sides, I am sure we all agree that it should be done with sterilized instruments.' Even if we can accept some rules of procedure as neutral because they are anodyne, the leading liberal values of justice (as fairness), freedom, individual rights, and (some kinds of) equality are not at all anodyne. The very contention that they are neutral components of any tenable theory of justice involves a substantive claim, and one which puts pressure on the underlying separation of the right from the good.

Rawls himself has tried two lines. In the first part of *A Theory of Justice* he mounted a universalist case for holding that rational and self-interested individuals would subscribe to his principles of justice, if they had to choose behind a veil of ignorance. Kantian liberalism, congruent with the moral point of view, was the best all-risks insurance policy. This case was squarely universalist, being mounted on what was universally rational for human beings with a universal human nature. It claimed to show that Rawls's conception of justice could lay title to being the true concept. But twenty years of reflection have convinced him that a metaphysical grounding, whatever its ultimate merits, is the wrong sort of justification. In *Political Liberalism*, the principles of justice are unchanged but they purport to encapsulate only a historical, more or less local liberal consensus and to have a foundation which is political, not metaphysical. In effect, we might say, he has withdrawn any universalist pretensions so as to forestall a charge of ethnocentricity, whether or not the charge finally sticks.

Dispensing with metaphysical support may widen electoral appeal. But it subverts the purpose of claiming neutrality for liberal values which are not platitudinous. Liberal declarations of human rights, for instance, are robust and sharp-edged moral declarations, intended to lay anyone who breaches them open to moral condemnation. Their neutrality, if they have it, is to do with their being so undeniably well-founded that they can be assumed in all further discussion of how a just society should be organized. This has to remain a claim to universal standing, even if one becomes coy about quite what lies behind it. Otherwise Amnesty International could not speak out globally. If declarations of rights bound only those who sign them, it would be ethnocentric to complain of behaviour by those who do not.

By this reckoning, consensual overlap is reassuring but neutrality goes with universalism. Declarations of rights may be disputable but they do not brook dissent. One can enquire whether equal rights for women include an equal right to serve in the front-line infantry in wartime; but the neutral answer is not that they do in all and only those nations which think so. What goes for dissenting regimes goes also for dissenting groups within a single society. One can ask what claim a mistress should have on a man's pension in Britain; but the neutral answer is not that it depends on which church the man belongs to. Neutrality is a universalist argument for insisting on certain values.

Whether an appeal to neutrality has special force depends on the robustness of liberal distinctions between procedural and substantive values and between the right and the good. Neither distinction seems very robust to me. If procedural values extend to questions of basic income and what counts as equal opportunity, they cannot be kept off limits; and skirmishes with communitarians have resulted in encroachments on the firebreak between the right and the good. In upshot, I see no way to secure liberalism by trying to put its core values beyond any but internal or consensual reasoning. The resulting slide into relativism leaves a disastrous parallel between 'liberalism for liberals!' and 'cannibalism for cannibals!'

There may still be good reasons to claim neutrality in some form and to construe procedural values in a way which helps with the difficult question of what to regard as private in a liberal society. But liberalism has to remain a fighting creed with universalist pretensions. It can refine its weapons and stress its toleration of the tolerant. It can include values which must be spread by persuasion, rather than by decree. But there are also some which it is committed to enforcing and these need a fighting defence against a charge of ethnocentricity. It has to take a universalist and objectivist moral stand at home and abroad.

III

The moral of Chesterton's man of universal goodwill is not that there are no procedural values but that they are not solely, so to speak, adverbs of manner, prescribing how without restricting what. They may be schematic but they are not indefinite. They comprise a minimal universal morality, yet one with a cutting edge. They weigh in somewhere between telling cannibals to use a knife and fork and forcing them to turn vegetarian. This fuzziness is prone to leave liberals either defending too little or claiming too much. To introduce a new pair of terms and a new threat, there is an awkward question about universality to be raised by asking whether liberal values are 'thick' or 'thin'.

To flesh out this contrast, I shall borrow partly from *Thick and Thin* by Michael Walzer[8] and partly from *Ethics and the Limits of Philosophy* by Bernard Williams.[9] Between them, they make an attractive suggestion about the nature of ethics, one fertile for our understanding of citizenship and, at the same time, unnerving for liberals. The next two paragraphs sketch a theme from Walzer and the third adds one from Williams.

Walzer opens *Thick and Thin* with a vignette of people marching through the streets of Prague in 1989, carrying placards which say simply 'Truth' or 'Justice'. These are concepts with universal appeal: everyone can pile in behind them. But they do universal service only because they barely restrict what is done locally in their name. They have minimal and maximal meanings. Justice, for instance, means minimally giving everyone their due and that is as requisite in a caste system as in a meritocracy or commune. It also has maximal meanings, many of them, which fill in the minimum in local and incompatible ways. Different cultures, and subcultures within them, construct different goods by attaching local meanings and values to aspects of life. 'Distributive justice is relative to social meanings' (p. 26, quoting *Spheres of Justice*, ch. 1). To demand justice is to join a universal parade but to speak up for and thereby reinforce some particular understanding of what it means.

Philosophers like to fancy that moral terms start thin and then thicken locally. They can thus maintain that the minimal, universal meaning is a core or foundation, from which only (variants of) one maximal elaboration can be properly extracted. But the minimum is not free-standing in this way. 'It simply designates some reiterated features of particular thick or maximal moralities' (p. 10). It may have its uses for generating solidarity or arming critics; but cannot help in defending what matters to people and motivates their specific actions. This is the work of thickly conceived values, for instance those of social democracy, market freedom, republican virtue, public decency, in short those marking out some thick idea of the good life. Hence a thin proceduralism is not the partner of cultural pluralism, since it has no grip on communality and cultural difference. 'Cultural pluralism is a maximalist idea, the product of a thickly developed liberal politics' (p. 17).

This all goes nicely with Bernard Williams's remarks on thick and thin in *Ethics and the Limits of Philosophy*. Thick concepts are those with social and emotional resonance for people with a specific way of life. They operate close to ground level, so to speak, as familiar terms to describe and assess action. Whether an action is cowardly is a matter of fact with moral import. Other examples are 'treachery', 'promise', 'brutality', 'courage', 'coward', 'lie', 'brutality', 'gratitude'. By blending the empirical and normative, they give their users their bearings through life. 'We may say, summarily, that such concepts are action-guiding' (p. 140). Thin concepts, by contrast, are abstract and, so to speak, etherial. Examples are the prescriptive 'ought', 'right', or 'good', dear to moral philosophers, which supposedly reward the reflective search after universal truth and explain what it is about action, described thickly, that accounts for its rightness or wrongness. But this is philosophical illusion, since they are too thin to serve as guides. (It avails nought to be told to be good or to do what is right.) Indeed, they are even a hindrance, since they tend to provoke reflection, thereby weakening the moral import of their thick concepts. By asking one question too many, people cease to know their way about and lose their sense of where they belong. As Williams puts it in an arresting phrase, 'reflection can destroy knowledge' (p. 148).

Taken together, Walzer and Williams set liberals a neat ambush. If only maximal moralities, rich in thick concepts with local resonance, can give guidance, then the minimal, universal core of liberalism is idle decoration. For example, it cannot debar a local justice where it takes the evidence of two women to disprove the evidence of one man. Local justice can satisfy the minimal demands of giving everyone their due and still treat men and women differently, for instance by giving women an education which excludes them from most careers. To make headway, liberals might be lured by Walzer's suggestion of 'a thickly developed local politics'. But the thick concepts employed would be sure to have less resonance than those it sought to displace. And, if we believe Williams, any power to guide action thereby acquired would belong wholly to thick concepts not in the minimal, universal core. In short, a 'thickly developed local politics' would forfeit universal standing without acquiring local muscle. Indeed, it is close to a contradiction in terms.

Liberals can best avoid the ambush, I think, by showing that thin concepts are not too thin to guide action and then offering a *thinly* developed local politics. Here is how they might go at it.

Consider Walzer's other placard, 'Truth'. Minimally, it demands only that what authority states to be the case shall indeed be the case. It calls for an end to lies and misrepresentations. Perhaps it extends to carelessness about evidence or to official self-deception. But it is essentially simple. It is not given pause by the thought that facts are often unclear, statistics ambiguous, and the effects of policy obscure. Nor does it care about arguments concerning the ultimate character of logic and evidence. Nor does it wait upon philosophical disputes among adherents of the Correspondence, Coherence, Pragmatist, and Performative theories of truth.

Yet there are 'maximalist' disagreements on such matters. They range over the nature of logic, evidence, and interpretation. They challenge the very idea of knowledge and rational belief, the possibility of objectivity as standardly conceived. For example, the thesis that all facts involve interpretation is sometimes held to imply that judgements of fact cannot be disentangled from judgements of value.[10] If that were true, and if judgements of value could not be objective, the call to political action in the name of Truth might lose its clarion universality. Indeed, it would lose it, if Walzer were right about the relation of thick to thin. But, short of a radical relativism, thick concepts of truth are not of merely local validity and do not do merely local work. Rival maximalist ideas compete to offer the true elaboration of truth.

Similarly, a liberal theory of justice is too dense for a placard and too contentious for all humanity to march behind. Yet it is squarely in competition with rival accounts of what it is to give everyone their due. Some of its rivals claim an impregnable, because only local, validity. But this move requires a relativism more radical than any endorsed by Walzer or Williams. Walzer insists that he has left scope for internal criticism of a maximal morality to bring it down by exposing 'internal tensions and contradictions'.[11] He points out that most regimes give hostages to external criticism, for instance by setting their public faces against torture. He argues for a kind of knowledge which is objective without being universal, as when architects learn objective lessons from existing buildings without supposing that there can be any universal or perfect design. The same goes, he says, for experiments in democracy. On the other hand, he does not explain how these nods to objectivity can be valid unless thick concepts with local meaning and standing can be invalid. Liberals should not hesitate to ask him.

Williams is radically sceptical about reason in ethics. But this is a scepticism 'more about philosophy than it is about ethics' (p. 74) and his book ends with an 'optimistic belief in the continuing possibility of a meaningful individual life' (p. 201). In the nuanced intervening chapter on 'Relativism and Reflection', he firmly rejects any short-order, vulgar relativism, because it is 'implausible to suppose that ethical conceptions of right and wrong have a logically inherent relativity to a given society' (p. 158). He also rejects as confused any variant of relativism which issues in 'a non-relativistic morality of universal toleration' (p. 159). To live a meaningful life one must be a someone who belongs somewhere and takes care not to ask 'one question too many'. One must not ask for a philosophical justification of one's whole way of life, and thus fall prey to the kind of reflection which 'can destroy knowledge'. But, short of that, a relative objectivity is possible. On the other hand, Williams seems to me enough of a relativist to imply that any integrated society, whose members accept their place and identity, is beyond criticism. Can he avoid the implication? The question gives liberals somewhere to start.[12]

Meanwhile, I see no neat divide between thick and thin. If the philosopher's 'ought' is thin and 'treachery' thick, what about 'just', 'virtuous', and 'rational', 'duty', 'honour', 'tolerance', 'generosity', and 'kindness'? All are action-guiding, even if more strongly in some contexts than in others. (Duty, once thick in Sparta, is thin in Los Angeles; honour melts in the light of reason, except perhaps among thieves.) Williams is no doubt right to say that 'the thicker kinds of ethical concept have less currency in modern society' and that 'there is no route back from reflectiveness' (p. 163). But the thinner kind have always served as reasons for action, even if imprecisely; and I draw the same lesson from Walzer's efforts to give social critics a chance. Relativism about what does motivate people says nothing about what should; nor does it prevent liberals sticking to reason through thick and thin.

By arguing that the thinner concepts are still action-guiding, liberals can open the way to a *thinly* developed local politics. The way will not be untroubled. For instance, individualism and a regulative ideal of individuality are vulnerable to communitarian thoughts about what differentiates people (and peoples). Such universals do not differentiate. In so far as liberals need to recognize difference, they are nudged towards a socially embedded self, or at least towards qualifying the idea that 'the self is prior to the ends which are affirmed by it.'[13] As noted above, the citizens who are party to the 'fair system of cooperation between free and equal persons' deployed in *Political Liberalism* are more social beings than the schematic individuals who assembled at the start of *A Theory of Justice*. Whether there is a notion of 'reasonable persons' able to hover between heaven and earth is a metaphysical crux for a thinly developed liberal politics. But trouble does not mean disaster, and I cite the example only to preface some concluding remarks on universalism and ethnocentricity.

The front-line liberal case for there being some universal values is, I think, normative: there are values which everyone should recognize. A charge of ethnocentricity can then be met in two ways. One is empirical: there are values which everyone does recognize. This is dubious but not indefensible. Everyone pays at least lip-service to much of what is in the UN Declaration and it is hard to avoid practising a little of what one preaches. Better, societies are unviable without trust and hence without normal running which includes virtues like truthfulness and promise-keeping. But an empirical defence soon shades into a metaphysical one, needed in any case to sustain the normative front line. The other defence is, therefore, a contentious, objectivist universal story about, for example, human nature, human interests, the fundamentals of law, the conditions of flourishing for civil society, or the character of citizenship. This has to be metaphysical, because to leave it ungrounded is to hand over to a politics where reason cannot prevent victory to the sharp elbows of those in positions of power.

Which values shall liberals defend as universal? The standard answer is procedural values backed by a separation of the right from the good. This answer may or may not pick out the smallest set with the best-entrenched defences. In any event, it needs substantive support. Procedural values which extend to a distributive principle of social justice and a robust view of what counts, for purposes of drawing a circle round every human being, as harm to others, call for reasoning which strains any separation of the right from the good. In short, even if muted for reasons of tact or tactics, a liberalism which believes in freedom, justice, inalienable rights, and equality is still a fighting creed.

What does a minimal universalism imply about relativism and pluralism? Even an explicitly fighting version can come to terms with a relativism which finds relevant differences in some varieties of culture and circumstance. It cannot do so across the board, however, since it cannot forfeit its minimal values at home nor its *locus standi* in speaking out against illiberal regimes abroad. Hence it is incompatible with any version of relativism which, to recall Bernard Williams, holds that right and wrong have a logically inherent relativity to a given society or which issues in a non-relativistic morality of universal toleration. This leaves murky areas further to explore, especially when multiculturalists endorse a practice in the name of ethnic identity and difference and liberals are unsure whether their minimal case objects. For example, are special rights of representation for minorities to be welcomed?[14]

This all makes for edgy relations between liberals and pluralists. They sound like allies, at least until liberals deny that liberalism is but one position among many, all equally authoritative. Pluralists are inclined to thoughts about incommensurability which favour either many ultimate values or none. Liberals offer an alliance which gives their minimal position universality before allowing plurality. Both parties presumably agree that a society is viable only where shared values engender trust. But does trust require the liberal minimum or can it be secured by illiberal values and practices? This prickly question turns thoroughly awkward when it comes to multiculturalism, minorities, and citizenship.

Finally, then, is universalism ethnocentric? There are certainly ethnocentrics about. But they do not include every group of people who claim universal, objective truth for what they believe. To secure a conviction, it is not enough to point out that the defendants' beliefs serve to privilege their way of life or suit their interests. No doubt belief in the white man's burden strengthens the white man's sense of identity and hence his power, but more is needed. The prosecution must show that the claim to universality is unwarranted and that failure to recognize this is due to cultural myopia.

These Olympian conditions seem unreasonable and question-begging. It sounds unreasonable to call for a balance of warranted belief in matters of, for instance, religion, ethics, or metaphysics. Indeed, even to moot it suggests an ethnocentric belief in the universality of Western scientific reasoning covertly at work. But the argument has been on a more abstract level. I have been careful neither to define a canon of scientific reasoning nor to suggest a scientific monopoly of rational deliberation. My line has been only that what Reason requires in theoretical and practical matters is an objective question.

That still sounds question-begging. How could there possibly be a Mount Olympus at the centre of the world, from whose summit the wise can see what is in the world? Is universalism itself not ethnocentric? For a final answer, I am tempted to slip into the clever-clever mode which relativists hate and their critics love: universalism is ethnocentric only if ethnocentricity is universal. But, since this tends to be sterile here is a better reply. Pluralists and multiculturalists must be able to argue that groups denied recognition or resources have been *wrongly* excluded. Since they do not propose that everyone, from racists to sexists, should be included, they need a standpoint which is not cognitively arbitrary. Since they too need to see what is in the world, reflexivity is too dangerous a petard to toss at universalism.

Even so, is liberalism in particular ethnocentric? I have argued that liberals cannot duck the question by claiming to articulate only a local, mainly Western consensus. They must fight for at least a minimalist, procedural thesis about freedom, justice, equality, and individual rights. This has to be itself a substantive thesis and, given the seepage between the right and the good, not so very minimalist anyway. It needs concepts, thin and thicker than thin, which make for a prickly conference on multicultural citizenship. But liberals remain children of the Enlightenment with something intolerant to say about truth, virtue, and happiness.

Since their opponents can dispute one brand of universalism only in the name of another, we have a brisk answer to the original question: No.

NOTES

I would like to thank Timothy O'Hagan warmly for his helpful comments on an earlier draft.

1. M. de Condorcet, *Historical Sketch for the Progress of the Human Mind*, Xth Stage, 1795.
2. Edward Said, *Orientalism* (New York: Random House, 1978). Page references are to the Vintage Books 1979 edn.
3. R. Rorty, 'Solidarity or Objectivity?', in M. Krausz (ed.), *Relativism: Interpretation and Confrontation* (Notre Dame, Ind.: University of Notre Dame Press, 1989): 35–50, 44.
4. For instance, Lord Curzon, on becoming viceroy of India, declared that the British were there 'in obedience to what I call a decree of Providence for the lasting benefit of millions of the human race.'
5. J. S. Mill, *On Liberty*, ch. 1.
6. *Principles of Political Economy*, Bk. V, ch. ix, sec. 2.
7. J. Rawls, 'Justice as fairness: political not metaphysical', *Philosophy and Public Affairs*, 14 (1985): 238 and *Political Liberalism* (Columbia University Press, 1993): 9 and 26.
8. Michael Walzer, *Thick and Thin: Moral Argument at Home and Abroad* (Notre Dame Ind.: University of Notre Dame Press, 1994).
9. *Ethics and the Limits of Philosophy* (London: Fontana Books, 1985).
10. For example by Catherine Elgin in 'The Relativity of Fact and the Objectivity of Value', in M. Krausz (ed.), *Relativism: Interpretation and Confrontation* (Notre Dame, Ind.: University of Notre Dame Press, 1989): 86–98.
11. *Thick and Thin*: 47, and, more generally, the rest of ch. 3 on 'Maximalism and the Social Critic'.
12. I have pressed harder in 'The Shape of a Life', in J. Altham and R. Harrison (eds.), *World, Mind and Ethics* (Cambridge: Cambridge University Press, 1995): 170–84. See also Williams's reply on 210–16.
13. John Rawls, *A Theory of Justice*: 560.
14. For instance, when the elders of the Innuits in Canada deny that ordinary Innuits should be allowed to appeal to the Canadian judicial system against their rulings, which way should liberals jump? See Will Kymlicka, *Multicultural Citizenship* (Oxford: Clarendon Press, 1995). I also recommend the discussion and examples in Timothy O'Hagan, 'An Unsolved Dilemma of Liberalism', *Praxis International*, 11/3 (1991): 299–308.

3

'Nous' et 'les Autres' The Politics of Complex Cultural Dialogue in a Global Civilization

SEYLA BENHABIB

The question 'Is Universalism Ethnocentric?' betrays an anxiety accompanying the West since the conquest of the Americas. This is the nagging thought that western ways of life and systems of value are radically different from those of other civilizations. This widespread anxiety rests upon false generalizations about the West itself, the homogeneity of its identity, the uniformity of its developmental processes, and the cohesion of its value systems. Very often the suggestion that 'universalism is ethnocentric' presupposes a homogenizing view of other cultures and civilizations, with the consequence that elements of these cultures and civilizations which may be perfectly compatible with, or which may themselves lie at the root of the West's own discovery of universalism, are neglected.

Consider the following episode in the rise of Renaissance culture: after the division of the Roman Empire in AD 395 and the fall of its western part in AD 476, Greek philosophy, the thought of Plato and Aristotle, were forgotten in the West. It is well known that Arab and Jewish philosophers of the Middle Ages, Ibn Sina (Avicenna), Ibn Rushd (Averroes), Maimonides, and Ibn Gabirol (Avicebron) kept the classical tradition alive.[1] In the thirteenth century in Anatolia the poet Yunus Emre developed a form of mystical Neoplatonism which anticipated not only elements of Renaissance humanism, but also pantheistic philosophies of the nineteenth century. Yunus Emre advocated the view that the human person is at the centre of a divine chain of being, of ascending complexity, beauty, and perfection, and that we reach the height of our spiritual capacities insofar as we partake through our minds of the divine order of these forms. Emre, who is one of the great mystical poets of Islam, blended Plato's teaching of the forms with Aristotelian ontology. Galileo's claim that 'the book of nature was written in mathematics'[2] has much in common with Yunus Emre's belief that the universe is an intelligible, ordered hierarchy of forms.

When we pose the question 'Is Universalism Ethnocentric', do we take account of this complex global dialogue across cultures and civilizations? Or do we rest satisfied with the gesture of self-criticism emerging out of the radical doubt and uncertainty which European culture, in particular, began to experience about itself at the end of the eighteenth century and increasingly in the nineteenth century? The question 'Is Universalism Ethnocentric' pre-supposes that we know who the 'West and its others', or in Tzvetan Todorov's famous words, 'Nous et les autres', are.[3] But who are we? Who are the so-called others? Are they really our others?

In recent debates on cognitive and moral relativism, more often than not, a holistic view of cultures and societies as being internally coherent, seam-less wholes has dominated. This mode of posing the problem has prevented us from taking stock of complex global civilizational dialogues and encoun-ters which are now increasingly our lot, and has encouraged the binarisms of 'we' and 'the other(s)'. Current concerns about multiculturalism and multicultural citizenship are bringing to an end this particular phase of relat-ivism/universalism discussions which had been dominated by strong theses of 'incommensurability' and 'untranslatability'. Nevertheless, and despite the waning of the epistemological relativism of Jean-François Lyotard and Richard Rorty, false assumptions about 'cultures', their coherence and purity, con-tinue to influence the work of multicultural theorists like Will Kymlicka, who advocate 'group-differentiated citizenship rights'. My contribution is a plea for the recognition of the radical hybridity and polyvocity of all cultures; cultures and societies are polyvocal, multilayered, decentred, and fractured systems of action and signification. Politically, the right to cultural self-expression needs to be grounded upon, rather than being considered an alternative to, universally recognized citizenship rights.[4]

UNIVERSALISM IN CONTEMPORARY PHILOSOPHICAL DEBATES

The term 'universalism' can stand for several clusters of views.

1. Universalism may signify the philosophical belief that there is a fundamental human nature or human essence which defines, in the most significant sense, who we are as humans. Some may say, as did most philo-sophers of the eighteenth century, that this human nature consists of fixed and uniform passions and dispositions, instincts, and emotions, all of which can be studied through observation and reflection. Thomas Hobbes, David Hume, and Adam Smith but also Helvetius and d'Holbach come to mind here. Others may argue that there is no such fixed human nature (Rousseau), or that even if there were one, it would be irrelevant for determining what is most essential about us as humans (Kant): namely our capacity to formulate and to live by universalizable moral principles. Still others, like Jean-Paul Sartre, for example, may repudiate empirical psychology, philosophical anthropology, and rationalist ethics, and maintain that what is universal about the human

condition is that we are doomed to choose for ourselves and create meaning and value through our actions in a universe which would otherwise be devoid of both. Although most philosophical universalists are essentialists, as the example of Sartre shows, they need not be. They can be existentialists as well.

2. Universalism in contemporary philosophical debates has come to mean, most prominently, 'a justification strategy'. In these disputes the lines are drawn around another set of issues: hermeneuticists like Hans-Georg Gadamer, strong contextualists like Richard Rorty, postmodern sceptics like Jean-François Lyotard, and power/knowledge theorists like Michel Foucault question whether there can be an 'impartial', 'objective', and 'neutral' philosophical reason. They maintain that all justificatory strategies, all pretences to philosophical objectivity are inevitably mired in historical horizons and contexts of cultural, social, and psychological forces. In Thomas McCarthy's words, these are the advocates of a 'critique of impure reason'.[5]

Opposed to them are universalists like Karl Otto-Apel, Hilary Putnam, Jürgen Habermas, Ronald Dworkin, Thomas Nagel, Thomas Scanlon, and John Rawls (at least of *A Theory of Justice*). These *justificatory universalists* may or may not be essentialist: they may entertain very few rock-bottom beliefs about human nature and psychology, but they all share strong views about the 'normative content of human reason', about the validity of those procedures of inquiry, evidence, and questioning which are the cognitive legacy of Western philosophy since the Enlightenment. Impartiality, objectivity, critical inquiry, intersubjective verification of results, arguments and data, consistency of belief, and self-reflexivity would minimally define this normative content.

3. Universalism is not only a term in cognitive inquiry, equally significantly it has a moral meaning. I would associate it with the principle that all human beings, regardless of race, gender, sexual preference, ethnic, cultural, linguistic, and religious background are to be considered moral equals and are thus to be treated as equally entitled to moral respect. The hard question in philosophical ethics today is whether one can defend moral universalism without supporting strong cognitive universalism in the senses either of 1 or 2.

4. Finally, universalism may have a legal meaning. Many who are sceptical about human nature or rationality, or about philosophical justifications may none the less argue that the following norms and principles ought to be accorded universal respect by all legal systems: all human beings are entitled to certain basic human rights; these would include minimally the rights to life, liberty, security, due process before the law, rights of speech and freedom of association, including freedom of religion and conscience. Some would prolong this list by adding socio-economic rights, others would insist on participatory, democratic rights.

Richard Rorty's defence of 'postmodernist bourgeois liberalism', for example, fits this bill.[6] John Rawls's position in *The Law of Nations*[7] is quite consistent with it, as are Jacques Derrida's many interventions against apartheid, and on behalf of minorities and civil rights.[8] Rorty, Rawls, and Derrida all attempt to disassociate legal universalism from essentialism. They attempt to show that *universalism*, like justice, can be *political without being metaphysical*.[9]

Although I believe that universalism without metaphysics is possible, I question whether moral and legal universalisms can be defended without a strong commitment to the normative content of reason. Most advocates of philosophical relativism intermingle cognitive with moral and legal issues.

THE CHALLENGE OF RELATIVISM[10]

Contemporary philosophical arguments about relativism proceed from insights developed in the philosophy of language. Incommensurability, incompatability, and untranslatability claims are usually formulated with reference to linguistic systems and in particular about communication across the latter. For Jean-François Lyotard a 'phrase' is the most elementary unit of analysis, which is 'constituted according to a set of rules (its regimen)'.[11] Thus a genre of discourse, like teaching, can entail phrase regimens of knowing, interrogating, showing, ordering, or classifying. Phrase regimens and genres of discourse always exist in the plural; furthermore, and this is crucial, genres of discourse are not only plural, but also 'heterogeneous', irreducible to a common or comprehensive discourse. This is the problem of the 'différend'. A differend is a case of a conflict between two parties that cannot be equitably resolved for lack of a rule of judgement applicable to both cases.

Lyotard's vision is that of a quasi-Nietzschean metaphysic of struggle and the will to power extending throughout our linguistic, symbolic, cognitive, and political universe. He writes of phrase 'regimens', the 'civil war of language', the impossibility of 'subjecting' heterogeneous phrase regimens to a common law except forcibly. The vision is one of contestation, struggle, battle, the ubiquitous presence of power everywhere. 'To speak,' wrote Lyotard earlier, 'is to fight.'[12]

Yet there is also something remarkably brief, impatient, almost *stàccàto* in these formulations. The premiss of the absolute heterogeneity and incommensurability of regimens and discourses is never argued for; it is simply posited. It corresponds to what Richard Bernstein has called a 'pervasive amorphous mood'.[13] Incommensurability is the central epistemic premiss of Lyotard's philosophy of language and also its weakest. Lyotard nowhere distinguishes between incommensurability, heterogeneity, incompatibility, and untranslatability. He assembles under the heading of '*le différend*' a range of meanings extending from radical untranslatability in language to the sense of unfairness or injustice experienced when the language of the victor is invoked to describe the wounds of the vanquished.[14]

The thesis of radical untranslatability of genres of discourse and phrase regimens is no more meaningful, however, than the thesis of the radical incommensurability of conceptual frameworks. If frameworks, linguistic or conceptual, are so radically incommensurable with each other, then we would not be able to know this; for our ability to describe a framework as a framework in the first place rests upon the possibility of being able to identify, select, and specify certain features of these other conceptual networks as being sufficiently like ours so that they can be characterized as conceptual activities in the first place. Radical incommensurability and radical untranslatability are incoherent notions, for in order to be able to identify a form of thought, a language—and we may add: a culture—as the complex meaningful human systems of action and signification that they are, we must be in a position at least of recognizing that concepts, words, rituals, and symbols in these other systems do have a meaning and reference which we can specify, select, and describe in a manner intelligible to us. This implies that there cannot be radical incommensurability and untranslatability: if radical incommensurability were the case, we would not even be able to identify certain units of thought in other cultures as being concepts as opposed to, say, exclaim if radical untranslatability were true we could not even recognize the other set of utterances as part of a language, that is, a practice that is more or less rule-governed and shared in fairly predictable ways by a certain group of humans. Likewise, if cultures were so radically divergent, we would not be in a position to isolate complex human activities with their myths, rituals, and symbols as meaningful and intelligible wholes and describe these as a marriage ceremony, a feast, or a prayer. As Hilary Putnam has pointed out:

It is a constitutive fact about human experience in a world of different cultures interacting in history while individually undergoing slower or more rapid change that we are, as a matter of universal human experience, able to *do* this; able to interpret one another's beliefs, desires, and utterances so that it all makes some kind of *sense*. (Emphasis in the text).[15]

If phrase regimens and genres of discourse were so radically heterogeneous, disparate, untranslatable, then indeed it would be impossible to account for one of the most usual competencies of language users: namely that in the course of the same conversation, we can move from teaching to advertising, from informing to seducing, from judging to ironizing. As competent users of a language we can negotiate these nuances of meaning, shifts of style, suggestions of innuendo, playfulness, and irony. But if ordinary language use and performance suggest that phrase regimens and genres of discourse are not insular and unbridgeable units, what becomes of the thesis of their absolute heterogeneity?

Whereas for Jean-François Lyotard the question of cultural relativism is but an aspect of the larger problem of the incommensurability of discourses and language games, Richard Rorty maintains that even the very terms of this debate as between 'universalism' and 'relativism' are outmoded today; 'they are remnants of a vocabulary which we should try to replace.'[16] Rorty sees his own commitment to the values of 'liberalism' as reflecting the choice of a certain self-description, and not as being defensible in terms of any foundational or essentialist arguments. At times Rorty, like Lyotard, argues that the narratives of our cultures do what they do without any need for further justification, 'we do not need to scratch where it does not itch.'[17] At other points, he acknowledges that liberal culture institutionalizes the search for justification in science, ethics, aesthetics, jurisprudence, and politics but refuses to attribute to this fact any gain in rationality. For Rorty the attempt to question and to challenge the values and norms of one's own culture or that of any other in terms which transcend the self-understanding of this culture is illusory.[18]

Yet unlike Lyotard, Rorty rejects radical incommensurability and untranslatability. In 'Solidarity or Objectivity' he writes: 'the distinction between different cultures does not differ in kind from the distinction between different theories held by members of a single culture . . . The same Quinean arguments which dispose of the positivists' distinction between analytic and synthetic truth dispose of the anthropologists' distinction between the intercultural and the intracultural.'[19] The consequences of this argument are much more radical for Rorty's position than he acknowledges. If in effect there is no asymmetry between disputations among members of one culture and disputations among members of different cultures; if it is a matter of the degree and extent of divergent belief systems subscribed to by different groups, then Rorty's talk about 'us' v. 'them', about 'our ethnocentrism' v. 'theirs' is profoundly misleading as well as self-contradictory. The lines between us and them do not necessarily correspond to the lines between members of our culture and those of another. The community with which one solidarizes is not ethnically or ethnocentrically defined; communities of solidarity may or may not be ethnically established. There is no necessary overlap between solidarity and ethnocentrism but only a contingent one.

By Rorty's own philosophical admission, all that the pragmatist is warranted to say is that 'Among human beings there are those who can be actual or potential participants with me in a community of conversation and those who are not and may never be.'[20] Yet this community of conversation has a shifting identity and no fixed boundaries. It is not coincident with an ethnos, with a homogeneous 'we'. Membership in this community is defined through the topic of the conversation, the task at hand, and the problem being debated. For a true pragmatist, the formation and definition of identity would follow suit upon the identification of a set of shared interests, be they scientific, artistic, cultural, linguistic, economic, or national. We are all participants in different communities of conversation as constituted by the intersecting axes of our different interests, projects, and life situations. A consistent pragmatist could only say that all inquiry, whether scientific or moral, all justification, whether in aesthetics or jurisprudence, and all demonstrations, whether in banking or in physics, are conversations that can only occur in the presence of others who share enough of my beliefs such as to enable us to communicate with one another.

In his continuing references to 'they' v. 'us', 'their' vs. 'our' group, Rorty ignores that most of us today are members of more than 'one' community, one linguistic group, one ethnos. Millions of people the world over engage in migrations, whether economic, political, or artistic. Every nation-state in Europe today is facing the challenge of multiculturalism and multi-nationalism. True nations, pure linguistic groups, and unsullied ethnic identities are 'imagined' communities.[21] They were created through the imagination of nineteenth-century poets, novelists, historians, and of course statesmen and ideologues. Who are 'we'? And what is 'ours'?

THE PARTIAL TRUTH OF CULTURAL RELATIVISM: FROM COMMUNITIES OF CONVERSATION TO COMMUNITIES OF INTERDEPENDENCE

Even if views of radical incommensurability and untranslatability, inspired by philosophies of language, are ultimately untenable, many of us still want to insist that there is some deep truth in the cultural relativist position. Where does this intuition derive from? What does it reflect? The intuition that some aspects of cultural relativism may be true derives from features of our modern world: we know infinitely more than the eighteenth and nineteenth centuries did about the sheer variety, multiplicity, and incongruity of human cultures, systems of belief, value hierarchies, and modes of representation. As our knowledge of other cultures and of ourselves increases, our sense of relativity does as well. Paradoxically, the more we understand the more we can forgive. Indeed, in the study of human culture and society it seems that '*Tout comprendre c'est tout pardonner*.' I want to call this the 'hermeneutic truth in cultural relativism'.

All understanding, be it of the past, of a different culture, or of a work of art, begins with a methodological and moral imperative to reconstruct meaning as it appears to its producers. But there can be no such reconstruction of meaning without interpretation, without placing the object of one's study in the context of some other framework within which what is studied 'makes sense'. In this process of 'making sense', the belief system studied and one's own framework meet, enter into dialogue, challenge each other. Hans-Georg Gadamer has introduced the wonderful phrase of a '*Horizontverschmelzung*', a melting or merging or a blending into one another of horizons, to describe this process. In this sense all understanding is interpretation,[22] and all interpretation is a transcultural conversation. If the interpretation of cultures and interpretation across cultures is possible, then we reach a conclusion already attained in the previous section, namely that strong incommensurability and untranslatability are untenable.[23]

This conclusion still does not answer the question: even if every act of understanding and interpretation implies a *'Horizontverschmelzung'*, do we know which set of presuppositions, which horizon, is the most reasonable and correct one? Some of the most difficult issues facing us today arise primarily from the real confrontations between cultural horizons. The distinction between the periphery and the centre has been superseded; the periphery is at the centre. The condition of global interdependence in which we find ourselves has practically transformed all cross-cultural communication and exchange into a real confrontation. Bernard Williams's insight that the notion of real confrontation is to some extent a sociological notion is crucial.[24]

As a consequence of the worldwide development of means of transportation and communication, in the wake of the emergence of international markets of labour, capital, and finance, with the multiplying and increasing effects of local activities on a global scale—take the case of ecological damage —the real confrontation of different cultures has produced not only a *community of conversation* but also a *community of interdependence*. It is not only what we say and think but also what we eat, burn, produce, and waste that has consequences for others of whom we may not have the foggiest idea but whose lives may be affected by our actions.

In this context, the articulation of a *pluralistically enlightened ethical universalism* on a global scale emerges as a possibility and as a necessity.

1.   The interpretation of cultures as hermetic, sealed, internally self-consistent wholes is untenable and reflects what can be called the 'poor man's sociology'.

2.   This view of cultures as self-consistent wholes is also refuted by philosophical arguments concerning the impossibility of radical incommensurability and untranslatability.

3.   If all understanding and interpretation of the other(s) must also make sense to us from where we stand today, then the boundaries of the community of conversation extend as wide as those ever-widening attempts at understanding, interpreting, and communicating with the other(s).

We have become moral contemporaries, caught in a net of interdependence, and our contemporaneous actions will also have tremendous uncontemporaneous consequences. This global situation creates a new community, a 'community of interdependence'.

4. If in effect the contemporary global situation is creating real confrontations between cultures, languages, and nations, and if the unintended results of such real confrontation is to impinge upon the lives of others, then we have a pragmatic imperative to understand each other, and to enter into a cross-cultural dialogue.

5. Such a pragmatic imperative bears moral consequences. A community of interdependence becomes a moral community if it resolves to settle those issues of common concern to all via dialogical procedures in which all are participants. This 'all' refers to all of humanity, not because one has to invoke some philosophically essentialist theory of human nature, as Rorty seems to assume, but because the condition of planetary interdependence has created a situation of worldwide reciprocal exchange, influence and interaction.

6. All dialogue in order to be distinguished from cajoling, propaganda, brainwashing, strategic bargaining, and the like presupposes certain normative rules. Minimally formulated these normative rules entail that we recognize the right to equal participation among conversation partners; the right to suggest topics of conversation, to introduce new points of view, questions, and criticism into the conversation; and the right to challenge the rules of the conversation insofar as these seem to exclude the voice of some and privilege those of others. These rules of conversation can be summed up with the norms of 'universal respect' and 'egalitarian reciprocity'.[25]

7. In the context of cross-cultural, international, and global exchanges, but not only in such cases, these norms of 'universal respect' and 'egalitarian reciprocity' are counterfactual guides to action. The limits of universal respect are always tested by the differences among ourselves, as well as from others; egalitarian reciprocity is likely never to be complete in a world community where states and peoples are at different levels of technological, economic, and military development, not to mention the fact that they are also subject to different social, historical, and cultural structures and constraints, and dispose over widely divergent reasons. What these norms of 'universal respect' and 'egalitarian reciprocity' articulate, however, is a limit for our intuitions.

CONTEMPORARY MULTICULTURALISM DEBATES

My goal so far has been to clear up the philosophical underbrush, those epistemological and methodological assumptions that have dominated debates in the 1980s about universalism/relativism. Contemporary debates about 'multiculturalism and the politics of recognition',[26] to use Charles Taylor's felicitous phrase, begin from the epistemological vantage point that cross-cultural dialogue and coexistence are real, unavoidable, and necessary. The confrontation between various currents and understandings of Islam and the varieties of the Western tradition, to name but one case, is no longer merely a 'notional confrontation'. It is being carried out every day in a variety of forms, in a myriad of different countries: from debates about Koran schools in Germany, to struggles about the rights of young Muslim women in the Pakistani community of Bradford, England to refuse arranged marriages, to the desire of girls of Islamic faith to wear the chador in French public schools and not to have to participate in gymnastic classes—the clash of cultures is right here in our cities, parliaments, market places, and public spheres. 'Complex cultural dialogue' is not only a sociological reality but also an epistemological vantage point with methodological implications for social science and moral inquiry. What consequences does such a viewpoint bear for current multiculturalism debates? I will focus on Will Kymlicka's definition of 'culture' to show that the same kind of holistic assumptions concerning culture and society, which I have criticized above, are at work in his defence of the rights of cultural minorities as well.

WILL KYMLICKA'S CONCEPT OF CULTURE

It is the great merit of Will Kymlicka's recent contributions to have articulated one of the most compelling cases for group-differentiated citizenship rights from within liberal moral and political theory. Kymlicka argues that the basic principles of liberalism are principles of individual freedom, and that 'liberals can only endorse minority rights insofar as they are consistent with respect for the freedom and autonomy of individuals.'[27] Kymlicka attempts to soften clashes which may occur between these liberal principles of freedom and a specific cultural group's practices by distinguishing between 'internal restrictions' and 'external protections'.[28] While the first concerns claims a group makes upon its own members, the latter kinds of rights and claims refer to those directed by members of the same group against the larger society. Kymlicka plausibly concludes that 'liberals can and should endorse certain external protections, where they promote fairness between groups, but should reject internal restrictions which limit the right of group members to question and revise traditional authorities and practices.'[29] None the less, the definition of culture which Kymlicka gives as well as his privileging of cultural forms of collective identity over other possible identity markers—gender or sexual preference—will force him into a more acquiescent acceptance of relativist forms of cultural difference.

Kymlicka proposes to focus on what he calls a 'societal culture'. This is a culture 'which provides its members with meaningful ways of life across the full range of human activities, including social, educational, religious, recreational, and economic life, encompassing both public and private spheres. These cultures tend to be territorially concentrated, and based on a shared language.'[30] I would like to suggest that there are *no* such 'societal cultures'.

Kymlicka has conflated *institutionalized forms of collective public identities* with the concept of *culture*. There are British, French, Algerian nations and societies which are organized as states; but there are no British, French, Algerian 'societal cultures' in Kymlicka's sense. Why?

Any complex human society, at any one point in time, is composed of material and symbolic practices with a history. This history is the sedimentation and repository of struggles for power, symbolization, naming, and signification, in short for cultural and political hegemony carried out among groups, classes, and genders. There is never a *single* culture, as a coherent system of beliefs, significations, symbolizations, and practices, which extends 'across the full range of human activities'. Social institutions are not only culturally but also structurally and organizationally determined. Societal culture does not define the working of the international stock market or of the NYCE average in Hong Kong and Tokyo differently from the way it does in New York or London, for example. The practices of individual stockbrokers in informal ways, in the private sphere, in everyday ritual interactions may all be culturally determined, but as stock traders they follow the same logic of instrumental-purposive action. I would plead for a stronger differentiation than Kymlicka allows for between social action systems on the one hand, cultures and personality structures on the other. Kymlicka's definition of societal cultures is holistic, monochronic, and idealistic in that it confuses social structure with social signification.

What are the consequences of this definition of culture for Kymlicka's normative position? The strong distinction which Kymlicka wishes to draw between national minority rights and the rights of immigrant groups collapses. According to Kymlicka, 'we should aim at ensuring that all national groups have the opportunity to maintain themselves as a distinct culture, if they so choose.'[31] Immigrants' claims to equal access to a societal culture can be met by enabling them to integrate into the 'mainstream cultures'. This can be achieved 'by providing language training and fighting patterns of discrimination and prejudice'.[32] Except for Sunday closing laws and certain dress codes for immigrant groups, polyethnic cultural rights are to be subordinated to assimilation to mainstream national cultures. Hence Kymlicka's position would justify the requirement that the children of immigrants from a former French colony, like the Côte d'Ivoire, for example, be only schooled in French and that their parents' wishes to school these children in English would be overridden by the rights of the distinct national cultures, in this case the Québècois one. There may be historical reasons, specifically in the case of Canada, for wanting to retain the tripartite social contract of the country among the Anglophone, Francophone, and Aboriginal nations. Yet reasons of *historical precedence* must not be confused with *philosophical arguments* as to why a set of identity claims emerging out of one set of markers, i.e. the cultural ones, should be privileged over others. Cultures are not homogeneous wholes; they are self-definitions and symbolizations which their members articulate in the course of partaking of complex social and significative practices. Cultural practices rarely reach the level of coherence and clarity which a theorist is able to tease out of these first-level articulations and engagements. Any collective experience, sustained over time, may constitute a culture. Why privilege institutionalized cultures over ones which may be more informal and amorphous, less recognized in public, and perhaps even of more recent origin?

Kymlicka falls into the trap of culturalist essentialism when he argues that

Given the enormous significance of social institutions in our lives, and in determining our options, any culture which is not a societal culture will be reduced to ever-increasing marginalization. The capacity and motivation to form and maintain such a distinct culture is characteristic of 'nations' or 'peoples' (i.e. culturally distinct, geographically concentrated, and institutionally complex societies). Societal cultures, then, tend to be national cultures.[33]

With this admission, Kymlicka's multicultural liberalism comes to resemble varieties of nineteenth-century nationalism, in that he is compelled by the logic of his own argument to confuse *societal culture* with the *dominant culture*, and to plead for the preservation of such cultures.[34] His definition of culture and his privileging of societal cultures marginalize and disenfranchise other forms of collective identity formations which coalesce around different identity-markers. This is an illiberal conclusion.

Remember Kymlicka's thesis which reconciles political liberalism with the right to the maintenance of societal cultures. Liberalism rests on the value of individual autonomy, that is of allowing individuals to make free and informed choices about their lives, 'but what enables this sort of autonomy', according to Kymlicka, is the fact that our 'societal culture makes various options available to us. Freedom, in the first instance, is the ability to explore and revise the ways of life which are made available by our societal culture.'[35] To ensure freedom and equality public institutions and policy should make available 'equal membership in, and access to, the opportunities made available by the societal culture'.[36]

If culture is valuable from the standpoint of political liberalism because it *enables* a meaningful range of choices in the conduct of our lives and because it *forms the horizon* for developing a life-plan in the first place, then objectively there is no basis for deciding among national cultures or ethnic cultures, the cultures of religious groups, or those of social movements. *The value of culture for political liberalism is to enable condition for individual choice. To proceed from this premiss to the conclusion that only in societal cultures can such a value be realized for the individual is reifying ontology.* If the right to culture derives from individual autonomy, then no differentiations can be allowed among the value or worth of those cultures except as expressed through the activities of individuals. It is individuals and groups who determine, through their activities, the value of such cultural allegiances.

The goal of any policy for the preservation of cultures must be the empowerment of the members of cultural groups to appropriate, enrich, and even subvert the terms of their own cultures. The right to cultural membership entails the right to say 'no' to the various cultural offers made to one by one's upbringing, one's nation, one's religious or familial community. The exercise of autonomy is inconceivable if it entails only cultural reproduction; it must also entail cultural struggle and rejection through which the old is transformed and new cultural horizons are articulated.

Arguing from different premises I am reaching a criticism which Rainer Forst has recently raised against Kymlicka as well:

Yet if one starts from a form of moral autonomy that needs to be respected by *any* culture . . . thus requiring recognition of this form of autonomy is not an imposition of a liberal way of life, but an insistence on a basic form of respect no culture can deny to its members so long as it claims to be normatively accepted by those who belong to it.[37]

THE POLITICS OF CULTURAL PRESERVATION

In conclusion, let me consider two sets of arguments brought forth by strong defenders of group-differentiated cultural rights: let me call the first set of arguments 'communitarian multiculturalism', and the second 'constitutional pluralism'.

Communitarian multiculturalists, like Bhikhu Parekh, disagree that culture can be viewed as a context of choice alone, instead they see culture as defining individual identities.[38] Culture is the context within which we need to situate the self, for it is only in virtue of the interpretations, orientations, and values provided by culture that we can formulate our identities, say 'who we are' and 'where we are coming from'. Stated very generally this is of course true. Yet, communitarian multiculturalism falls into the same trap as the concept of a 'societal culture'. It homogenizes, flattens out contradictions and struggles, and disregards interpretive strands and contestations which constitute cultures. Alasdair MacIntyre's insight that we must conceive of cultures not in the image of some glass sphere into which we can fit all our value-commitments but rather as 'interpretive narratives', which are multivalent and span generations, is crucial.[39] In fact, the vitality of a culture is constituted by the narrative struggles among generations who focus on how, where, and when to transmit it. Culture is this multivalent and polyvocal conversation across generations which unites past, present, and future through contested narratives.

When culture is viewed interpretively and hermeneutically, its identity-constitutive function would be realized in that it allows individuals and communities maximum chances for interpretation, renovation, and recreation.

It is not the task of the state or of the legislatures to anchor in individuals a sense for the sacredness of culture. Politics should provide culture with the conditions of its own regeneration within the institutions of a free civil society and a free public sphere. Communitarian multiculturalism misunderstands the 'narrative indeterminacy' which is at the heart of the transmission and reproduction of cultures under conditions of modernity.

With the disenchantment of the world of values comes both danger and beauty, as we know from Max Weber as well as Martin Heidegger. The danger is that a fragmented value universe will be unable to regenerate and recreate itself and fall increasingly into scholasticism on the one hand and incoherence on the other. The possible beauty of cultural regeneration is that out of the seemingly incoherent, lifeless, and jagged fragments of culture a new narrative, a new reconfiguration, or in Walter Benjamin's sense, a new constellation will emerge. Under conditions of modernity cultures are less like the crystal balls of the soothsayers and fortune tellers but more like the images in a kaleidoscope: with each turn we reconfigure the pieces and are amazed by the novelty and vitality of each new configuration.

Precisely because the work of culture is, at best, the successful reconfiguration of fragments, or the retelling of narratives, it is not convincing to anchor the rights of ethnic and cultural groups at the constitutional level. Citizenship rights should not be *constitutionally group-differentiated*; ethnic, cultural, and linguistic groups can be given special privileges and immunities by the constitution precisely in order to assure the fulfilment of their universal citizenship claims. Group-differentiated claims to language, land, and representation are in general defended in order to realize the benefits of universal citizenship for groups involved. Let us consider as examples the Aboriginal peoples, who have been subject to Anglophone, Francophone, and Hispanic colonialism in the Americas; or the Gypsies of Europe who have been persecuted, tortured, and exterminated by the Nazis, or the Kurdish people whose language, history, and distinct identity are being denied them in contemporary Turkey. In these cases, special group rights can be seen as fulfilling the promise of universal citizenship rather than creating enclaves of maintaining particularistic forms of identity.

Unless we defend with strong arguments the norm of universal citizenship, the recognition of such group rights would otherwise inevitably lead to the clash of 'internal freedoms' and 'external protections'. For if our goal is the preservation of ethnic, cultural, and linguistic diversity for its own sake, we risk sacrificing moral autonomy to aesthetic plurality. Forms of life which are unjust, which are cruel, which are authoritarian, can also be beautiful, interesting, and fascinating. We must decide whether the aesthetic value of the plurality of cultural life-forms, like those of the Aboriginal peoples, the Gypsies, and Kurdish tribes, should be placed ahead of the freedom, justice, and dignity to be accorded to all their members, and in particular, their women.

In each of these cases, the traditional life-form is based upon patriarchal structures which presuppose the oppression, and in some cases, even the sale and physical coercion of women.

The task of the liberal-democratic state cannot be to preserve the frozen beauty of these traditional life-forms. Rather, the state must assure the protection of each of its citizens, including the women of these ethnic, cultural, and linguistic minorities. This assurance, however, cannot take place through forceful intervention—this is the mistake of the Turkish military against the Kurdish people; nor can it take place through paternalizing social work—this is the attitude of contemporary Spanish and Czech governments towards the Gypsies on their territories. The liberal-democratic state can allow the realization of universal citizenship rights through creating in civil society and the public sphere those conditions of participation whereby these groups become members of a public conversation and dialogue, and represent to all involved and via the voices of all affected their own narratives of identity and difference.

Such dialogues are risky and unpredictable: they may generate further polarization or they may generate intercultural and interlinguistic understanding. They may also result in the dissolution of traditional life-forms or in their renaissance—as seems to be happening with Islam in contemporary Europe. There is no gain in the moral universe without some loss. Moral autonomy and cultural pluralism need not always conflict, but when they do it is important to know where one stands.

In a recent review of the great Indian director, Satyajit Ray's life and films, Amartya Sen has written:

The difficulties of communication across cultures are real, as are the normative issues raised by important cultural differences; but these difficulties do not require us to accept the standard divisions between 'our culture' and 'their culture'. Nor do they give us reason to overlook the demands of practical reason, and of political and social relevance, in favour of faithfulness to some alleged historical contrasts. The celebration of these differences—the 'dizzying contrasts'—is far from what can be found in laboured generalizations about the unique and fragile purity of 'our culture', and in the vigorous pleas to keep 'our culture', 'our modernity', immune from their culture, their modernity.[40]

NOTES

1. See brief entry, 'Medieval Philosophy', Paul Vincent Spade, *The Oxford History of Western Philosophy* (Oxford: Oxford University Press, 1994): 82 ff. Majid Fakhry, 'Philosophy and History', in *The Genuis of Arab Civilization. Source of Renaissance* (London and Cambridge Mass.: Eurabia Publishing and MIT Press, 1983): 55–77.

2. Galileo Galilei, *Dialogue of the Two New Sciences* (1638), in *Great Books of the Western World*, Mortimer J. Adler (ed.) (Chicago: Enclyopaedia Britannica Inc., 1994, 5th edn.): 125–260.

3. Tzvetan Todorov, *On Human Diversity: Nationalism, Racism and Exoticism in French Thought*, trans. Catherine Porter (Cambridge, Mass.: Harvard University Press, 1993).

4. See the volume, *Relativism. Interpretation and Confrontation*, ed. with an Introduction by Michael Krausz (Notre Dame, Ind.: University of Notre Dame Press, 1989) for relativism debates of the 1980s.

5. T. A. McCarthy, 'The Critique of Impure Reason: Foucault and the Frankfurt School', *Ideas and Illusions. On Reconstruction and Deconstruction in Contemporary Critical Theory* (Cambridge, Mass.: MIT Press, 1991): 43–76.

6. Richard Rorty, 'Postmodernist Bourgeois Liberalism', *Journal of Philosophy*, 80 (1983): 583–9.

7. In Oxford Amnesty Lectures, 1993.

8. See most recently Derrida's reflections on Europe, *The Other Heading. Reflections on Today's Europe*, trans. by Pascal-Anne Brault and Michael B. Naas (Bloomington, Ind.: Indiana University Press, 1992).

9. It may appear that there is no difference between positions 3 and 4, insofar as any defence of a legal system based upon the recognition of universal human rights—no matter how short or long their list—would involve a moral view of the human person as a being entitled to such rights. I agree; in that sense legal universalism without moral universalism is an incoherent position. None the less, there are attempts in contemporary philosophy to give a weaker, more political and pragmatic, justification of legal universalism. The question is whether this is a defensible philosophical option. My own view is that position 4 inevitably slides into position 3 which then leads to some form of 2.

10. Parts of this discussion have previously appeared in, S. Benhabib 'Cultural Complexity, Moral Interdependence, and the Global Dialogical Community', in Martha C. Nussbaum and Jonathan Glover (eds.) *Women, Culture, and Development* (Clarendon Press: Oxford, 1995): 235–59.

11. Jean-François Lyotard, *The Differend. Phrases in Dispute*, trans. by Georges Van Den Abbeele (Minneapolis: University of Minnesota Press: 1988).

12. Jean-François Lyotard, *The Postmodern Condition: A Report on Knowledge*, trans. by Geoff Bennington, *Theory and History of Literature*, vol. 10 (Minneapolis: University of Minnesota Press, 1984): 10.

13. R. J. Bernstein, 'Incommensurability and Otherness Revisited', in *The New Constellation* (London: Polity Press, 1981): 117.

14. In *The Postmodern Condition* Lyotard is more explicit about the link between claims of conceptual incommensurability and the issues raised by the encounters of cultures. Lyotard concludes that the epistemologically enlightened postmodernist, as opposed to the imperialistically oriented Eurocentric scientist, does not seek legitimation, but instead assumes the attitude of the curator of a conceptual museum and 'gaze(s) in wonderment at the variety of discursive species, just as we do at the diversity of plant or animal species' (see *The Postmodern Condition*: 26–7).

15. Hilary Putnam, 'Two Conceptions of Rationality', *Reason, Truth and History* (Cambridge: Cambridge University Press, 1981): 117.
16. Richard Rorty, *Contingency, Irony and Solidarity* (Cambridge: Cambridge University Press, 1986): 44.
17. R. Rorty, 'Habermas and Lyotard on Postmodernity', *Praxis International*, 4/1 (1984): 34; see also *Contingency, Irony, and Solidarity*: 54.
18. Rorty, *Contingency, Irony, and Solidarity*: 59.
19. Richard Rorty, 'Solidarity or Objectivity', *Post-Analytic Philosophy*, ed. by John Rajchman and Cornel West (New York: Columbia University Press, 1985): 9.
20. It is inconsistent, after his admission that there is no essential asymmetry between *intercultural* and *intracultural* disputes, for Rorty to continue to assert that

> the pragmatist, dominated by the desire for solidarity, can only be criticized for taking his own community too seriously. He can only be criticized for ethnocentrism, not for relativism. To be ethnocentric is to divide the human race into the people to whom one must justify one's beliefs and others. The first group—one's ethnos—comprises those who share enough of one's beliefs to make conversation possible. (Richard Rorty, 'Solidarity or Objectivity', p. 13)

This manner of putting the issue is misleading. The word 'ethnos' since Aristotle refers to those who share a certain *ethike*, a certain way of life and a certain set of values. In our days, this word had also come to designate a certain linguistic and cultural descent. Thus, in the United States today we speak of Italian Americans, Jewish Americans, Chinese Americans, Afro-Americans, and others as constituting 'ethnic' groups. Certainly, it would be a moral and political calamity if what Rorty meant was that Italian Americans needed to justify their views and beliefs only to other Italian Americans. This kind of justification of solidarity would only be a philosophical whitewash for all sorts of ethnic and cultural prejudice and racism to run rampant in society. Rorty does not mean this; his political statements make clear that this is not his intention. Why then does he continue to write and speak in ways which on the one hand echo older forms of hermetic, and pre-Davidsonian cultural relativism, while on the other hand, rejecting radical cultural relativism and incommensurability? Distinguishing between the general idea of a 'community of conversation' and a culturally specific ethnic community would help sort out some of Rorty's contradictions.

21. See Benedict Anderson, *Imagined Communities. Reflections on the Origin and Spread of Nationalism* (London: Verso Books, 1983). I am indebted to Lorenzo Simpson's trenchant critique of Rorty in, *Technology, Time and the Conversations of Modernity* (New York and London: Routledge, 1995): 95–135.
22. See Hans-Georg Gadamer, *Truth and Method* (New York: Seabury Press, 1975), Georgia Warnke, *Gadamer, Hermeneutics, Tradition and Reason* (Cambridge: Polity Press, 1987), and David Hoy, *The Critical Circle. Literature, History and Philosophical Hermeneutics* (Berkeley, Calif.: University of California Press, 1978).
23. I find Alasdair MacIntyre's claim that such a transcultural conversation may force us to revise forms of theory and practice embodied within our own tradition and that this is a demand of rationality quite compelling.

Rationality, understood within some particular tradition with its own conceptual scheme and problematic, as it always has been and will be, nonetheless requires qua rationality a recognition that the rational inadequacies of that tradition from its own point of view . . . may at any time prove to be such that perhaps only the resources provided by some quite alien tradition . . . will enable us to identify and to understand the limitations of our own tradition; and this provision may require that we transfer our allegiance to that hitherto alien tradition. (Alasdair MacIntyre, 'Relativism, Power, and Philosophy', in *After Philosophy. End or Transformation*, ed. by Kenneth Baynes, James Bohman and Thomas McCarthy (Cambridge, Mass.: MIT Press, 1987): 408)

My only disagreement with this formulation would be that traditions, like cultures, are not unities with clearly definable borders but hybrid conversations and argumentations, so that when we 'transfer allegiances', what we are really doing is less like choosing to become the fan of a new soccer team but more like positioning ourselves in an 'in-between space' of narration, where we can hear and impersonate many and divergent conflicting voices and stories. MacIntyre has defended this view of traditions as 'conversations in crisis' in other works, including 'Epistemological Crises, Dramatic Narrative and the Philosophy of Science,' *The Monist*, 60 (1977): 433–72.

24. In *Ethics and the Limits of Philosophy*, Bernard Williams introduces a distinction between 'real' and 'notional' confrontations among cultures which sheds some light on the interdependence of understanding and evaluation.

A real confrontation between two divergent outlooks occurs at a given time, if there is a group of people for whom each of the outlooks is a real option. A notional confrontation, by contrast, occurs when some people know about two divergent outlooks, but at least one of these outlooks does not present a real option. The idea of a 'real option' is largely, but not entirely, a social notion. (B. Williams, *Ethics and the Limits of Philosophy* (Cambridge, Mass.: Harvard University Press, 1985): 161)

Williams calls relativism seen in this way *the relativism of distance* (Ibid. 162).

25. For an elaboration of the justification and content of discourse or communicative ethics and for a discussion of where I differ from Jürgen Habermas and Karl-Otto Apel in their formulations, see my *Situating the Self. Gender, Community and Postmodernism in Contemporary Ethics* (London and New York: Routledge, 1994), Introduction and ch. 1 in particular.
26. Charles Taylor, 'Multiculturalism and the Politics of Recognition', in *Multiculturalism. Examining the Politics of Recognition*, ed. by Amy Gutmann (New Jersey: Princeton University Press, 1994): 25–75.
27. Will Kymlicka, *Multicultural Citizenship* (Oxford: Clarendon Press, 1995): 75.
28. Ibid. 35.
29. Ibid. 37.
30. Ibid. 76.
31. Ibid. 113.
32. Ibid. 114.
33. Ibid. 80.
34. Consider for a moment 'diasporic cultures'. Some of the most significant cultural achievements of human history and civilization have been brought forth by the experiences of groups of people who were not 'territorially concentrated',

and institutionally represented. All of Jewish culture preceding, and much of it even following, the establishment of the State of Israel is 'diasporic' culture. Anglo-Indian, Franco-Caribbean, and Hispano-American cultures are all outstanding examples of such diasporic achievements. Should not our concept of culture be fine-tuned enough to bear testimony to such civilizational achievements?

35. Will Kymlicka, 'Do We Need a Liberal Theory of Minority Rights', in *Constellations*, 4/1 (1997): 75.
36. Ibid. 75.
37. Rainer Forst, 'A Theory of Multicultural Justice', in *Constellations*, 4/1 (1997): 70.
38. Bhikhu Parekh, 'Dilemmas of a Multicultural Theory of Citizenship', in *Constellations*, 4/1 (1997): 60 ff.
39. Alasdair MacIntyre, *After Virtue* (Notre Dame, Ind.: University of Notre Dame Press, 1984).
40. Amartya Sen, 'Our Culture, Their Culture. Satyajit Ray and the Art of Universalism', *New Republic*, 1 April 1996: 34.

II

Does Multiculturalism Threaten Citizenship?

4

Cultural Pluralism and Partial Citizenship

JEFF SPINNER-HALEV

A multiculturalism that tries to create a society with several distinct cultures deeply threatens citizenship. In this kind of multicultural society, people are not interested in citizenship; they are not interested in making the state a better place for all; they care little about how public policies affect most people or about their fellow citizens. Even the term 'fellow citizen' might strike them as strange. What they have are fellow Jews, or fellow blacks, or fellow Muslims, or fellow Sikhs. Citizens, however, are not their fellows. These multiculturalists might be interested in the state, but only so they can convince it to give them support, financial and otherwise, to further their own goals. The advantage of a society where group membership is prior to citizenship is that groups have a reasonable chance of maintaining a robust version of their identity. However, this thick multiculturalism is not the most usual form of multiculturalism. The more typical forms of multiculturalism are much more innocuous and, ironically, are only weakly multicultural. The typical multiculturalist claims are about members of minority groups pressing for inclusion into the dominant culture. They want the history of their group recognized as important; they want to be able to retain some sort of traditional dress while serving their country; or perhaps they want recognition and want elected officials to recognize their communities by visiting them and participating in their holiday celebrations. These claims are about expanding citizenship. Though this inclusive multiculturalism may harm some people's narrow notions of citizenship, constricted ideas of citizenship often ought to be expanded.

I investigate the relationship between multiculturalism and citizenship in this essay. There are two reasons for doing so. First, a common criticism of multiculturalism is that it will lead to the Balkanization of society. If we think of ourselves in terms of groups, this criticism runs, the idea of citizenship will wane in the face of separate group life. Second, political theorists (especially but not exclusively liberal theorists) have increasingly talked about citizenship and issues of difference, diversity, and multiculturalism. I want here to connect these two discussions by answering the following question: does multiculturalism threaten citizenship? I will argue that strong forms of multiculturalism tend to threaten citizenship, while inclusive multiculturalism usually enhances citizenship. Yet there is a third model, one that is derivative from the strong multicultural model but does not harm citizenship. Insular groups that maintain a cohesive group identity do not threaten citizenship when they make few claims on the state and so members of these groups should be not thought of as full citizens. After discussing citizenship and inclusive multiculturalism, I spend some time discussing the case of 'partial citizenship' because it illustrates the difficulty in maintaining a distinct culture in a way that does not harm citizenship. I then explain why the stronger forms of multiculturalism usually threaten citizenship. I also discuss why the reaction to inclusive multiculturalism actually imperils citizenship more than multiculturalism does. I conclude with a brief discussion of why citizenship matters.

A problem with any discussion of multiculturalism is that the term is used so widely that it connotes many different things. I'm interested here in two kinds of groups, those that want to protect their cultural practices in a way that requires considerable separation from others, and groups that want their cultural practices accepted in and by the larger culture. When the former happens, this thick multiculturalism can be thought of as cultural pluralism. When the latter occurs, this inclusive multiculturalism can be thought of as one aspect of the diversity of a society. Diversity is partly about the plurality of beliefs and doctrines that people hold and partly about the different cultural practices that people have. The latter are practices that people do not want to serve as barriers to inclusion into mainstream society. (I will sometimes refer to inclusive multiculturalism as diversity, even though the two are not synonymous.) These practices are shared with others and sometimes shed by the people who originally hold them as they take on new cultural practices. A diverse society has many different kinds of practices and beliefs that are part of its mainstream culture, practices and beliefs that shift among and between people.[1] A society that is marked by cultural pluralism has groups that do not want to share their cultural practices with others.

Like many dichotomies, the one I'm painting between cultural pluralism and diversity masks the many shades of grey that lie in between the two poles. To show that this dichotomy is indeed too simple, I will touch upon a few of these shades of grey below. Yet this dichotomy is useful because it illustrates when multiculturalism threatens and when it enhances citizenship.

I. INCLUSIVE MULTICULTURALISM

Liberal citizenship

I want to suggest that there are two levels of citizenship; the first is a legal requirement, while the second is a moral one. The first level of citizenship insists that all citizens treat each other in a non-discriminatory fashion in public and in most of the institutions of civil society and do not harm one another.

In the private realm discrimination can abound, but people must tolerate one another. This means at the least that no one can physically harm another without due cause such as self-defence. In some cases, this first level of citizenship applies to non-citizens as well. Citizens typically shouldn't discriminate against non-citizens. In fulfilling contracts and serving customers all should be treated equally, regardless of their citizenship status. This part of citizenship overlaps with a common notion of human rights: no one should face discrimination based on ascriptive characteristics. I want to say, however, that non-discrimination is part of citizenship for two reasons. First, in the USA (and parts of Europe) it was citizens—women, workers, blacks—who fought for the right to be treated equally. Second, non-citizens can face discrimination in some cases where citizens should not. Liberal citizenship's legal requirements give citizens certain rights, like the right to vote, to run for office, and to petition the government. Further, some institutions can discriminate against non-citizens, as in the realm of employment, admissions to schools, and in government programmes. Discrimination against non-citizens isn't required in all these realms. A liberal government could decide that resident aliens should be allowed to vote, but it need not.[2]

Though liberal laws insist upon non-discrimination, laws are flouted all the time. Since laws are not enough to stop people from discriminating, liberals hope that people will voluntarily follow these legal conditions of citizenship. Unfortunately, these hopes are often dashed as it seems that fulfilling these demands is rather hard. If it were easy to refrain from discrimination, we'd have a lot less racism and sexism than we currently do. Still, this is part of the ideal of citizenship that is needed if a state attempts to become liberal.

The second requirement of citizenship are demands on citizens, demands that are moral, as opposed to legal, since the state can encourage them in its citizens but cannot legally require them. A liberal democracy will work best if citizens are able to talk to one another, if they are willing to compromise, and if they are willing to not only look out for their private interests, but for the public good as well. While it is too much to ask for citizens to be motivated exclusively by public concerns, if all citizens routinely looked out only for their narrow self-interest, injustices would multiply. If citizens were unwilling to think about and pursue the common good, politics would become a game where the strongest won. Citizens must be willing to look out for the common good some of the time if there is to be a chance to end injustice.

This leads to the virtues of good liberal citizens: they are able to cooperate with one another, they understand the importance of listening to others in democratic discussions, they are willing to compromise, they think, they keep at least an occasional eye on the political world, and when they contact their elected officials it is not to get a better job, but to insist on better policy-making. These virtues help citizens to create a more just world and help them to keep an eye on the government to make sure it doesn't overstep its bounds. These liberal virtues have become more important since liberalism has become coupled to democracy.[3] These virtues can be encouraged in a variety of ways by the institutions of society, but they can hardly be mandated. Some citizens will shy away from these virtues; if a majority of citizens do so then the state is in danger of not being so liberal. Certainly, however, the liberal state can survive and even thrive if some citizens eschew these liberal virtues.

Multiculturalism and cosmopolitanism

Inclusive multiculturalism, which is probably the most prevalent kind of multiculturalism, is about fulfilling the second level of liberal citizenship. This brand of multiculturalism wants people who are excluded from the cultural norms of society to be included. These people want to be included in democratic discussion as full and equal citizens; they want to be listened to, and they want to be treated fairly in social and political life and in the schools. When members of excluded groups, who are forced out of mainstream society, argue that its history is wrongly neglected from history textbooks, they are not attempting to maintain a distinct cultural identity. Rather, they want their history to be included in the country's historical narrative. They want to make their history part of the country's history. When black history and Jewish history and Italian American history are taught in schools as part of American history, as they should be, these histories can be claimed by all Americans. All Americans can be inspired by Martin Luther King, Jr., not only black Americans.

Similarly, when Martin Luther King, Jr. Day became a national holiday, it became a day for all Americans to celebrate. King then is not only a special figure to the black community, but studied in schools and officially celebrated nationally, he becomes a special figure to all Americans. This version of multiculturalism isn't about celebrating different cultures. It is about changing the current conception of citizenship to include the formerly excluded. It is about celebrating and affirming the diversity of American society. The people who ought to be most concerned about this change are not the defenders of citizenship, but the members of the black community who want to cherish the memory and teachings of King. Once King becomes a figure for all Americans, the black community will have little control over how his memory and teachings will be used. Since the holiday has been established, we no longer see celebrations of King's birthday only in black churches; now, white churches, synagogues, civic organizations, and government offices organize celebrations on King's birthday. This may be a good thing for citizenship and diversity, but it certainly does not do much to help maintain distinct cultural boundaries in society.[4]

Other forms of inclusion are not so thin but still retain a veil of multi-culturalism. When Jews want to wear their yarmulkes (skull caps) while in the military, or Sikhs want to wear the turbans while serving as Canadian Mounties or in school, these people want to retain something of a distinct identity. I say 'something' here because what they are after is not maintaining a robustly distinct identity. Jews that want to be radically different from non-Jews don't join the American army; they stay in the yeshiva. None the less, serving in the army with a yarmulke or a turban is showing a form of cultural identity that distinguishes the wearer from (some of his) fellow citizens. Diversity does not entail the eradication of all cultural differences, but the differences that are preserved are typically less robust than the similarities that coexist with it. Indeed, this inclusive multiculturalism is often quite like cosmopolitanism. When a devout Sikh serves as a Canadian Mounty, eats hamburgers at home, attends Toronto Blue Jay baseball games on the weekends, and when his children attend the University of Toronto where they partake in their own form of the cosmopolitan life, then he and his family are living the cosmopolitan life, one that draws on several cultural traditions. These citizens have both their fellow Sikhs and their fellow citizens. Occasionally this combination will cause a conflict of some sort, but usually most can combine both identities with little problem.

Problems of accommodation

Sometimes problems of accommodation will arise when people with different practices immigrate to a country that is unfamiliar with the cultural practices of the immigrants. Devout Muslims, for example, want to be able to pray in a mosque several times on Fridays. This is not very different from Christians wanting to pray on Sundays or Jews on Saturday, but many more businesses, government offices, and schools are closed at the weekend than on Friday. The work week is an accident of history, and so there is no principled reason to deny accommodation to those who come into the picture after the work week has been established.

The work week can be defended on grounds of convenience; it does accommodate the majority of people in Western democracies, since most citizens in them are Christian (though some may have more Muslims than Jews) and when it was established there was no intent to discriminate against Muslims. But it's not clear why intent should matter. The original intent behind some laws may not be able to keep up with certain changes in society. Laws that penalize people for taking more than two weeks off from a job a year may be couched in neutralist language that originally was meant to apply to all workers. Yet such a law could clearly penalize pregnant women, who typically want considerably more time off right before and after they give birth. Many countries have made attempts to accommodate these women so they can bear children without penalty. As citizenship expands to encompass more than white men, some of the norms and laws of society should change as well to avoid unfair discrimination.

Devout Muslims should be accommodated, since it is not fair that Muslims have to work on their weekly holy day but Christians and Jews do not. This accommodation will have to be done on a case-by-case basis, but certainly imagination will often be needed when doing so. Still, there will undoubtedly be limits to accommodation and even the idea of accommodation means that some people may be singled out or at certain disadvantages at work. (It may be harder to get a promotion if the boss sees less of you and more of others.) Those with beliefs that were not considered (or were outvoted) when the work week and holidays were established will still prove to be more of a burden to them than to others. I do not think there is a way around this problem. It's hard to see how the work week can accommodate everyone equally. If 95 per cent of the population wants to take off Sunday and 5 per cent wants Friday off, many offices and businesses will structure themselves around the majority.

We should also expect accommodation to be slow, difficult, and occasionally impossible. For a few jobs it may be that everyone has to work at the same time, and that those who feel obligated to leave work on a day that everyone else wants to work cannot be accommodated. Still, many times accommodation will be possible, though figuring out the best way to accommodate new cultural or religious practices will often take some time. Accommodation will not, however, harm citizenship. It will allow more people to be first-class citizens while adhering to their particular practices and beliefs.

II. CULTURAL PLURALISM AND PARTIAL CITIZENSHIP

Inclusive multiculturalism often leads to a kind of cosmopolitanism that makes it harder for groups to maintain a distinct cultural identity. The route to cultural preservation in an egalitarian liberal democracy lies in separation, something that religious groups tend to do best. Unfortunately, much of the talk surrounding cultural diversity and difference skips over religious groups, though it is these groups that are typically the most culturally distinct. Groups that set up clear and important markers that distinguish them from others are the ones that are most likely to maintain a distinct identity. People that believe they are following God's will by living a certain way are less likely to make compromises than those who are trying to live a certain way of life out of, say, respect for the past. It is groups like the Amish, Hutterites, and ultra-orthodox Jews that are the most distinct in the USA and Canada. While other groups that are not religious also try to retain their own identity, my claim is that these groups are less successful, not that they are unsuccessful. The Amish, for example, have a more distinct way of life than do Italian-Americans.

Following God's will, members of the Amish, the Hutterites, and ultra-orthodox Jews shun many of society's mainstream institutions. They don't attend the universities and colleges that others do. They don't aspire to work for large corporations or get a government job. They don't ask to have their history taught in public schools or have others come into their community to learn about them. Members are expected to follow the norms of the community; if they don't, they will be shunned and excluded. Unsurprisingly, members of these groups look among themselves as their primary community. They fail the moral requirements of liberal citizenship. They are not particu-larly interested in knowing much or thinking about politics (with some ultra-orthodox Jews being an exception, something I discuss below). Being good participants in democratic discussions doesn't interest them. This is the model of cultural pluralism: distinct communities with particular cultural practices that are rarely shared with others.

When these groups also try to ignore the state, however, and simply live among themselves, they do not harm citizenship. If people live in an insular community that ignores the moral requirements of liberal citizenship, and they make few or no public claims, this is not cause for worry. When this hap-pens, the members of these groups are what I call partial citizens.[5] When members of these groups do not involve themselves in politics, when they do not press the state for financial favours or funds to establish institutions for themselves, when they do not ask for things that will harm other citizens, they need not be thought of as full members of the state. These communities must supply economic opportunities for their members, support their elderly, educate their children, and supply a satisfying spiritual life and fill their members' leisure time. It may be that there will be some reliance on the state, perhaps for educating its young. There also may be some interaction, usually economic, between the community and the outside world. The separation from the state and the mainstream culture is not complete, but it is large; it is con-siderably and obviously larger than it is for others. It is also difficult. If a large percentage of the population became partial citizens, there might be cause for worry, but to shun many institutions of the modern world is something that few people will be able to do. It's no accident that many of these groups' members were born into their group. They didn't have to unlearn much of what they learned at an early age to become a member. It is hard to imagine the number of partial citizens becoming very large.

By using the idea of partial citizenship I want to recognize the ambiguous relationship members of some insular communities have with the state and other citizens. Partial citizenship rests upon something of a bargain: as long as the group stays away from the common life of the country, and doesn't try to eat at the public trough, then society can agree that citizenship has fewer claims on them than on others. I do not think the idea of partial citizenship should be introduced directly into law, though it may have legal ramifications. Rather, I would encourage the state's official to recognize that groups like the Amish and the Hutterites are unlike other citizens, and sometimes they should accommodate these groups. This accommodation will be largely based at the second level of citizenship: the state need not worry about trying to instil the liberal virtues in partial citizens. Of course, not all requests for accommodation should be granted, but as long as the accommodations do not violate the first level of citizenship, and members of the group pay the same taxes as others and do not harm others, they can be accommodated.

A few examples can illustrate the possibilities and limits of accommodation for partial citizens. Partial citizens can be accommodated when it comes to education. They should certainly have to teach (or have the state teach) their children basic skills, but they do not have to teach them the sorts of critical thinking skills we want future citizens to have. The Amish travel by horse and buggy and so traffic officials should plan to accommodate their slow means of transportation. Yet partial citizens should not be exempt from taxes. Partial citizens receive protection from the state's military and police, benefit from its regulation of air and water, and receive other public goods. Since all citizens, partial or not, benefit from public goods, all should have to pay for them. Moreover, partial citizens still compete economically with other citizens, and they should not be given an unfair economic advantage over their competitors by paying fewer taxes.

Just as partial citizens should pay taxes, so too should they contribute in times of war. If they refuse to fight, accommodation means that alternative service should be found for them; they should not be allowed to skip service altogether. Besides paying for public goods, limits on accommodations are important so they do not give people an incentive to become partial citizens. It should be hard to be a partial citizen, otherwise citizenship might be threatened. Accommodations should allow partial citizens to live in their own community, but they do not live in their own state, and so they must pay Caesar his due.

Partial citizens contribute to a multicultural society. Having a very different way of life, sometimes speaking a different language, often wearing different sorts of dress, occasionally shunning some conveniences of modern life, these groups are clearly culturally different from the rest of us. Though members of these groups never think in public terms like good citizens do, thinking of them as partial citizens allows us to see that they don't threaten citizenship. They don't vote, run for office, or involve themselves in policy debates. They may not think in public terms, but because they don't make public demands it is not a matter of concern that they do not act like good citizens.

The right to exit

By now, nearly everyone knows that the Amish do not want to send their children to public high schools. Because their children will not have the option to become astronauts or pianists, some argue, they are harmed. If people want to become Amish, this argument runs, they ought to choose this way of life; they shouldn't be trained for it. The steady flow of people who leave the Amish community, however, suggests that the Amish are more autonomous than many realize.[6] Still, this worry about the Amish is the right one: no one should be forced, or nearly forced, to live a certain kind of life. People born in insular communities ought to be able to leave if they wish.

I can best illustrate the dilemmas of the right to exit with the Hutterites. Like the Amish, the Hutterites are an Anabaptist group that fled Europe to avoid persecution. Most Hutterites live in Western Canada where they live in small colonies of about a hundred people. When a colony gets too big, about 150 people, it splits into two with the mother colony taking on half of the daughter colony's debt. Everyone works according to his or her abilities, and everyone's needs (which are defined minimally) are cared for. Everything in a colony is owned communally. There is absolutely no private or personal property, except what is kept by stealth. People get to keep a few things as their own, like clothes and some personal effects, but they are not owned by the users. The Hutterites are farmers and because they work hard and reinvest much of their earnings into farm equipment, their colonies are often quite wealthy. They don't use the wealth for luxury items, or even for items that most North Americans consider essential, because they live simple lives.[7] Saved money that is not used for new farming equipment or for kitchen appliances is used to help begin new colonies.

The difficulty here is one of having the economic means to exit, which a court case illustrates. In the early 1960s four members—all brothers—of a Hutterite colony began to stray from the faith, as they became converted to the beliefs of the Radio Church of God. When this became apparent, the Hutterites tried to show the Hofer brothers the error of their ways. The brothers, however, showed no remorse and in fact began to practise their new beliefs in the colony, flouting many of the colony's rules. The Hutterites expelled the brothers from the colony and the brothers retaliated by suing, saying they deserved their share of the colony's assets.[8]

The force of the Hofer's contention is clear: they worked hard in the colony, and it is unfair that because they changed their mind on a few religious matters they became penniless and homeless. The colony had a legal charter (as all Hutterite colonies do) stating that members who are expelled have no claim on the colony's property. A strictly legalistic approach, however, won't do.[9] A legal document that says in exchange for work you will be given food, along with clothes and shelter but no money makes the coercion of members quite possible. A member may feel unable to leave the colony since he can't take any money or possessions with him. Without any assets, a member's choices are quite restricted. A liberalism committed to giving people choices about their lives ought to be concerned when the choice to leave one's community is severely circumscribed. The liberal state ought to be wary of a contract that means a person will work hard in his adult life (and part of his adolescence) but receive no money. Not all contracts are legal in the liberal State. No one can agree to become a slave or an indentured servant. While the Hutterites are neither, they give up considerable rights as members of their community.

Yet the Hutterite community cannot remain true to its religious ideals if it must give every member a proportionate share every time someone leaves. If every person who left received a proportionate share of the colony, many colonies would collapse. Since colonies are small, it would take only a few members to leave at around the same time for the colony to disintegrate. If liberals side with the Hofers in their case (which they lost), this would reveal the extent that toleration is predicated on an individualistic conception of property. Groups that had a communal view of property would find themselves out of luck in the liberal state. No one can be forced to be a good liberal citizen, however, and liberal tolerance means that the state should allow those who want to live differently. No one forced the Hofer brothers to work in the Hutterite colony after they became adults. They could have left when they were younger, and worked outside the colony.

Some may wonder if the Hutterites really understand that they can leave the colony; almost certainly they do. Few members of insular groups are unaware of the outside world. The lure of modern culture is rather powerful, and it's hard to hide people from it. People who try to shield their children from outside influences rarely completely succeed. Furthermore, small groups must routinely deal with outsiders for many reasons. The Hutterites regularly make trips to town to sell their goods, buy various items, to meet other Hutterites, and sometimes go to the bar to drink. The Hutterites don't baptize children, but wait until adulthood to do so, which means the decision to remain part of the Hutterite community must be a deliberate one. Moreover, while Hutterite children attend school with other Hutterites in the colonies, they are taught by non-Hutterite state teachers. On many days of the week, Hutterite children are taught about the world from a very worldly perspective.

Despite these outside influences, it is difficult for someone raised in a colony to refuse to become a Hutterite, since doing so means leaving the colony; one's family and the world one knows best are left behind as well. This certainly is not easy to do, but this is not a problem peculiar to Hutterite children. Many children have difficulty straying from the path their parents set out for them. Hutterite parents are not the only ones who try to influence their children to follow their path. The fact that the Hutterites (or the Amish) heavily influence their children should not bother liberals. Nor should their education because the Hutterites are educated by state teachers. Some may object to the lack of diversity in Hutterite schools, but their nearest neighbours are rarely close so the only option is busing over long distances, which is hardly an attractive alternative.

One key difference between Hutterite parents and others is that the choice Hutterites give their children is a stark one. They say, in effect, 'either you live like us, or you are severed from our community.' Since the Hutterites prescribe the way one lives in a rather detailed fashion, if one chooses the Hutterite way, one is giving up a considerable part of one's individuality. Yet if one rejects their way of life, one's ties to the community are usually completely severed. A stark choice indeed.

Other families that successfully influence their children rarely give their children such a severe choice. They may influence their children, but when the children are grown they will probably choose their own clothes to wear, what they want to eat each day, and where they want to live. They can decide what movie or television show to watch (unlike the Hutterites, they can choose to watch movies and television). They may choose their occupation and perhaps deviate from how their parents worship. Few families present their children with the sort of choice that the Hutterites do. A stark choice, however, is still a choice: as uneasy as liberals may be with the choice the Hutterites give their children, there are no liberal grounds for insisting that the Hutterites give their children more options. Doing so would interfere in the way the Hutterites run their affairs. As long as they do not physically harm their members or prevent people from leaving, the liberal response to the Hutterites has to remain rather muted.

Another reason why groups like the Hutterites make liberals uneasy is that while the Hutterites may understand that there is another world out there, and they may see it from afar and occasionally from up close, they are always spectators of this world. The Hutterites surround themselves with fellow believers; they are not members of multiple groups. Their children have no meaningful interaction with non-Hutterite children. Yet here too liberals cannot do very much. If parents want to raise their children in a sheltered environment, the liberal State cannot prevent them from doing so. It is one thing if parents refuse to let their children leave the house, do not teach them how to read and write, and raise their children so they are incapable of understanding the world outside their home. But this does not describe the Hutterites; even if they do raise their children in a sheltered way, that's true for many parents in liberal states.

Still, the issue of the right to exist from insular communities dangles. Without any money or much knowledge of how the outside world works, it must be a rather frightening and daunting experience to leave the community.[10] Many members may feel unable to leave. An older member may realize that he made a mistake joining the Hutterites, but he should not be forever bound to a decision made when he was 18. People ought to be able to change their mind. Without any money, however, the option to leave the community is severely restricted. The difficulties in finding their way in the outside world may lead some young adults to accept baptism in the community even though they prefer to leave. To enable people to leave by easing the transition from the Hutterites to the outside world, a small fund should be set aside by the Hutterites for members that leave their community. The amount of money given to someone who leaves the Hutterites should not be an incentive to leave, because then the state would be nearly closing down the community. No one should become wealthy by leaving, but a few thousand dollars would help members leave the community if they wish. Some money will give members the choice to leave. This money is not meant to be compensation for work. Though by the time they are 18 many Hutterites have worked for several years on the colony, many children work for family businesses for little compensation beyond the food, shelter, and clothing that we expect parents to supply their children.

The exit fund will allow members to leave, meaning that members who want to leave will have chosen to stay for as long as they remained members of the colony. Older members are compensated for their work by the food, shelter, and clothing they are given and by the intangible goods they receive by living in an unusual community. This may not be adequate compensation (that will depend on the kind of work done by the member) but the option to leave needs to be balanced with the right of a community to live differently in the liberal state. The Hutterites won't set up this fund voluntarily but they should be forced to do so.

It is difficult to leave other insular communities as well. But apostates in the Amish or ultra-orthodox Jewish communities can and do own property, so leaving doesn't have such harmful consequences as leaving the Hutterites does. They can plan to leave beforehand, and save up money to move if they wish. The Hutterites cannot do this. Still, there are two worries when it comes to exit. Young adults may own very little, know little about how to live in the outside world, and have few job skills. (This is more likely with ultra-orthodox Jews than with the Amish, who are usually raised on farms. Some ultra-orthodox Jewish boys know a great deal about Jewish texts, but little else.) The second worry arises with older members, who when they leave the community may find themselves pressured to sell their house at a cheap price, or find that the clientele to their business suddenly evaporated. To ensure that there really is a right to exit, organizations are needed to help members of communities of partial citizens to leave them if they wish. These organizations (they can be run by the government, but need not be) can help apostates leave their communities without becoming destitute by giving them legal advice, or advice on how to re-establish their businesses. They can help train young adults for jobs or help them go to college. Again, these organizations should not make people who leave wealthy, but ensure that the right to exit really exists. Just as some countries assist immigrants adjust to their new home, partial citizens (and full citizens in insular communities) who become full citizens need assistance as well. Partial citizens are not immigrants, but certainly there are resemblances between the two. We should not, however, expect these organizations to become very busy since leaving one's family and community behind is hardly an easy decision to make.

Though the Hutterites should be forced to create an exit fund, few other groups should be made to replicate them.[11] My larger point here is not about the Hutterites, though, but about the right to exit. Barring those groups that completely shield their members from the outside world, there is little liberals can do about ensuring that all people have the psychological resources to make a truly autonomous choice about whether they will follow the paths of their parents or not. Education is the place most liberals look at, and education certainly matters a lot (it matters enough for me to discuss it below), but as long as parents have a large influence over their children and private schools exist, education can only do so much to ensure that children will become autonomous.

Partial citizens must comply with the legal demands of liberal citizenship; the first level of citizenship applies to them and they must allow their members to become full citizens if they so choose. They must educate their children to a large enough degree so they can leave their community if they wish. This does not mean calculus courses and courses in French (the sort of things taught in the public schools many liberals wish existed in large numbers); it means teaching reading and basic knowledge in maths and science. Members of communities of partial citizens should have the basic skills to join the larger community of full citizens if they wish. Nor can partial citizens physically harm their children.

The right to exit from insular communities and their need to adhere to the first level of citizenship suggests some limits to the concept of partial citizenship. Partial citizens are not quite a 'nation within a nation' as Amy Gutmann suggests in her remarks critical of the idea.[12] This supplies some answers to some apparently difficult cases that arise in a multicultural society. What about groups that practise female circumcision? Or try to deny their children standard medical treatment, even if the alternative seems to be death? The problem here is not that these groups harm citizenship. The problem is that they harm particular citizens (even if their citizenship is partial). In these cases the solution is clear. Physical harm to children is simply not allowed in a liberal democracy, even in the name of diversity or tolerance. This sort of harm will give these children permanent pain unnecessarily for the rest of their lives. Women can opt for clitorectomies and adults can choose to forgo standard medical treatment. Liberal democracies should allow people to harm themselves, but not others, even their children. People that need not adhere to these standards of citizenship are those that live in non-liberal sovereign communities, those communities that really are nations within a nation.[13]

III. CULTURAL PLURALISM AND THE
THREAT TO CITIZENSHIP

The multicultural threat to citizenship comes when groups want to retain their identity like partial citizens do, but want the state to help them to do so. This is where the line between cultural pluralism and inclusive multiculturalism becomes blurred. Some groups aren't particularly interested in inclusion or citizenship. They simply want some of the benefits of citizenship without acting like citizens. I argued above that partial citizenship rests on something of a bargain: partial citizens make few public claims, but don't try to extract resources from the state. Some groups, however, make few public claims but try to get as many state resources as they can.

Kiryas Joel

A recent example of this is the case of the Kiryas Joel school district. All of the residents of the village of Kiryas Joel, New York, are members of the Satmar Hasidim, one of the branches of the Jewish Hasidic movement. Like all Hasidim, the Satmar distinguish themselves from secular society in clear ways. They look different. The boys wear black coats, pants and hat, white shirt, and have long side curls; the girls wear long dresses with long sleeves. Married women usually shave their heads and wear wigs, and sometimes hats. They speak Yiddish among themselves, and study and pray in Hebrew. For most, English is their third language. They are not interested in popular American culture. They rarely watch television, listen to the radio, or see movies; they read Yiddish newspapers. They do not attend secular institutions of higher learning. Most work as teachers in their community, in low-skilled jobs, or have small businesses that mostly (but not always) cater to their community. They don't hold public office outside the communities they control. They are interested in living a pious, religious life, a life that is inspired by their leader, the rebbe, and his predecessors and that centres around the study of sacred Jewish texts.

  In many ways the Satmar appear to be partial citizens. Separate from the secular world to a large degree, the Satmar try to keep to themselves. Unsurprisingly, nearly all the schoolchildren in the village of Kiryas Joel attend private yeshivas, as do most Satmar children in the USA. However, some of the children are disabled and so teaching them requires more money than teaching the able-bodied. To get more funds, the Satmar established a school for the disabled in their community that was taught by public school teachers. In response to two Supreme Court rulings, however, the state removed its teachers, and told the Satmar their children would have to attend a secular school near by.[14] The Satmar eventually refused to do this, but still wanted the extra state funds available to teach the disabled. To get more funds, the village convinced the New York state legislature and then Governor Mario Cuomo to create a public school district for itself. This was despite state educational policy that called for consolidating small school districts into larger ones instead of maintaining (not to mention creating) smaller districts that are relatively expensive to run. The school initially had only about fifty full-time students, with only half of them from Kiryas Joel. Eventually the school grew to 138 full-time and 200 part-time students, with over half of the students from communities other than Kiryas Joel.[15] This small school wasn't a school for the disabled in Kiryas Joel; it was a school for Satmar disabled children. The school, however, was not a yeshiva. The subjects were secular, and the community's rabbis granted a special exemption to the students so they could sit together in co-educational courses. For the Satmar these were important concessions, though liberals take it for granted that public schools teach a secular curriculum to boys and girls in the same classroom. The US Supreme Court struck down the school district in 1994 as unconstitutional. However, the state legislature rewrote the law to reinstitute the school district.[16]

The advantage of this law is that it generously supports cultural pluralism. The problem with the school district is that it harms citizenship with public support and funds. Part of the purpose of public schools is to get children from different backgrounds together. Heterogeneous schools allow different students to learn about one another and to learn how to work together. When students learn these sorts of things they make for better citizens. Part of good citizenship is knowing how to work with others and learning about people who are different. Good citizens do not only think of themselves or their primary group (if they have one) when they act as citizens. Rather, they will think of the people who will be affected by different public policies and laws and consider them when taking a position on an issue. They will learn that others have interests, and sometimes democracy calls for a compromise between those with different interests. Even if schools are not enough to create good citizens, they help do so in important ways.

The Satmar, however, are not interested in the virtues of citizenship. They worry about the effects of having their children mix with those different from them. The parents did not want to send their children to a secular school because of the 'panic, fear, and trauma [the children] suffered in leaving their own community and being with people whose ways were so different.'[17] The reason why Satmar children should attend public schools from the point of view of citizenship is precisely why the Satmar didn't want their children to attend these schools.

Because the Satmar want to use public funds to educate their children as Satmar and only Satmar and not as citizens they break away from being partial citizens. By trying to lay claims to public funds, the insularity of the Satmar begins to crack. The Satmar are not partial citizens for other reasons as well. Despite their desire for insularity they take public funds in several ways.

While some Satmar are quite wealthy businessmen, and give generously to their community, others are very poor and receive food stamps and live in public housing.[18] The Satmar also vote. It is because they vote that politicians are willing to listen to their desire for a special school district. The Satmar usually vote in a bloc (though this is not always the case), following the wishes of their rebbe; a high percentage of them vote as well.[19] Their religious views make them a potent political force, though in Kiryas Joel they are only mildly concerned with politics. Because their involvement in public life is limited, however, the Satmar in Kiryas Joel could become partial citizens relatively easily. If they chose this route, however, the issue of public funding for their school district would never come up.

Public funds should be used for things that are in the public interest. Encouraging citizenship is in the public interest and on this count the separate school district for the Satmar fails. Some argue, though, that there is also a public interest in supporting different forms of life.[20] This is a little too strong. There is a clear public interest in supporting citizenship; different forms of life can be supported *if* this support doesn't harm citizenship. Forms of life that violate the first level of citizenship should not be supported. If liberal society will only support educational systems that work to create liberal citizens with liberal values, then there will be a loss of a certain kind of pluralism. The Satmar illustrate that there sometimes is a trade-off between citizenship and cultural pluralism.

When this trade-off does appear the USA should choose to support citizenship over multiculturalism. The state has a vital interest in encouraging citizenship, and it should not go out of its way to do otherwise. While public funds for a Satmar school threatens citizenship only mildly, there are other groups in the USA that would like the same kind of public support that the Satmar receive. The problem in the USA is that public institutions are increasingly under siege; private schools are growing in the USA and many would like public funds. The increased privatization of public life, of which this is a part, is a threat to citizenship. The principle used to support the special school district for the Satmar may very well be used by others who also want public funds to support their group, a move that would greatly threaten citizenship and public institutions. It is often religious groups that want public resources for their parochial schools, but they are not the only ones. One version of Afrocentricity popular in some public schools teaches the 'African people as being the wellspring of creativity and knowledge on which the foundation of all science, technology and engineering rests.'[21] This Afrocentric curriculum not only teaches many lies but is aimed only at black students. Just as the Satmar should not have their own public schools neither should Afrocentrists like these.

To be sure, some religious schools and private schools of all kinds do an excellent job of teaching the virtues of citizenship. Some private schools, however, are more interested in raising Christians or orthodox Jews than citizens.

Furthermore, if more public funds leaked over to private schools, then even more public schools would be left with only poor students or children of adults who care little about education. These sorts of schools rarely teach much to their students.

The best way to ensure that citizenship is taught well in schools is to restrict the use of private schools. In the USA, though, this suggestion will not go very far and not only for private reasons. In the nineteenth century Protestants used the public schools to marginalize Catholics by insisting on using the King James bible in schools; segregated twentieth-century schools served many students badly. There is also the obvious concern that many public schools are in rather poor shape, but if all students had to attend public schools they would get more support as more parts of society had a clear stake in them. We would see a more concerted effort to make public schools better. Still, the history of the public schools in the USA suggests that having an escape route for dissenters is an important option to retain. Moreover, this option will allow for a more pluralistic society. Since schools in the USA are run by local governments, there is not too much danger of a centralized government insisting upon homogeneity in the schools. Still, local governments must be secular, while the most robust form of difference in society is religion. Giving religions the space to run their own schools will mean that liberal tolerance will allow for religious diversity.

The danger is that private schools will tug liberal society towards the model of cultural pluralism and decreased support for public institutions and citizenship. If this happens, the disadvantaged in society will be in even more trouble than they are currently. Some private schools harm citizenship; others do not. But all (good) public schools buttress citizenship. The more support the state gives private schools, the fewer good public schools we will have, and the more private schools we will have, many of which will have little concern for citizenship. This means that we should retain the option of private schools but the state should not support them. Similarly, this means that the state shouldn't fund public schools designed and used only for particular groups. Refusing the Satmar their school district hardly means that the Satmars' way life is no longer sustainable; it merely means that the public will not support it. Non-liberal forms of life that adhere to the requirements of the first level of citizenship should be allowed in the liberal state, but they are not entitled to state subsidy.

IV. THE REACTION TO MULTICULTURALISM AND THE RIGHT TO CULTURE

My argument does not rest on the belief that people have a right to culture. People do have a right to culture (it's hard to imagine how people can live without one) but they do not have a right to a particular culture, even if it is their own. If a group wants to protect its culture, its members should live in an insular community where they cannot expect state support. Liberal tolerance means that if they do this they can live as they please, as long as they follow the strictures of the first level of citizenship. If a group wants to live in mainstream society, have access to public institutions and resources, and make public claims, then it may have to change some of its cultural values. The problem with the claim that people have a right to a particular culture is that most cultures have anti-liberal democratic values in them. Implementing inclusive multiculturalism and fulfilling the claims of citizenship will in fact change American culture (and many others) considerably. The argument for inclusive multiculturalism is not predicated on the idea that black or Jewish or other hyphenated Americans have been denied a right to live in their culture. Rather, the argument is that the mainstream culture has erected barriers that exclude many groups, and that many of these barriers should fall. If these walls do come down, then both the mainstream culture and the formerly excluded cultures will change. Indeed, it is often the case that some parts of the culture of excluded groups have arisen precisely because of their exclusion, just as the mainstream society's culture is predicated on this exclusion.[22]

One way inclusive multiculturalism changes the culture of a society is by asking people to lose their grip on particular images of citizenship they have, something that is not easy to do. But images of citizenship have changed in the past and they can change again. Women are now citizens in the Western democracies. Black Americans are now legally equal citizens. These and other changes in citizenship, though, took a considerable amount of time, and caused a burden on many outsiders clamouring to get in. A static image of citizenship is more of a threat to citizenship than most forms of multiculturalism. Unfortunately, many of the fights to hold onto an exclusive version of the citizenship that took place in the USA during the massive immigrant waves between 1880 and 1920 are being repeated, both in the USA and in Europe. It is this reaction to inclusive multiculturalism, rather than multiculturalism itself, that threatens citizenship. Some in the USA want laws that say that bureaucrats must conduct state business in English, or they want to keep the curriculum unchanged from the old, racist, and sexist days of the 1950s. In France the state has decided that Muslim schoolgirls cannot wear head scarfs in public schools; some of these girls do not want to give up their head scarfs and so are denied a public education. By refusing to accommodate the Muslim girls the French government has pushed many of them further into the arms of the Muslim community, and away from full French citizenship. Britain funds some religious schools that adhere to the standards of a national curriculum, but no Muslim school has been able to receive government funding. While I doubt the British government should fund any religious schools, as long as it does it should fund Muslims schools. Funding these schools enhances citizenship because it means treating Muslims equal to other citizens. It also ensures that students at these schools will learn the national curriculum and not one centred only around Islam.[23]

V. WHY CARE ABOUT CITIZENSHIP?

While liberals will usually opt for strengthening diversity and inclusive citizenship over cultural pluralism, this begs an important question: why care about citizenship more than cultural pluralism? One can understand the trade-off between the two and decide that protecting the integrity of different cultures, even illiberal ones, is more important than fortifying citizenship.[24] Citizenship has become increasingly important to political theorists, who have rediscovered the citizen over the past decade or so. My argument here that liberal citizens have certain virtues is grounded in many of these recent discussions.[25] The virtues that liberals call for are not meant to increase loyalty to the state or a blind devotion to the common good, but to encourage people to use democratic processes wisely. Since citizens have power in the liberal democratic state if they don't use that power in liberal ways, the state over time will become something other than liberal, and possibly undemocratic as well. Not every citizen needs to have all the liberal virtues for the liberal state to remain so—this is why illiberal forms of life can exist in the liberal state—but if enough stray away from liberal principles, then a worry about the liberal state's future sets in.

Still, I don't think citizenship should automatically be supported over cultural pluralism. I think that this should usually be the case, but it's possible to imagine cases where cultural pluralism trumps citizenship. In a state where strong support for public institutions exists, some support for small cultural communities might not threaten citizenship. In a state where other citizens would not look at the Satmar case as a possible precedent to enable them to use public funds for their own private uses, supporting the Satmar school district wouldn't threaten citizenship. A Satmar community in, say, the homogeneous Sweden of old could probably have been supported without a threat to citizenship. The Swedes would not have been obligated to support the Satmar, but they could have done so without too much worry.

In states with an extensive immigrant tradition and with considerable diversity, however, and where support for public institutions is sometimes weak, supporting citizenship becomes important. In a diverse society people have to work harder to understand one another and to act together politically. Cooperation and trust can't be assumed among citizens; these virtues must be encouraged. Perhaps one of the most dangerous threats to citizenship, however, comes from inequality in wealth and power; when combined with cultural differences this threat is sometimes deadly. In one model of politics, each group tries to get as many resources from the state as possible. When some Hasidic Jews try to use state resources to help their own they can be seen as simply engaging in time-honoured interest group politics. This form of politics, however, where groups are only interested in using public resources for private purposes results in a race for state resources that is won by the people with the most political muscle. Since political muscle is often tied to wealth, this is the sort of formula that will usually favour the rich or the powerful and hurt the poor.[26] This sort of politics happens under guises other than multiculturalism and happens all too frequently. One can realize that private interests will almost certainly always have a role in politics while understanding that if private interests are the only force in politics, citizenship is threatened.

This politics where the wealthy and powerful take what they want from the government and ignore those more needy, or where they decide they don't need public government and establish their private governments with walled-in neighbourhoods, letting in only those with the proper identification, is the sort of politics that threatens citizenship. Those outside the walls are sometimes white but are often black or Muslim. Inclusive multiculturalism is right to fight for including those who are excluded because they have some different cultural practices, and sometimes this will be enough for citizenship. Frequently, however, the route to inclusion and to enhancing citizenship needs to include ways to get over—or reduce—the barriers of wealth and power. Accepting the diversity that multiculturalism is a part of will allow more people to enter what the walls, but the poor will still remain outside. A robust version of citizenship, however, will work towards ensuring that everyone can build walls with the neighbours and friends. It will also ensure that the walls have many doors.

NOTES

This essay was written while I was a Visiting Laurence S. Rockefeller Fellow at the University Center for Human Values at Princeton University over the 1995–6 academic year. Many thanks to the Center for providing the ideal space to think about and write this paper. Earlier versions of this paper were presented at the Political Philosophy Colloquium at Princeton University, February 1996 and at the European University Institute, Conference on Multiculturalism, Minorities and Citizenship, Florence, Italy, April 1996. Audiences at both places provided helpful comments and questions. The comments of an anonymous reviewer for Oxford University Press also helped me improve this essay.

1. This definition of diversity is taken from Jeff Spinner-Halev, 'Difference and Diversity in an Egalitarian Democracy', *Journal of Political Philosophy* 3/3 (Sept. 1995): 262. In my discussion I will not discuss groups that have a reasonable claim and aspire to some sort of political sovereignty. Typically, groups like the Quebecois should be thought of in terms of nationalism, not multiculturalism.

2. I also believe that in the first level of citizenship should have a guarantee of what John Rawls calls primary goods—housing, food, and so on—but since this is not important for my argument here I will be silent on this aspect of citizenship.

3. I explain the demands of citizenship since liberalism has become attached to democracy in Jeff Spinner, *The Boundaries of Citizenship: Race, Ethnicity and Nationality in the Liberal State* (Baltimore: Johns Hopkins University Press, 1994), 92–5. See also Stephen Macedo, *Liberal Virtues: Citizenship, Virtue, and Community in Liberal Constitutionalism* (Oxford: Oxford University Press, 1990).

4. A black minister recently complained to me that in his city the Jewish temple celebrated King's birthday, which always drew a big crowd. This angered him, since he saw King's birthday as a holiday whose celebration should be led by black people. But once it became a national holiday, 'ownership' of it spread to the whole political community.

5. I introduced this idea in Spinner, *Boundaries*: ch. 5. See also Stephen Macedo, 'Liberal Civic Education: The Case of God v. John Rawls?,' *Ethics*, 105 (Apr. 1995).

6. Amy Gutmann argues that the Amish should have to go to public high schools in 'Civic Education and Social Diversity', *Ethics*, 105 (Apr. 1995). About 20% of the Amish leave their communities, however, which shows a considerable degree of autonomy.

7. The Hutterites don't own televisions or radios; each colony has a few cars and trucks so members can go into the city when needed. They wear simple clothes, live in community-built housing, and eat together in the common dining hall. They rarely take long trips. To a large degree, the colonies are self-sufficient. While they buy certain large items that they can't make themselves, they build their own housing and furnishing, weave their own clothes, and make their own wine.

8. *Hofer* v. *Hofer* (1970) 13 D.L.R. (3d) 1 (Supreme Court of Canada).

9. Although the colony should be treated like a corporation when it comes to its interactions with outsiders. For example, when it comes to liability issues if the colony isn't treated like a corporation people with claims against a member of the colony wouldn't be able to collect anything. There would be no way to tax the colony's income. Other similar issue may arise, meaning that in the colonies' external relations with others we should think of them as a corporation.

10. While Hutterites are aware of the outside world, this does not mean they have the necessary knowledge to navigate through it very well. How to find a place to stay for the night, how to look for a job, how to open up a bank account— mundane matters like these which are necessary to live in the world outside the colonies aren't known by most Hutterites.

11. Few groups hold property communally. One that does, Israeli kibbutzim, give departing members some form of compensation.

12. See Gutmann, 'Civic Education': 570.

13. I'm thinking here of native peoples in the USA and Canada. Native Americans and First Peoples in Canada are better thought of as sovereign communities. Because many of their communities have been damaged by white people, the issue of sovereignty is a complicated one. Many of these communities are too small to hope to become self-sustaining in the near future; other communities are so poor that they need help from the USA and Canada to survive. Sovereignty may be the appropriate goal for these communities, but their actual situations may mean that this is a goal that may take many years to be achieved.

14. *Aguilar* v. *Felton*, 473 US 402 (1985) and *School District of Grand Rapids* v. *Ball* 473 US 373 (1985).

15. Jerome R. Mintz, *Hasidic People: A Place in the New World* (Cambridge: Harvard University Press, 1992): 320, 324.

16. The old law singled out Kiryas Joel as a separate school district. The new law is written in general language, but it just so happens that the only village to meet all the 'general' criteria laid out in the new law is Kiryas Joel. This new law has been struck down by in New York State courts. It has not yet been appealed to the Supreme Court.

17. *Board of Education of Kiryas Joel* v. *Grumet* 114 US 2490 (1994).

18. Some public housing in Brooklyn was specially designed for the Satmar. This housing has two sinks in each apartment, so the Satmar can keep their strict dietary rules. Some public housing also has 'Sabbath elevators', which automatically stop on each floor on Saturdays. This relieves the Satmar from actually causing the elevator to stop on a particular floor, which would violate their interpretation of how one is to keep the Sabbath holy.

19. The Satmar are not always monolithic. Sometimes, disputes within the community arise and people defy the rebbe. This happened in the mid-1980s, after the death of the old, revered rebbe. Some people disliked the new rebbe, and opposed him in a variety of ways. Over time, however, this opposition has waned though it still persists. The opponents to the rebbe ultimately have two choices. They can leave the community or make peace with the rebbe. Rebbe elections do not happen at regular intervals.

20. This argument is made by Avishai Margalit and Moshe Halbertal, 'Liberalism and the Right to Culture', *Social Research*, 61/3 (Autumn 1994).

21. Irving M. Klotz, 'Multicultural Perspectives in Science Education: One Prescription for Failure', *Phi Delta Kappa*, 75/3 (1993). Klotz provides a devastating criticism of one popular but deeply flawed version of Afrocentricity.

22. I elaborate on this claim in Spinner-Halev, 'Difference and Diversity'.

23. A worry about Muslim schools is that many are segregated by sex. The concern here is that these segregated schools will just increase the control of Muslim men over their daughters. The response to this, however, is to ensure that Muslim schools for girls do a good job teaching the national curriculum. There is nothing inherently subordinate about a girls' school. The case for this inequality needs to be made, not assumed.

24. Chandran Kukathas, 'Cultural Toleration', in *Ethnicity and Group Rights*, ed. Will Kymlicka and Ian Shapiro (New York: New York University Press, 1996).

25. Ronald Beiner, *Theorizing Citizenship* (Albany: SUNY, 1995); Stephen Macedo, *Liberal Virtues: Citizenship, Virtue and Community in Liberal Constitutionalism* (Oxford: Oxford University Press, 1990); Amy Gutmann, *Democratic Education* (Princeton: Princeton University Press, 1989); William Galston, *Liberal Purposes: Goods, Virtues and Diversity in the Liberal State* (Cambridge: Cambridge University Press, 1991).

26. Being rich and powerful often go together, but the Satmar show that political power can also rest on organization and the ability to deliver votes; wealth helps in this regard, but is not necessary.

5

The Paradox of Multicultural Vulnerability: Individual Rights, Identity Groups, and the State

AYELET SHACHAR

Marriage is a union between *two* persons—*one* man and *one* woman. . . .
Both give themselves to each other forever, because they give themselves
to each other wholly. . . .
　　The conception of marriage involves that the women who surrenders her
personality shall at the same time surrender the possession of all her property and her exclusive rights in the state. . . . To the state both husband and
wife appear as only one person; what the one does is as valid as if the other
has also done it. All public legal acts are performed only by the husband . . .
　　Women, therefore, do really exercise the right of suffrage—not immediately, however, in their own person, . . . but—through the influence which
results from the nature of the marriage relation.

> J. G. Fichte, 1762–1814, *The Science of Rights*

Custom may familiarize mankind with the violation of their natural rights
to such an extent, that even among those who have lost or been deprived of
these rights, no one thinks of reclaiming them, or is even conscious that they
have suffered any injustice.
　　Certain of these violations . . . have escaped the notice of philosophers
and legislators, even while concerning themselves zealously to establish the
common rights of individuals of the human race, and in this way to lay the
foundation of political institutions. For example, have they not all violated
the principle of equality of rights in tranquilly depriving one-half of the human
race of the right of taking part in the formation of laws by the exclusion of
women from the rights of citizenship?

> Marie-Jean-Antione-Nicolas Caritat, Marquis de Condorcet, 1743–1794,
> *The First Essay on the Political Rights of Women*

I. PRELIMINARY REMARKS

Multicultural accommodation in its various legal manifestations (e.g. exempting group members from certain laws, or awarding identity groups some degree
of self-governance) aims to ensure that identity groups have the option to
maintain what Robert Cover calls their *nomos*: the normative universe in

which law and cultural narrative are inseparably related.[1] The move towards
multicultural accommodation is generally justified in terms of promoting
the 'participation and inclusion . . . [of] groups with different circumstances
or forms of life . . . without shedding their distinct identities.'[2] Multiculturalism
presents a threat to citizenship, however, if pro-identity group policies, aimed
at levelling the playing field among minority groups and the larger society,
systematically allow the maltreatment of certain categories of group members,
such as women, effectively annulling their citizenship status.

The following discussion considers one significant way in which multiculturalism threatens citizenship, examining the deleterious effects of multicultural accommodation policies upon women. More specifically, the analysis
highlights the tension between family law accommodation and citizenship
rights which arises when an identity group member's rights *as a citizen* are
violated *by her identity group's family law practices*, a phenomenon I call the
'paradox of multicultural vulnerability'.

II. THE MULTICULTURAL CITIZENSHIP MODEL

From the time of antiquity, citizenship has been defined as the legal status
of membership in a political community. This status entitled every citizen to
'whatever prerogatives and . . . whatever responsibilities that [we]re attached to
membership.'[3] Already under Roman jurisprudence, '[a] citizen came to mean
someone free to act by law, free to ask and expect the law's protection.'[4]
With the creation of the nation-state, criteria were established to specify the
conditions for acquiring and maintaining full citizenship. As a legal status,
citizenship connotes a unique, reciprocal, and unmediated political relationship between the individual and the political community.[5] In democratic societies, citizens are endowed with political rights and individual liberties; and it
is on their behalf that the state is understood to act.

Due to the anti-*ancien regime* legacy of modern conceptions of citizenship, individual rights are generally prioritized over assertions of legal entitlements based on subnational group affiliation. Thus liberal, civic republican,
or ethnocultural models of membership all share in common a basic mistrust
of 'identity groups' as a relevant component of citizenship theory. (The term
'identity groups' here refers to a range of religious, ethnic, racial, or tribal
groups which are recognizable by virtue of their *nomos*.)[6] Proponents of a
multicultural understanding of citizenship, on the other hand, are concerned
with the power of the state to erode identity groups. This concern derives
from a philosophical position which stresses the role of culture and group
affiliation in constituting a person's 'understanding of who they are, of their
fundamental defining characteristics as [a] human being.'[7] Charles Taylor, in
his influential essay *The Politics of Recognition*, argues that we form our
identities and our conceptions of ourselves as free and equal agents through
a dialogical process, using certain given 'cultural scripts'.[8] Culture, under this

view, 'is not just something that we use to understand and evaluate the world, it is also part of us.'[9] Will Kymlicka also holds that membership in an identity group and participation in its cultural expressions—rather than mere 'blood' ties—provide individuals with 'an intelligible context of choice, and a secure sense of identity and belonging.'[10] This emphasis on the links between culture, identity and group membership stands at the core of various quests for a move towards a multicultural understanding of citizenship.[11]

Under this new understanding, 'persons would stand forth with their differences acknowledged and respected'[12] and could participate in the public sphere 'without shedding their distinct identities.'[13] This new multicultural understanding of citizenship stresses the interaction among three components—individuals, identity groups, and the state (a trichotomy), rather than the two components of traditional citizenship—the individual and the state (a dichotomy).[14] This new understanding of citizenship departs from the colour-blind ideal and aims to carve out a philosophical and legal rationale for recognizing identity groups as deserving of special or 'differentiated rights'.[15] The multicultural understanding of citizenship therefore departs from the perception of all citizens as individuals who are merely members of a larger political community, and instead views them as *simultaneously* having equal rights as individuals and differentiated rights as members of identity groups.

Hence in legal terms, the move towards a multicultural citizenship model raises potential conflicts among *three* components, identity groups, the state, and individual rights. Schematically, six prototypical legal conflicts can arise under a multicultural citizenship model: individual v. individual; individual v. state; identity group v. identity group; identity group v. state (the most often-discussed legal conflict under multiculturalism); 'outsider' v. identity group (as for example, in affirmative action cases)[16]; and 'insider' v. identity group. My discussion focuses on the final category of legal conflict: that which occurs between a citizen-insider and her own identity group. In such conflicts, multicultural accommodation policies which grant identity groups *carte blanche* legal powers tacitly sanction the maltreatment of certain categories of insiders, of them women, within their own identity groups.

How do proponents of the multicultural citizenship model handle this phenomenon, the 'paradox of multicultural vulnerability'? That is, what types of, how many, and whose citizenship entitlements should be put at risk in the interest of accommodating a given identity group's *nomos*? To answer this question, first we need to distinguish between what I call the 'strong version' and the 'weak version' of the multicultural citizenship model.

III. 'STRONG' AND 'WEAK' MULTICULTURAL MODELS

The strong version of the multicultural citizenship models calls for a fundamental shift in our understanding of citizenship. This shift grants identity groups strong formal, legal, and constitutional recognition and permits them to govern their members 'in accord with their customs and views.'[17] The strong multicultural model is based on the notion that the constitution (and the individual rights it protects) are, as James Tully puts it, 'an imperial yoke, galling the necks of the culturally diverse citizenry.'[18] Under the strong model, the state should free identity groups from the injustice of an alien form of rule by two means: first, by creating islands of self-governance for identity groups; and second, by officially including the diverse voices of identity groups within the constitutional framework and within public discourse.

The strong multicultural model, however, focuses almost exclusively on the problem of intergroup injustice: individual rights and the state are no longer the central components of citizenship as they were in the traditional citizenship models; rather, the central entities become identity groups and the state. Yet in its crusade to integrate identity groups into the public sphere in a fair and equal manner, respecting their differences, the strong multicultural model tacitly conceals the phenomenon of intragroup oppression. It obscures the power relations *within* identity groups while highlighting the conflicts that exist *among* identity groups or *between* identity groups and the state.[19] Therefore, the strong model oversimplifies the relationship among identity groups, the state, and individual rights (or the trichotomy) into another too easy (albeit more modern) dichotomy.

The weak version of the multicultural model more effectively addresses the intragroup impacts of multicultural accommodation: it acknowledges the potential tension between recognizing different cultures and protecting the rights of group members as citizens. While proponents of the weak multicultural model disagree about the justifications for adopting accommodationist policies (these justifications range from 'autonomy-based/valorization of choice' arguments to 'tolerance/respect for diversity' reasoning), they agree on the proposition that a morally adequate treatment of identity groups must seek ways to provide multicultural accommodation *without* abandoning the protection of individual rights.[20] Will Kymlicka, a prominent representative of the weak version, expresses this goal in the following way:

I believe it is legitimate, and indeed unavoidable, to supplement traditional human rights with minority rights. A comprehensive theory of justice in a multicultural state will include both universal rights, assigned to individuals regardless of group membership, and certain group-differentiated rights or 'special status' for minority cultures.[21]

Moreover, Kymlicka argues that the real test of the multicultural model of citizenship lies in its ability to 'explain how minority rights coexist with human rights, and how minority rights are limited by principles of individual liberty, democracy, and social justice.'[22]

The strong multicultural model fails Kymlicka's test because it emphasizes solely the rights of identity groups. The weak version, however, to some degree mediates among the components of the *trichotomy*. Unfortunately, the weak multicultural model also contradicts its own central tenet—that 'minority rights are limited by principles of individual liberty, democracy and social justice' —because there are circumstances under which it upholds *carte blanche* accommodation, even when the delegation of legal powers to the identity group systematically exposes certain group members, such as women, to violations of their state-guaranteed individual rights.[23]

Thus in certain situations, the move towards multiculturalism actually threatens citizenship rights[24]—at least for many women, who are caught at the intersection of *multiple* membership affiliations. Certainly citizenship has a long and troubling history of excluding those deemed 'unfit' for full membership on the basis of their gender, race, tribal affiliation, or national origin: only quite recently, towards the end of the twentieth century, have *all* categories of adults been extended full citizenship rights.[25] Ironically, now the that all adults, regardless of their gender, race, national, or tribal affiliation, can boast equal access to citizenship rights, women are being barred from fully exercising those rights in the context of current multicultural accommodation policies.

Although women may accrue some benefit from accommodation policies, as individuals with 'other' identities, they bear disproportionate costs for preserving their group's *nomos*. That is, the multicultural focus on 'identity'— as embedded in religious, racial, ethnic, or tribal affiliation—fails to capture the multiplicity of group members' affiliations; and even more importantly, it is blind to the particular vulnerability that certain traditionally subordinated classes, such as women, may suffer in the context of their own cultures.

The tension between multiculturalism and citizenship is even further aggravated when the state's delegation of self-governance powers to identity groups in certain legal arenas is accompanied by a 'non-intervention' policy[26]. The term 'non-intervention' refers to a legal policy traditionally associated with two different arenas: *laissez-faire* economics and 'family privacy'.[27] The policy of state non-intervention in the market place is based on the assumption that the market 'naturally' reflects actual supply and demand. A non-interventionist economic policy typically assumes that the market place is autonomous and therefore can function independently of the state.[28] In the multicultural context, a non-intervention policy thus defers to a group's traditions, even in instances of the 'paradox of multicultural vulnerability', when a group's practices might systematically injure certain categories of at-risk group members, such as women.

Politically, the term 'non-intervention' is misleading: it re-enforces the myth that identity groups, if only given the chance, could exist as autonomous entities bearing no relation to the state. Of course, if this were the case, then there would be no need to envision a multicultural model of citizenship: for the very logic of this project is to have the state change the *background rules* affecting the status of identity groups. Even if a perfect system of non-intervention could be established, the state would still at some level be involved in setting policies which would greatly affect identity groups.[29] After all, even under a 'non-interventionist' accommodation policy, some entity must define the criteria by which groups will be recognized, accommodated, and awarded group-differentiated rights. Significantly, the state itself plays a crucial role in determining which groups are allowed some degree of 'self-governance', and who is authorized to speak for a given culture.[30]

On what basis should the state make these crucial decisions? Will Kymlicka argues that self-government rights—which require the delegation of legal powers to national minorities—should be awarded only to a limited class of identity groups, primarily to groups of indigenous peoples. These groups, he explains, had governed themselves until they were incorporated (often involuntarily, through conquest or colonialization) into the state.[31] Members of immigrant, ethnic, or religious groups who have voluntarily 'uprooted themselves'[32] do not fall, in Kymlicka's view, into the category of national minorities.[33] Rather, they are loosely defined as ethnic groups and are entitled instead to polyethnic rights.[34] Polyethnic rights refer to a range of legal measures, varying from antidiscrimination laws to forms of public funding for ethnic and religious groups' cultural practices, but not to rights to autonomous self government.[35]

Certain types of identity groups fit neither into Kymlicka's 'indigenous' category nor into his 'immigrant' category, however. Religious identity groups, for example, which under Robert Cover's analysis would be recognized as paradigmatic candidates for state accommodation of their *nomos*, would fit neither into Kymlicka's definition of a national minority nor into his ethnic group category. Even under traditional citizenship models certain religiously defined identity groups have been recognized as deserving a limited sphere of autonomy in legal arenas which relate to cultural preservation, such as family law.[36]

Under traditional citizenship models, the state has actively sought parallel or partial control over these issues, however.[37] Should the state, under a *multicultural* citizenship model, grant total self-governance powers to identity groups over matters of family law, even if such accommodation increases the probability that certain citizens' individual rights will be damaged in intragroup spheres? To clarify and complicate the question of state intervention, I present the following situation A and B, two hypothetical examples of multicultural accommodation.

IV. TWO HYPOTHETICAL CASES

In situation A, the state grants an Indian tribe full discretion over matters of resource development in the community.[38] This allocation of powers strengthens the group's autonomy *vis-à-vis* the state, because decisions regarding resource development will be made by the group in accordance with its own decision-making mechanisms. For example, the tribe has been awarded full discretion over matters of resource development; a majority of its members have decided to open a gambling facility on the territory. A similar decision could not have been made under state law, because state law prohibits gambling activities. However, the justification for adopting the decision to open a casino was not dictated by what I call the group's 'essential traditions'.[39] In other words, providing gambling opportunities to the tribe and its visitors is not an identity-preserving imperative dictated by the group's authorities or inside courts in the name of protecting the group's *nomos*.

The tribe's decision to open the facility will no doubt have both an economic and social impact on tribe members. Although a successful casino would accrue financial benefit to tribe members, certain members, compulsive gamblers, for example, might be better off if the facility were not opened. Thus, random majority policy decisions can potentially injure certain group members. However, the infringements upon members in such cases are accidental rather than encoded in a group's sanctioned traditions, as they are in following situation B.

In situation B, an identity group is awarded exclusive jurisdiction over a matter substantive to its self-definition: family law. The group is given authority to construct its membership boundaries: to decide who by marriage or by birth is eligible for group membership, and to shape legal relations between spouses within the community. In other words, what is granted in situation B by the state is not an 'open-ended' policy issue to be determined by the group's decision-making mechanisms, such as whether or not to open a gambling facility. Instead, a well-defined 'text' of social and legal norms and practices (i.e. aspects of the group's essential traditions) is given authoritative status.[40] Thereafter, group members are bound to have their marital affairs adjudicated by 'inside' courts which apply the group's personal status laws, even if, as individuals, these citizen-insiders would have preferred to have such matters adjudicated by 'outside' courts, which would apply state laws.

In sum, the qualitative difference between situation A and situation B lies not in the state's granting a given identity group exclusive legal powers, but in whether or not the multicultural accommodation policy recognizes a group's self-governance powers over matters that are *already ascribed* in the group's 'essential traditions'.

Granting immunity to essential intragroup practices obscures, however, the fact that an identity group's 'essential traditions' are the outcome of a long, often contested, history. Consequently, the components that constitute the *nomos* of a group are never as fixed or stable as they may seem at any given moment. Over time, identity is negotiated, contested, transformed, defined, and redefined by group members through ongoing interactions both inside and outside the identity group. In this sense, nomoi groups are contingent, historical, and socially constructed entities, not the 'natural' or 'fixed' essences they are often thought to be.[41] Identity groups constantly redefine their 'essential traditions' in relation to inside or outside challenges. Most participants in the multi-cultural discourse recognize that inside–outside interaction is inevitable. In fact, this recognition actually serves as one of the strongest justifications for multicultural accommodation policies, particularly those that grant identity groups greater self-governance powers over their members' legal affairs.

V. 'ESSENTIAL TRADITIONS' AND VOICES FROM WITHIN

That identity groups might benefit from having their members bound by the group's traditions rather than by state law is, as I have noted, a perfectly sensible suggestion. Who, however, is allowed to define what the group's 'essential traditions' are? Which *voices from within an identity group* should be recognized by the state as 'representative' of the 'integrity of a group's culture'? Surprisingly, these questions, which skim the muddied anthropological, sociological, and ethnographic waters, have hardly been addressed in the multicultural literature. The paucity of available scholarship on the above questions contributes to a widespread blindness in the multicultural debate regarding the ways in which the state itself helps to 'constitute' group identities through its multicultural accommodation policies. In the family law arena, for example, multicultural accommodation policies which recognize the authority of religious communities to perform legally binding marriage and divorce ceremonies (in lieu of civil registration procedures), set standards which define *who* in the group has the legal power to solemnize religious marriage and divorce.[42] The accommodation of identity groups in the context of a larger political community, therefore, is never just an act of 'recognition'. Rather, given the interaction between 'inside' and 'outside' forces, and the diversity *within* identity groups, the state, whatever shape its accommodation policies takes, inevitably impacts intragroup power relations and legitimizes certain interpretations of an identity group's culture over other possible, competing, interpretations.

The state's sanctioned delegation of legal powers to the authorities within an identity group, when accompanied by a state 'non-intervention' policy, thus plays right into the hands of a group's acknowledged leaders: it allows those leaders to define any potential changes in the group's practices as 'corruptions' of a group's identity. In religious communities, female group members who attempt to bring about intragroup changes (by suggesting a less gender-biased reading of its family law practices, for example), are often accused by group leaders of *culturally betraying* their group's traditions. Such labelling effectively silences those citizen-insiders who dare to question standard readings of their group's essential traditions.[43]

Moreover, the so-called 'traditional' treatment of women sometimes becomes a cultural emblem symbolizing a group's 'authentic' identity. Not surprisingly, this phenomenon, which elsewhere I call 'reactive culturalism',[44] further complicates the relationship among identity groups, the state, and individual rights. In instances of reactive culturalism, any state intervention in issues related to family law, for example, is seen by the entire group as a threat to their '*nomos*'. Hence, enormous pressure is imposed on women insiders to 'give up' their state-guaranteed individual rights and to assert their group loyalty by accepting the standard interpretation of group doctrine as the only possible 'correct' reading of their group's family law traditions.

If we accept the proposition that power relations, hierarchies, and subordination exist not only *between* groups but also *within* groups, and that intragroup dynamics are often impacted by the relationship between the state and identity groups, then we should be aware that multicultural accommodation may do more than recognize a group's identity: in many ways, it indirectly partakes in the ongoing process of redefining the essential traditions that constitute a group's *nomos*.

Given that a group's essential traditions are more fluid than members are led to believe, it is theoretically possible for the group to 'reinterpret' those traditions if they systematically injure women. Changes are difficult to bring about in any established system, however. Moreover, as I have mentioned, sometimes a group's essential traditions become cultural emblems which distinguish the group's own culture from the world 'outside'. In such situations, injured group members are often punished when they call for changes in the group's 'essential' practices: their actions are taken as a betrayal of the group.

VI. FAMILY LAW AND THE CONSTRUCTION OF IDENTITY

An identity group's family law traditions, which undergird its requirements for 'legitimate' marriage, divorce, and adoption proceedings, and which set criteria for group membership, naturally stand at the very centre of a group's sense of its cultural uniqueness. Hence, family law is an arena in which the multicultural state is tempted to grant identity groups the maximum degree of control over their own affairs.

At the same time, family law is also a realm in which women have been systematically subordinated. Hence a multicultural accommodation policy which allows an identity group complete autonomy in its family law practices potentially exposes women to state-sanctioned violations of their basic rights, just when they are most in need of state protection over their entrenched individual rights as citizens. Significantly, unlike the other, arbitrary violations of members' rights which might occur within an identity group, violations of women's rights in the family law arena are *systematic* rather than accidental, and hence more

troubling. While in some cases the injurious effects of multicultural accommodation can reasonably be dismissed as the 'random' costs of accommodation upon various group members, the debilitating effects of accommodated
family law practices cannot be easily dismissed.

The following pages demonstrate more concretely how family law serves
a crucial function in preserving collective identities. Yet, I argue, in part because
a group's family law practices are central to its *nomos*, they are particularly
difficult to challenge: unfortunately, rules which systematically violate members' rights as citizens are often built into a group's most cherished cultural
scripts.

In order to understand the centrality of family law in preserving a nomoi
group's boundaries we need briefly to examine the two basic means through
which collective identities are maintained. The two means, which are often
intertwined, are generally categorized as 'the racial, ethnic, biological and territorial, on the one hand, and the ideological, cultural and spiritual on the
other.'[45] Anne McClintock stresses the former, emphasizing that collective
identities 'are frequently figured through the iconography of familial or
domestic space.'[46] She also observes that even the term 'nation' is closely
etymologically related to the verb *nasci* (Latin): 'to be born',[47] and that communities are also symbolically figured as domestic genealogies.[48] Benedict
Anderson also suggests that communities are best viewed as akin to families
or religious orders.[49] Such communities are understood by their members as
having 'finite, if elastic, boundaries.'[50] Defined in this fashion, group membership derives its meaning from a system of 'differences',[51] which must be
demarcated by membership boundaries.[52]

Nomoi groups demarcate their boundaries by engaging in sorting processes
which define who is inside and who is outside the group. Nomoi groups, unlike
nation-states, lack the institutional authority to formally determine who
belongs to the political community (for example, they lack the sovereignty
which would permit them to define citizenship or legal residency). Moreover,
groups struggling to preserve their differences within a nation-state—that is,
under a common citizenship status—lack the institutional means to oblige
members to claim membership. Nomoi groups cannot issue formal documents
of membership or force members to contribute taxes to the collective.
Instead, they attempt to maintain their membership boundaries by employ-
ing the biological descent and cultural affiliation criteria earlier mentioned.
This distinction between 'biological' and 'cultural' is itself oversimplified and
to some degree misleading. Yet groups attach varying degrees of significance
to each of these two elements. Some groups, for example, define themselves
primarily in cultural or linguistic terms. These groups are less exclusive than
those which define themselves solely in terms of biological descent. These
more exclusive nomoi groups often use *family law* as a central tenet in the
construction of their membership boundaries, and in asserting and preserving
their differences.[53]

Generally, family law demarcates membership boundaries in two related ways: first, by defining who, by way of marriage, can become a group member (which mixed marriages are recognized by the group), and second, by developing complex lineage rules that determine who, by virtue of birth, is eligible for acquiring full membership in the group.[54] Within this paradigmatic legal structure, there is space for specific nomoi groups to define the means through which membership boundaries are codified in the context of the group's essential traditions. Under the shared notion that group membership is legally transmitted by birth, various religious traditions have given different content to the 'membership transmission procedure'. The Jewish tradition, for example, dictates that membership by birth is transmitted along matrilineal lines, while other religious traditions, such as Islam, dictate that group membership is transmitted along patrilineal lines.

The emphasis in exclusive nomoi groups on marriage and membership by birth provides a strong impetus for the group to develop various social and legal mechanisms for controlling the personal status, sexuality, and reproductive activity of women; for women have a central and potentially powerful role in procreating the collective.[55] Intragroup control of women is achieved partially via the implementation of personal status laws and lineage rules which clearly define how, when, and with whom women can give birth to children so as to ensure that those children become legitimate members of the community. Legitimacy, in this context, refers not to the traditional common-law definition (i.e. a child born in a legal marriage), but to granting membership by birth only to a child born in accordance with the group's specific personal status laws and lineage rules.[56] Family law, then, effectively creates and maintains a group's membership boundaries, and also regulates the real life marriage and procreative choices of a group's members.

Given these constitutive, regulative, and sorting functions of family law, nomoi groups predictably express a strong interest in having exclusive control over their members' personal status. In moving towards a multicultural citizenship model, family law has therefore become a contested field in which the state and nomoi groups vie for control. That nomoi groups should struggle for autonomy in the family law arena is not surprising. But family law policies have a particular, often detrimental, effect on the citizenship status of women; for women stand at the fulcrum of a set of legal rules and policies that control their personal status, sexuality, and procreation, and are encoded in the group's essential traditions.

Nomoi groups often highlight women's responsibilities as the reproducers of legitimate children in accordance with the group's personal status laws and as primary socializers of the young.[57] In other words, women make an important contribution as bearers or transmitters of collective identity: '[o]n the one hand, they are acted upon as members of collectives, institutions or groupings, . . . On the other hand, they are a special focus of . . . concerns as a social category with a special role (particularly human reproduction).'[58]

A group's recognition of women's unique contribution to the collective could, in theory, grant women a powerful position within that group. In practice, in many religious communities, this conceptual deification of the female role of wife-mother-homemaker has done exactly the opposite.[59] Somewhat paradoxically, precisely because of women's contribution in transmitting a group's 'understanding of the world over time', women have been exposed to severe intragroup policing of their personal status, sexuality, and procreation.[60] Such policing, if encoded in the group's essential traditions, can lead to systematic sanctioned maltreatment of women in the intragroup spheres, which, ironically, might be tacitly endorsed by a state's multicultural accommodation policy.[61]

VII. THE ISRAELI TEST CASE

In the arena of family law, the 'paradox of multicultural vulnerability' is not merely a theoretical concern about the tension between group accommodation and the protection of certain group members' individual rights. Rather, the tension between multiculturalism and citizenship is part of the lived experience of millions of women who live in countries like India, Israel, and Kenya, which have already adopted accommodationist policies with reference to matters of personal status of their citizens. All Israeli citizens, for example, must have their marriage and divorce disputes resolved by their identity groups' personal status law, as interpreted by the religious courts of their respective communities.[62] Moreover, Israeli religious courts, which have been awarded different degrees of exclusive jurisdiction over matters of family law, are in principle immune from state intervention, even if they uphold group traditions which expose certain insiders, particularly women undergoing divorce proceedings, to systematic, gender-based oppression.

Jewish divorce law, for example, which is informed by a tradition that does indeed praise women's roles as wives and mothers, still permits a husband to 'anchor' his wife against her will; that is, he can force her to remain legally married to him even if their relationship has ended. Under Halakhic law, the giving and accepting of the *get* (divorce decree) is a private act between the spouses, which takes place under the supervision of a Jewish court. Unless both spouses agree to the divorce, the ultimate power to decide whether or not to dissolve the marriage remains in the husband's hands: until he declares that he is willing to grant his wife the *get*, there is no way for her to seek release from the marriage bonds.[63] Because such maltreatment of women is encoded in 'essential' Jewish family law traditions, Israel's multicultural accommodation policy does more than recognize the autonomy of religious courts in the family law arena. In effect, it also grants (state-authorized) religious courts a *carte blanche* licence to subordinate certain of their group members, namely women.[64] In the Israeli case, then, no rhetoric about women's equal citizenship status can compensate for the structural powerlessness a female group member suffers under an accomodation policy that defers to the exclusive jurisdiction of religious communities in matters of marriage and divorce.

As we have seen, marriage and 'legitimate' childbirth serve a crucial dual function: they create and maintain a group's membership boundaries, and, at the same time, perpetuate an unequal distribution of power between men and women in the group. Given this dual function of family law, it becomes extremely difficult for women to alter the gender-scripts ascribed in their group's essential traditions: attempts to reread a group's family law traditions in a less discriminatory way may be interpreted by the group's acknowledged leaders as an assault on family law's demarcation function. This tension is aggravated when a strict reading of a group's essential traditions with regard to the regulation of women's personal status, sexuality, and procreation, comes to serve as part of the group's manifestation of its 'authentic' collective identity.[65] In such instances, examples of what I call 'reactive culturalism', the allocation of legal powers to nomoi groups in the family law arena permits those in power in identity groups (most often, male authorities) to further employ an essentialist rhetoric to *silence* members who criticize their policies—by portraying 'connected critics'' efforts to reduce intragroup inequalities as interfering with the group's collective struggles to maintain its differences.[66] Such labelling obviously has a chilling effect upon women citizen-insiders. Moreover, certain groups view women as 'unfit' for political activity. In such cases, female group members, who may be gravely affected by multicultural accommodation, have no opportunity to shape the relationship between their identity groups and the state *from within*.

Hence in the case of family law women are more vulnerable than men to maltreatment within their own identity groups due to a gender-based subordination which is *encoded* in the group's accommodated, essential traditions. Unfortunately women's attempts to improve their intragroup status, whether by introducing internal reforms or by seeking 'outside' legal remedy, are often blocked.[67] Under such conditions, women's group affiliation weakens, if not altogether erases, their *gender* identity, although, ironically, it is precisely their 'womanhood' which subjected them to intragroup violations of their citizenship rights in the first place.

VIII. CONCLUSION: THE 'PRIVACY ZONE' FALLACY

As I have shown, the delegation of exclusive legal powers by the state to nomoi groups, tacitly if not explicitly, grants identity groups a licence to subordinate certain of their members, namely women, reinforcing what I call 'the paradox of multicultural vulnerability'. Moreover, a 'non-interventionist' accommodation policy permits identity groups to encircle themselves with barriers so inviolable that whatever happens *within* those groups, happens 'outside' the jurisdiction of state law. Hence, if a violation of individual rights occurs within an identity group, then the violation is categorized as a 'private affair': the state, as an 'outside' entity, has no business intervening. This binary opposition leads us astray, however, not only because it ignores the web of relations between inside and outside, and the fragility of these categorizations, but also because it obscures the fact that what constitutes a 'private affair' is in itself a construct of the state's regime of law.[68]

The (re-establishment) of a 'privacy zone' in the identity group context[69] is sometimes justified by an appeal to the so-called 'right of exit' argument.[70] The 'right of exit' argument, however, obscures the very real hardships of leaving one's identity group (economic hardship, lack of education, skill deficiencies, or emotional distress, for example),[71] and suggests that an injured insider, because she is maltreated in intragroup spheres, should abandon the very centres of her life, family, and community. Differently put, the 'right of exit' argument forces insiders into a cruel zero-sum choice: either accept all group practices—including those that violate your state-guaranteed individual rights—or leave. This perception echoes the troubling doctrine of 'implied consent', as it assumes that those who haven't used the 'exit' option have implicitly agreed to their own subordination by the group's practices. Ultimately, the right of exit argument resembles the nineteenth-century rhetoric that interpreted a woman's consent to marriage as implied consent to atrocities such as rape or battering by her spouse.[72] Given this historical background, it is troubling that after having abolished the 'implied consent' doctrine in state law, we find it resurfacing in the context of the contemporary multicultural debate.

As should be clear by now, the central question the multicultural citizenship model must address is not *whether* the state should intervene in identity groups. It inevitably will, as 'the paradox of multicultural vulnerability' demonstrates. Rather, the central questions are *how* the state should intervene, when, on whose behalf, and based on what criteria. In answering these complex questions, we need to begin to develop a 'reshaped' multicultural citizenship model, one which is sensitive to the diversity within groups, and takes into account not only the interests expressed by a group's acknowledged leaders, but also the *voices from within* expressed by group members, especially those who may be subject to systematic maltreatment by their group's accommodated traditions.[73] No democratic principle can justify a multicultural accommodation policy which does not hear the voices of those insiders who might, ironically, be damaged by the very policy that purports to assist them.

Given women's unique contribution to the collective, the long history of their intragroup vulnerability, and their relatively late entitlement to the full benefits of citizenship, it would be a grave mistake to disenfranchise them from their long-fought-for individual rights solely because they choose to participate in their own cultures. In other words, as identity group members, women should not have to give up their citizenship entitlements. Otherwise, why should theorists and legislators bother developing a *multicultural citizenship* model at all?

NOTES

1. Robert M. Cover, 'The Supreme Court 1982 Term, Foreword: *Nomos* and Narrative', *Harvard Law Review*, 97 (1983): 4. Cover defines 'nomos' as a normative universe in which law and narrative are inseparably related: '[n]o set of legal institutions or prescriptions exists apart from the narratives that locate it and give it meaning. For every constitution there is an epic, for each decalouge a scripture. Once understood in the context of the narrative that give it meaning, law becomes not merely a system of rules to be observed, but a world in which we live', ibid. 4–5. Cover focuses his analysis on religious identity groups which create 'alternative' nomian worlds in the constitutional state. As Abner Greene puts it, these groups 'sometimes called "nomoi", . . . are constituted of people who share a comprehensive world view that extends to creating a law for the community', Abner S. Greene, '*Kiryas Joel* and Two Mistakes about Equality', *Columbia Law Review*, 96 (1996): 1, 4.
2. Iris Marion Young, 'Polity and Group Differences: A Critique of the Ideal of Universal Citizenship', *Ethics*, 99 (1990): 250, 272.
3. Michael Walzer, 'Citizenship', in *Political Innovation and Conceptual Change*, Terence Ball *et al.* eds. (1989): 219; David Held, 'Between State and Civil Society: Citizenship', in *Citizenship*, Geoff Andrews, ed. (1991): 19.
4. J. G. A. Pocock, 'The Ideal of Citizenship Since Classical Times', repr. in *Theorizing Citizenship*, Ronald Beiner, ed. (1995): 29, 36.
5. See Rogers Brubaker, *Citizenship and Nationhood in France and Germany* (1992): 35–49.
6. Although what constitutes an 'identity group' is a controversial question, I will propose for the purposes of this discussion that such groups are marked by a unique history, a distinct culture, a set of essential traditions, collective memories, or an experience of maltreatment by mainstream society. My analysis deals only with groups which wish to maintain their identity as an alternative to full assimilation.
7. Charles Taylor, 'The Politics of Recognition', in *Multiculturalism: Examining the Politics of Recognition*, Amy Gutmann, ed. (1994): 25.
8. Ibid. 31.
9. J. M. Balkin, 'Ideology as Cultural Software', *Cardozo Law Review* (1995): 1221, 1229.
10. Will Kymlicka, *Multicultural Citizenship: A Liberal Theory of Minority Rights* (1995): 150.

11. The move towards the legal recognition of identity groups as entities deserving special or 'differentiated rights' is thoroughly discussed by Will Kymlicka, *Multicultural Citizenship* (1995). See also William A. Galston, 'Two Concepts of Liberalism', *Ethics*, 105 (1995): 516; Martha Minow, 'The Constitution and the Subgroup Question', *Indiana Law Journal*, 71 (1996): 1; Bhikhu Parekh, 'Cultural Pluralism and Limits of Diversity' *Alternatives*, 20 (1995): 43; J. Spinner, *The Boundaries of Citizenship* (1994); Charles Taylor, 'Shared and Divergent Values', in *Options for a New Canada*, 53–76; Ronald L. Watts and Douglas M. Brown eds. (1991); Charles Taylor, *The Politics of Recognition*; James Tully, *Strange Multiplicity: Constitutionalism in an Age of Diversity* (1995); Iris Marion Young, 'Polity and Group Difference: A Critique of the Ideal of Universal Citizenship', *Ethics*, 99 (1989): 250; Iris Marion Young, *Justice and the Politics of Difference* (1990); Vernon Van Dyke, 'The Individual, the State, and Ethnic Communities in Political Theory', *World Politics*, 29 (1977): 343.
12. Iris Marion Young, *Justice and the Politics of Difference*: 119.
13. Iris Marion Young, 'Polity and Group Difference': 272.
14. For a concise discussion, see Stephen Castles, 'Democracy and Multicultural Citizenship', in *From Aliens to Citizens*, Rainer Baubock, ed. (1994).
15. Kymlicka, for example, distinguishes between three forms of group-differentiated rights: self-government rights (the delegation of legal powers to national minorities); polyethnic rights (financial support and legal protection for certain practices associated with particular ethnic or religious groups); and special representation rights (guaranteed seats for national or ethnic groups within the central institutions of the larger society). See Kymlicka, *Multicultural Citizenship*: 6–7, 26–33.
16. In such cases, an outsider challenges the criteria which define an identity group or the legitimacy of distributing benefits based on those criteria for membership. See e.g. Regents of the *University of California* v. *Bakke* 438 US 265 (1978).
17. James Tully, *Strange Multiplicity: Constitutionalism in an Age of Diversity*; James Tully, 'Cultural Demands for Constitutional Recognition', *Journal of Political Philosophy*, 3 (1995): 111, 114.
18. Tully, *Strange Multiplicity*: 5.
19. See e.g. David Theo Goldberg, 'Introduction: Multicultural Conditions', in *Multiculturalism: A Critical Reader* (1994): 1–41.
20. See William A. Galston, 'Two Concepts of Liberalism'; Kymlicka, *Multicultural Citizenship*; Bhikhu Parekh, 'Minority Practices and Principles of Toleration'; Charles Taylor, 'Shared and Divergent Values'; Charles Taylor, 'The Politics of Recognition'; Iris M. Young, *Justice and the Politics of Difference*. As mentioned above, these scholars differ in their justifications for the move towards the recognition and accommodation of identity groups, yet they all share the commitment to protecting individuals' fundamental rights even under a multicultural citizenship model.
21. Kymlicka, *Multicultural Citizenship*: 6.
22. Ibid.
23. Kymlicka recognizes the potential tension between intergroup accommodation (or what he calls 'external protections'), and intragroup maltreatment within a given group (or what he calls 'internal restrictions'). However, Kymlicka asserts that in his view group-differentiated rights 'are primarily a matter of external

protections'. See Will Kymlicka, 'Three Forms of Group-Differentiated Citizenship in Canada', in *Democracy and Difference*, Seyla Benhabib, ed. (1996): 153,
160. It is precisely at this juncture that my analysis differs from his: I challenge
Kymlicka's presumption that the 'external' and 'internal' aspects of group accommodation can, or should, be considered separate. See Ayelet Shachar, 'Group
Identity and Women's Rights in Family Law: The Perils of Multicultural Accommodation', *Journal of Political Philosophy*, 6 (1998): 285–305.

24. I refer to 'citizenship' for the purposes of this discussion, in the following juris-
tic terms: as a legal status that defines membership boundaries in the body politic,
and entails a set of individual rights, as defined by state laws, which all citizens
can legitimately expect to posses and be subject to in a fair and equal manner.
This definition of citizenship does not imply that those who do not qualify as
citizens are not entitled to any legal rights *vis-à-vis* the body politic. I restrict
my analysis in this article, however, to the impacts of multicultural accommodation upon the status of *citizens*.

25. As the history of American citizenship laws illustrates, women and non-whites
have long been excluded from acquiring a full and equal citizenship status, even
when born in the USA. Similarly, immigration and naturalization policies have
restricted access to US citizenship based on explicit gender and racial criteria.
See Nancy F. Cott, 'Justice for All? Marriage and Deprivation of Citizenship in
the United States', in *Justice and Injustice in Law and Legal Theory*, Austin Sarat
and Thomas R. Kearns, eds. (1996).

26. Chandran Kukathas, for example, supports a non-interventionist policy even if
its consequences are intragroup violations of citizen-insiders' basic rights. See
Chandran Kukathas, 'Are There Any Cultural Rights?', *Political Theory*, 20 (1992):
105. Interestingly, a policy of non-intervention with regard to national minorities is also endorsed by Will Kymlicka, the prominent representative of the weak
multicultural model. This is surprising because Kymlicka asserts that liberal outsiders have a duty to support 'any efforts the community makes to liberalize their
cultures', and since he views the violation of insiders' basic rights by their own
group as morally unjust. See Will Kymlicka, 'The Rights of Minority Cultures:
Reply to Kukathas', *Political Theory*, 20 (1992): 140; see also Kymlicka,
Multicultural Citizenship: 166–70.

27. For a comprehensive discussion of the legal policy of non-state intervention, see
Frances E. Olsen, 'The Family and the Market: A Study of Ideology and Legal
Reform', *Harvard Law Review* 96 (1983): 1497; see also Frances E. Olsen, 'The
Myth of State Intervention in the Family', *University of Michigan Journal of Law
Reform*, 18 (1985): 835.

28. For a detailed historical analysis of the legal discourse on 'family privacy', see
Reva B. Siegel, ' "The Rule of Love": Wife Beating as Prerogative and Privacy',
Yale Law Journal, 105 (1996): 2117.

29. For a discussion of the impact of constitutional and institutional design on
ethnic groups in divided societies, see Donald L. Horowitz, 'Democracy in Divided
Societies', in *Nationalism, Ethnic Conflict, and Democracy*, Larry Diamond and
Marc F. Plattner, eds. (1994): 33–55.

30. Moreover, the 'walls' of identity groups are never absolutely sealed. Under a
multicultural 'non-intervention' policy the state may (and even should) indirectly

'intervene' in identity groups through measures such as tax exemptions, language programmes, or cultural preservation grants. A 'non-intervention' policy, however, actively prevents state intervention whenever such intervention might influence the group's status quo.

31. Kymlicka, *Multicultural Citizenship*: 6, 10–11.
32. Michael Walzer, quoted in Kymlicka, *Multicultural Citizenship*: 20.
33. Ibid. 14–15: 'Immigrant groups are not "nations", and do not occupy homelands. . . . [They] participate within the public institutions of the dominant culture(s) and speak the dominant language(s). . . . So while immigrant groups have increasingly asserted their right to express their ethnic particularity, they typically wish to do so within the public institutions.' For a different analysis of immigrant groups' claims, Bhikhu Parekh, 'Cultural Pluralism and the Limits of Diversity', *Alternatives*, 20 (1995): 431.
34. Ibid. 30–1.
35. Ibid. 20–1. Note that Kymlicka's model of multinational or polyethnic countries takes as its paradigmatic case the experience of countries like Canada, Australia, New Zealand, and the USA (which supposedly have been forced to establish multicultural arrangements to accommodate 'new' immigrants or ancient 'natives'). Interestingly, the distinction between the sorts of rights different identity groups are entitled to pivots around a concept which can be understood as 'ancient sin'. In case of national minorities, the sin that should guide the multicultural policy is the *involuntarily* incorporation of indigenous peoples by the colonializing state. In case of ethnic groups and religious minorities, it is their *voluntary* immigration as individuals to the new state that restricts the spectrum of claims they can raise against the state.
36. See Martha Minow, 'The Constitution and the Subgroup Question', *Indiana Law Journal*, 71 (1996): 1. Family law, as I later explain, establishes the group's 'genealogical line of membership', defining who by virtue of marriage or birth is recognized as a full member in the group.
37. For an illustration of this point in the American context of family law regulation, see e.g. Nancy F. Cott, 'Giving Character to Our Whole Civil Polity: Marriage and the Public Order in the Late Nineteenth Century', in *US History as Women's History*, Linda Kerber *et al.* eds. (1995): 107–21.
38. This is one of the examples given by Kymlicka, who discusses powers which are being gradually transferred by the USA and Canada to North American tribal/band councils. See Kymlicka, *Multicultural Citizenship*: 30.
39. What constitutes an identity group's 'essential tradition' is never fully fixed or immune to change. However, at any given period, a group's authoritative textual interpreters emphasize specific norms or practices as having a dominant (or in my terminology, 'essential') status.
40. Religious nomoi groups generally have a recognized corpus of 'texts' (e.g. holy scripts and their authoritative interpretations), which serve as their personal status laws, while ethnic and tribal groups might only have unwritten, customary personal status rules by which they regulate their members' behaviour. My reference to 'texts', however, also includes such customary personal status rules.
41. In asserting that identity groups are not to be conceived as 'natural', non-conflictual, or ahistorical entities, this chapter does not intend to imply that identity groups are fictional entities or that they are not constitutive of their

members' identities as 'encumbered selves'. However, I do not conceive identity as something which is 'virtually burnt into the genes of people'. For a similar position, see Steven Vertovec, 'Multiculturalism, Culturalism and Public Incorporation', *Ethnic and Racial Studies*, 19 (1996): 49, 51; for a critique of biologically or 'naturally' based conceptions of race encoded in law, Ian F. Haney Lopez, 'The Social Construction of Race: Some Observations on Illusion, Fabrication, and Choice', *Harvard Civil Rights-Civil Liberties Law Review*, 29 (1994): 1. See also Tessie P. Liu, 'Race and Gender in the Politics of Group Formation: A Comment of Notions of Multiculturalism', *Frontiers*, 7 (1991): 155. Liu describes the study of 'intercultural relations' as based on the rejection of the perception that 'the boundaries of group identity are fixed or at least readily apparent. Such an arrangement makes it difficult to conceptualize the relations between groups or how identities are mutually constructed in moments of contact.' The alternative, she argues, is to shift the focus of study 'toward examining the conceptual languages and activities that define the meaning of group membership', ibid. 157.

42. Since marital status has significant consequences not only for the involved parties but also for various third parties, the state sometimes requires a group to establish a register indicating the marital status of their members. When 'inside' officials control such tasks for the state, they may be subject to some 'outside' regulation. In Israel, for example, where matters of marriage and divorce fall under the exclusive jurisdiction of religious officials, state law regulates the terms of appointments of judges serving in religious courts. See the Dayanim Law of 1955, 9 LSI 74, which details the qualification for Rabbinical court judges; the Qadis Law of 1961, 15 LSI 123, which establishes the principles regarding the appointment of *qadis* to *Shari'a* courts in Israel; the Druze Religious Courts Law of 1963, 17 LSI 27. Note, however, that unlike the Jewish, Muslim, and Druze communities, the ten state-recognized Christian communities in Israel, which serve roughly less than 3% of Israel's total population, are free to organize, appoint judges, and legislate procedure according to ecclesiastical law, without regulation by the state.

43. In discussing 'the philosophical framework for the understanding of social criticism as a social practice', Michael Walzer suggests an alternative model to the 'detached critic' by calling attention to the important role of the 'connected critic'. Walzer asserts that '[c]riticism does not require us to step back from society as a whole but only to step away from certain sorts of power relationships within society. It's not connection but authority and domination from which we must distance ourselves'. See Michael Walzer, *Interpretation and Social Criticism*, (1987): 52.

44. Ayelet Shachar, *Multicultural Jurisdictions: Preserving Cultural Differences and Women's Rights in a Liberal State* (forthcoming), chap. 3.

45. Hedva Ben Israel, 'Nationalism in Historical Perspective', *Journal of International Affairs*, 45 (1992): 367, 393.

46. See Anne McClintock, 'Family Feuds: Gender, Nationalism and the Family', *Feminist Revue*, 44 (1993): 61, 62–3.

47. Note that the analogy I propose here between identity groups and nations is limited to the 'mechanisms' of biological and cultural reproduction. As I explained earlier, I focus here on the situation of identity groups which exist within the

framework of a larger political entity (the state). I will not examine the claims of groups seeking national independence/ sovereignty, or secession from the larger body politic. Rather, the identity groups, and in particular the nomoi groups, which I analyse seek accommodation for their 'differences' within the boundaries of the existing political entity—a state which is composed of a diverse citizenry.

48. McClintock, 'Family Feuds'.
49. Benedict Anderson, *Imagined Communities* (rev. edn., 1991).
50. Ibid. 7.
51. For a discussion about the construction of 'difference' as a relational term, see e.g. Andrew Parker *et al.* 'Introduction', in *Nationalisms and Sexualities*, Andrew Parker *et al.*, eds. (1992): 1, 5. More generally, see Martha Minow, *Making All the Difference: Inclusion, Exclusion, and American Law* (1990).
52. However, the multicultural justification for 'differences' *among* groups does not imply that 'actual inequality and exploitation' do not prevail *within* groups, as Anderson himself observes. See Anderson, *Imagined Communities*: 7.
53. Accordingly, family law loses its distinct role in legally defining membership boundaries if the group permits anyone interested in joining the group to become a full member.
54. Obviously there are other ways of acquiring membership in nomoi groups (e.g. by religious conversion), but in this chapter I focus on family law as a prime example of the above-mentioned situation B.
55. Men, too, are controlled by such laws, but as will be seen, not in a similarly discriminatory and subordinating fashion.
56. For these purposes, legal marriage is often a necessary but not sufficient condition. See e.g. the case of *Santa Clara Pueblo* v. *Martinez*, 436 US 49 (1978).
57. According to Halakhic family law, for example, group membership is transmitted along matrimonial lines. Hence, a child of a Jewish mother becomes a member in the Jewish community *by birth*. This religious affiliation is terminated, however, if the descendant converts to another organized faith.
58. Floya Anthias and Nira Yuval Davis, 'Introduction', in *Woman-Nation-State*, Nira Yuval Davis and Floya Anthias, eds. (1989): 6. Anthias and Yuval Davis's analysis of women's unique position is not aimed at 'essentializing' their role as 'biological reproducers' of collective identities (that is, as mothers) nor does it express the view that all 'reproduction' experiences of women are similar. Anthias and Yuval Davis therefore differ from cultural feminists who glorify mothering as the epitome of an 'ethics of care'. Compare e.g. Robin West, 'Jurisprudence and Gender', *University of Chicago Law Review*, 55 (1988): 1. For a critique of West's 'essential woman', see Angela P. Harris, 'Race and Essentialism in Feminist Legal Theory', *Stanford Law Review*, 42 (1990): 581.
59. See e.g. Saul J. Berman, 'The Status of Women in Halakhic Judaism', *Tradition* 14 (1973): 5.
60. Mary O'Brien argues that in Western history and political thought, men have attempted to provide their continuity over time by strictly controlling the legal and institutional forms (e.g. marriage) of women's 'legitimate' reproduction of children. Moreover, O'Brien claims that fathers' anxiety about paternity is the main source of women's sexual and social oppression: '[f]or men, sexuality is the basis of a free appropriative right, a power over women and children and a

power over time itself. It is also the basis of the radical uncertainty of that right, . . . and a lack of immediate recognition as progenitor. . . . The social relations of reproduction are relations of dominance precisely because at the heart of the doctrine of potency lies the intrasigent impotency of uncertainty, an impotency which colors and continuously brutalizes the social and political relations in which it is expressed', see Mary O'Brien, *The Politics of Reproduction* (1981): 191. See also Elizabeth M. Iglesias, 'Rape, Race, and Representation: The Power of Discourse, Discourses of Power, and the Reconstruction of Heterosexuality' *Vanderbilt Law Review*, 49 (1996): 869, 877: 'the root of women's sexual oppression is located not so much in male power as in the mechanisms through which men attempt to cope with, deny, and disguise their powerlessness'.

61. Clearly, however, not all women suffer intragroup injuries, even if they all are subject to the same family law code. This is partly because in nomoi groups, as elsewhere, women differ along various axes such as wealth, social status, or age. Family law, however, also serves other functions, such as the intergenerational transmission of power and resources (e.g. social status and property). My analysis here is limited to gendered aspects of the allocation of power and resources via nomoi groups' marriage and divorce laws.

62. In Israel, when both spouses belong to the same religious community, they must, by state law, pursue matters of marriage and divorce in a religious court. Thus, no 'unified' (civil) law applies to all Israeli citizens in matters of personal status. Instead, each community's religious court applies its personal law (i.e. the group's essential traditions). Therefore, '[i]n matters affecting their families, Israelis *must* function as Jews, Muslims, Druzes, etc.'. See Martin Edelman, *Courts, Politics, and Culture in Israel* (1994): 121 (emphasis mine). See also Isaac S. Shiloh, 'Marriage and Divorce in Israel', *Israel Law Review*, 5 (1970): 479.

63. For a clear summary of Halakhic divorce law, see Menachem M. Bayer, 'The Role of Jewish Law in Pertaining to the Jewish Family', in *Jews and Divorce*, Jacob Freid, ed. (1968). See also Frances Raday, 'Israel—The Incorporation of Religious Patriarchy in a Modern State', *International Review of Comparative Public Policy*, 4 (1992): 209.

64. Not only Jewish women but also Muslim, Christian, and Druze women are potentially subject to intragroup controls by their own group's traditions under the auspices of Israel's accommodationist family law policy. Muslim Shari'a courts, for example, have exclusive jurisdiction over *all* matters of personal status of Muslim Israeli citizens. This wide jurisdiction, of course, brings up a host of other problems that cannot be addressed here. For a concise account of Muslim personal status laws, see Aziza Y. al-Hibri, 'Marriage Laws in Muslim Countries', *International Review of Comparative Public Policy*, 4 (1992): 227.

65. This phenomenon is found in various religious communities which assert their identity in 'reaction' to outside changes, e.g. modernity or secularism. In the context of Muslim communities which have been ruled by Western colonial regimes, this 'reactive' assertion of identity had a specific, anti-imperialist tone. For further discussion, see Deniz Kandiyoti (ed.) *Women, Islam and the State* (1991); Valentine M. Moghadam (ed.) *Gender and National Identity* (1994).

66. I am using the term coined by Michael Walzer in *Interpretation and Social Criticism* (1985). The 'connected critic' is a group member who speaks from *within*,

sometimes at considered personal risk, objects, protests, and remonstrates against injustice in the community, ibid. 33. See also Kimberle Crenshaw, 'Demarginalizing the Intersection of Race and Sex: A Black Feminist Critique of Antidiscrimination Doctrine, Feminist Theory and Antiracist Politics', *University of Chicago Legal Forum* (1989): 139, 140.

67. This problem is particularly visible under accommodation regimes which follow the non-intervention rationale, as in the case of India, Israel, and Kenya. I critically evaluate such accommodation regimes in Ayelet Shachar, '(How) Should Church and State be Joined at the Altar?: Women's Rights and the Multicultural Dilemma' in *Citizenship in Diverse Societies*, Will Kymlicka and Wayne Norman, eds. (forthcoming 1999).

68. For a detailed account of the legal construction of the privacy discourse, see Siegel, 'The Rule of Love'.

69. Ironically, the concept of a 'privacy zone' here rests upon the same questionable logic that grants family law the greatest degree of autonomy in the multicultural state, mistakenly assuming that 'the family is capable of existing in some sense apart from state activity, as a natural formation rather than . . . as a creation of the state.' see Olsen, 'The Family and the Market': 1504.

70. See e.g. Kukathas, 'Are There Any Cultural Rights?'

71. See Martha Mahoney, 'Exit: Power and the Idea of Leaving in Love, Work, and the Confirmation Hearings', *Southern California Law Review*, 65 (1992): 1283; see also Kymlicka's 'Reply to Kukathas'.

72. See e.g. Siegel, 'The Rule of Love'. In a somewhat different context a woman who married a spouse of a different nationality was understood to have given her implied consent to be expatriated. Virginia Sapiro, 'Women, Citizenship, and Nationality: Immigration and Naturalization Policies in the United States', *Politics & Society*, 13 (1984): 1–26.

73. Space will not permit me to describe what a 'reshaped' multicultural policy in the family law arena, one which accommodates identity groups but does not systematically impose the costs of 'respect for groups' upon certain, less powerful insiders, might look like. For such a description, see Ayelet Shachar, 'Group Identity and Women's Rights in Family Law: The Perils of Multicultural Accommodation', *Journal of Political Philosophy*, 6 (1998): 285–305.

REFERENCES

Anderson, Benedict, *Imagined Communities*, London: Verso (rev. edn., 1991).

Balkin, J. M., 'Ideology as Cultural Software', *Cardozo Law Review* (1995): 1221–33.

Bayer, Menachem M., 'The Role of Jewish Law in Pertaining to the Jewish Family', in *Jews and Divorce*, Jacob Freid (ed.), New York: Ktav Publishing House (1968): 1–33.

Ben Israel, Hedva, 'Nationalism in Historical Perspective', *Journal of International Affairs*, 45 (1992): 367–97.

Berman, Saul J., 'The Status of Women in Halakhic Judaism', *Tradition*, 14 (1973): 5–28.

Brubaker, Rogers, *Citizenship and Nationhood in France and Germany*, Cambridge, Mass.: Harvard University Press (1992).

Castles, Stephen, 'Democracy and Multicultural Citizenship', in *From Aliens to Citizens: Redefining the Status of Immigrants to Europe*, Rainer Bauböck (ed.), Aldershot: Avebury (1994): 3–27.

Condorcet, Marie-Jean-Antoine-Nicolas de Caritat, Marquis de, 'On the Admission of Women to the Rights of Citizenship', *The First Essay on the Political Rights of Women*, trans. Alice Drysdale Vickery, Letchworth: Garden City Press (1912).

Cott, Nancy F., 'Giving Character to Our Whole Civil Polity: Marriage and the Public Order in the Late Nineteenth Century', in *US History as Women's History* Linda Kerber *et al.* (eds.), Chapel Hill: University of North Carolina Press (1995): 107–21.

—— 'Justice for All? Marriage and Deprivation of Citizenship in the United States', in *Justice and Injustice in Law and Legal Theory*, Austin Sarat and Thomas R. Kearns (eds.), Ann Arbor: University of Michigan Press (1996).

Cover, Robert M., 'The Supreme Court 1982 Term, Foreword: *Nomos* and Narrative', *Harvard Law Review*, 97 (1983): 4–68.

Crenshaw, Kimberle, 'Demarginalizing the Intersection of Race and Sex: A Black Feminist Critique of Antidiscrimination Doctrine, Feminist Theory and Antiracist Politics', *University of Chicago Legal Forum* (1989): 139–67.

Edelman, Martin, *Courts, Politics, and Culture in Israel*, Charlottesville: University Press of Virginia (1994).

Fichte, J. G., *The Science of Rights*, trans. A. E. Kroeger, London: Trubner & Co. (1889).

Galston, William A., 'Two Concepts of Liberalism', *Ethics*, 105 (1995): 516–34.

Goldberg, David Theo, 'Introduction: Multicultural Conditions', in *Multiculturalism: A Critical Reader*, Oxford: Blackwell (1994): 1–41.

Greene, Abner S., '*Kiryas Joel* and Two Mistakes about Equality', *Columbia Law Review*, 96 (1996): 1–86.

Haney Lopez, Ian F., 'The Social Construction of Race: Some Observations on Illusion, Fabrication, and Choice', *Harvard Civil Rights-Civil Liberties Law Review*, 29 (1994): 1–62.

Harris, Angela P., 'Race and Essentialism in Feminist Legal Theory', *Stanford Law Review*, 42 (1990): 581–616.

Held, David, 'Between State and Civil Society: Citizenship', in *Citizenship*, Geoff Andrews (ed.), London: Lawrence & Wishart (1991): 19–25.

Horowitz, Donald L., 'Democracy in Divided Societies', in *Nationalism, Ethnic Conflict, and Democracy*, Larry Diamond and Marc F. Plattner (eds.), Baltimore: Johns Hopkins University (1994): 35–55.

Iglesias, Elizabeth M., 'Rape, Race, and Representation: The Power of Discourse, Discourses of Power, and the Reconstruction of Heterosexuality', *Vanderbilt Law Review*, 49 (1996) 869–992.

Kandiyoti, Deniz (ed.), *Women, Islam and the State*, London: Macmillan (1991).

Kukathas, Chandran, 'Are There Any Cultural Rights?', *Political Theory*, 20 (1992): 105–39.

Kymlicka, Will, 'The Rights of Minority Cultures: Reply to Kukathas', *Political Theory*, 20 (1992): 140–6.

Kymlicka, Will, *Multicultural Citizenship: A Liberal Theory of Minority Rights*, Oxford: Clarendon Press (1995).

—— 'Three Forms of Group-Differentiated Citizenship in Canada', in *Democracy and Difference: Contesting the Boundaries of the Political*, Seyla Benhabib (ed.), Princeton: Princeton University Press (1996): 153–70.

Liu, Tessie P., 'Race and Gender in the Politics of Group Formation: A Comment of Notions of Multiculturalism', *Frontiers*, 7 (1991): 155–74.

McClintock, Anne, 'Family Feuds: Gender, Nationalism and the Family', *Feminist Review*, 44 (1993): 61–78.

Mahoney, Martha, 'Exit: Power and the Idea of Leaving in Love, Work, and the Confirmation Hearings', *Southern California Law Review*, 65 (1992): 1283–319.

Minow, Martha, *Making All the Difference: Inclusion, Exclusion, and American Law*, Ithaca: Cornell University Press (1990).

—— 'The Constitution and the Subgroup Question', *Indiana Law Journal*, 71 (1996): 1–25.

Moghadam, Valentine M. (ed.), *Gender and National Identity*, London: Zed Books (1994).

Nasir, Jamal J., *The Islamic Law of Personal Status*, London: Graham & Trotman (1986).

O'Brien, Mary, *The Politics of Reproduction*, Boston: Routledge & Kegal Pual (1981).

Olsen, Frances E., 'The Myth of State Intervention in the Family', *University of Michigan Journal of Law Reform*, 18 (1985): 835–64.

—— 'The Family and the Market: A Study of Ideology and Legal Reform', *Harvard Law Review*, 96 (1986): 1497–578.

Parekh, Bhikhu, 'Cultural Pluralism and the Limits of Diversity', *Alternatives*, 20 (1995): 431–57.

—— 'Minority Practices and Principles of Toleration', *International Migration Review*, 30 (1996): 251–84.

Parker, Andrew, *et al.* (eds.), *Nationalisms and Sexualities*, New York: Routledge (1992).

Pocock, J. G. A., 'The Ideal of Citizenship Since Classical Times', repr. in *Theorizing Citizenship*, Ronald Beiner (ed.), Albany: SUNY Press (1995): 29–52.

Raday, Frances, 'Israel: The Incorporation of Religious Patriarchy in a Modern State', *International Review of Comparative Public Policy*, 4 (1992): 209–25.

Sapiro, Virginia, 'Women, Citizenship, and Nationality: Immigration and Naturalization Policies in the United States', *Politics & Society*, 13 (1984): 1–26.

Shachar, Ayelet, 'Group Identity and Women's Rights in Family Law: The Perils of Multicultural Accommodation', *Journal of Political Philosophy*, 6 (1998): 285–305.

—— '(How) Should Church and State be Joined at the Altar? Women's Rights and the Multicultural Dilemma', in *Citizenship in Diverse Societies*, Will Kymlicka and Wayne Norman (eds.), Oxford: Oxford University Press (forthcoming 1999).

—— *Multicultural Jurisdictions: Preserving Cultural Differences and Women's Rights in a Liberal State* (Cambridge: Cambridge University Press, forthcoming).

—— and Ran Hirschl, 'What We Talk about When We Talk about Multiculturalism', paper presented at the *Nationalism, Multiculturalism and Liberal Democracy Colloquium*, Amsterdam, Royal Netherlands Academy of Arts and Sciences (26–8 Nov. 1997).

Shiloh, Isaac S., 'Marriage and Divorce in Israel', *Israel Law Review*, 5 (1970): 479–98.

Siegel, Reva B., '"The Rule of Love": Wife Beating as Prerogative and Privacy', *Yale Law Journal*, 105 (1996): 2117–207.

Smith, Rogers M., *Civic Ideals: Conflicting Visions of Citizenship in U.S. History*, New Haven: Yale University Press (1997).

Spinner, Jeff, *The Boundaries of Citizenship: Race, Ethnicity, and Nationality in the Liberal State*, Baltimore: Johns Hopkins University Press (1994).

Taylor, Charles, 'Shared and Divergent Values', in *Options for a New Canada*, Ronald L. Watts and Douglas M. Brown (eds.), Toronto: University of Toronto Press (1991): 53–76.

—— 'The Politics of Recognition', in *Multiculturalism: Examining the Politics of Recognition*, Amy Gutmann (ed.), Princeton: Princeton University Press (1994): 25–73.

Tully, James, 'Cultural Demands for Constitutional Recognition', *Journal of Political Philosophy*, 3 (1995): 111–32.

—— *Strange Multiplicity: Constitutionalism in an Age of Diversity*, Cambridge: Cambridge University Press (1995).

Van Dyke, Vernon, 'The Individual, the State, and Ethnic Communities in Political Theory', *World Politics*, 29 (1977): 343–69.

Vertovec, Steven, 'Multiculturalism, Culturalism and Public Incorporation', *Ethnic and Racial Studies*, 19 (1996): 49–69.

Walzer, Michael, *Interpretation and Social Criticism*, Cambridge, Mass.: Harvard University Press (1987).

—— 'Citizenship' in *Political Innovation and Conceptual Change*, Terence Ball *et al.* (eds.), Cambridge: Cambridge University Press (1989): 211–19.

West, Robin, 'Jurisprudence and Gender', *University of Chicago Law Review*, 55 (1988): 1–77.

Young, Iris Marion., 'Polity and Group Differences: A Critique of the Ideal of Universal Citizenship', *Ethics*, 99 (1990): 250–74.

—— *Justice and the Politics of Difference*, Princeton: Princeton University Press (1990).

Yuval Davis, Nira, and Anthias Floya (eds.), *Woman-Nation-State*, London: Macmillan (1989).

6

Comments on Shachar and Spinner-Halev: An Update from the Multiculturalism Wars

WILL KYMLICKA

Political theorists have only begun addressing issues of ethnocultural accommodation in a serious way in the last ten years or so, after decades of neglect. But we can already see a significant shift in the debate, a shift that is reflected in the chapters by Shachar and Spinner-Halev. Since I agree with most of what Shachar and Spinner-Halev say, my aim in this commentary will be to situate their arguments in the larger debate, and to take stock of where the debate is heading.

The first wave of writings on multiculturalism was primarily focused on assessing the *justice* of claims by ethnic groups for the accommodation of their cultural differences.[1] This reflected the fact that opposition to such claims has traditionally been stated in the language of justice. Critics of multiculturalism had long argued that justice required state institutions to be 'colour-blind'. To ascribe rights or benefits on the basis of membership in ascriptive groups was seen as inherently morally arbitrary and discriminatory, necessarily creating first- and second-class citizens.

The first task confronting any defender of multiculturalism, therefore, was to try to overcome this presumption, and to show that deviations from difference-blind rules which are adopted in order to accommodate ethnocultural differences are not inherently unjust. Several authors took up this task, attempting to defend the justice of certain kinds of multicultural accommodations, or 'differentiated citizenship', or group-specific rights.[2] These authors used a variety of arguments to make their case, but these arguments can be seen as resting on a common strategy. They all claim that while 'difference-blind' institutions purport to be neutral amongst different ethnocultural groups, they are in fact implicitly tilted towards the needs, interests, and identities of the majority group, and this creates a range of burdens, barriers, stigmatizations, and exclusions for members of minority groups. The adoption of explicitly multicultural policies, it is argued, helps to remedy the disadvantages which minorities suffer within difference-blind institutions, and thereby promotes fairness. Multiculturalism policies do not constitute unfair privileges or invidious forms of discrimination, but rather compensate for unfair disadvantages, and so are consistent with, and may indeed be required by, justice.

In my view, this first stage in the debate is over, and the multiculturalists have won the day. I don't mean that the defenders of multiculturalism have been successful in getting their claims accepted and implemented, although there is a clear trend throughout the Western democracies towards greater multiculturalism in public policy. Rather I mean that multiculturalists have successfully redefined the terms of public debate in two profound ways: (a) few thoughtful people continue to think that justice can simply be *defined* in terms of difference-blind rules or institutions. Instead, it is now widely recognized that difference-blind rules and institutions can cause disadvantages for particular groups. Whether justice requires common rules for all, or differential rules for diverse groups, is something to be assessed case by case in particular contexts, not assumed in advance; (b) as a result, the burden of proof has shifted. The burden of proof no longer falls solely on defenders of multiculturalism to show that their proposed reforms would not create injustices; the burden of proof equally falls on defenders of difference-blind institutions to show that the status quo does not create injustices for minority groups.

The first wave of multiculturalists have, in other words, punctured the complacency with which liberals used to dismiss claims for minority rights, and have successfully levelled the playing field when debating the merits of multiculturalism. It's an interesting question why multiculturalists have been so successful in changing the public debate so quickly. In part, I think, it reflects a growing acknowledgement of the many ways that mainstream institutions implicitly favour the majority—e.g. by using the majority's language, and by adopting a work-week that is based on the majority's religion. Moreover, as Spinner-Halev notes, it is difficult to see how all of these biases could be overcome. The idea that public institutions could genuinely be neutral amongst languages or religious calendars seems increasingly implausible.[3]

But the success of multiculturalists also reflects a growing awareness of the importance of certain interests which have typically been ignored by liberal theories of justice—e.g. interests in recognition, identity, language, and cultural membership. If these interests are ignored or trivialized by the state, then people will feel harmed—and indeed will be harmed—even if their civil, political, and welfare rights are respected. If state institutions fail to recognize and respect people's culture and identity, the result can be serious damage to people's self-respect and sense of agency.[4]

So the original justice-based grounds for blanket opposition to multiculturalism have faded. This has not meant that opposition to multiculturalism has disappeared, or even significantly diminished. But it now takes a new form. Or rather it takes two forms: the first questions the justice of specific multiculturalism policies in particular contexts, focusing on the way particular policies may entail an unjust distribution of the benefits and burdens associated with identity and culture; the second shifts the focus away from justice towards issues of citizenship, focusing not on the justice or injustice of particular policies, but rather on the way that the general trend towards multicultural-ism threatens to erode the sorts of civic virtues and citizenship practices which sustain a healthy democracy.

The chapters by Shachar and Spinner-Halev can be seen, I think, as a reflec-tion of these two new battlefronts in the multiculturalism wars. Shachar's is an excellent example of the first type of argument, about the (in)justice of particular policies; Spinner-Halev's is an important contribution to the second debate, about the impact on citizenship. I will discuss each of these new debates in turn, and where they are likely to lead in the next few years.

1. Justice in context

Some critics accept that the justice of multicultural demands must be evalu-ated on a case-by-case basis, and so focus on the potential injustices of par-ticular multicultural proposals in particular contexts, rather than making global claims about the inherent injustice of group-specific policies. These sorts of context-specific arguments are, I think, essential, and reflect real progress in the debate.

At the level of particular cases, the debate focuses, not on whether multi-culturalism is right or wrong in principle, but rather on a range of more prac-tical issues about the distribution of the benefits and burdens of specific policies—e.g. what exactly is the disadvantage which a minority faces within a particular institutional structure? Will the proposed multiculturalism reform actually remedy this disadvantage? Are the costs of a particular multicultural-ism policy distributed fairly, or are some individuals inside or outside the group being asked to shoulder an unfair share of the costs? Are there alternative policies which would remedy the disadvantage in a more effective and less costly way?

A good example of this sort of debate is the recent work on affirmative action in America. Whereas older debates focused almost entirely on whe-ther race-based preferences in admissions or hiring were morally wrong in principle, there is increasing recognition that this is too simple. It is widely accepted that African-Americans and other minorities face real disadvantages in certain institutional contexts, despite the professed colour-blind nature of these institutions, and that something needs to be done to remedy these disadvantages. The objection to affirmative action, therefore, is not that any deviation from colour-blind rules is unjust in principle, but rather that current affirmative action policies do not actually benefit the people who are most in need (i.e. they help middle-class blacks, but not the inner-city poor), that the costs of affirmative action are borne disproportionately by one group (i.e. young white males, some of whom may themselves be disadvantaged), and that there are alternative policies which would be more effective (i.e. improved funding for inner-city schools). Others respond that affirmative action has been demonstrably successful, and that no alternative policy has been nearly as effective.[5]

This new debate on affirmative action in the USA remains unresolved, to say the least, but at least it is the right *kind* of debate. It focuses, not on slogans about a colour-blind constitution, but on how particular educational or employment institutions do or do not disadvantage the members of particular groups, and on how proposed group-specific policies would or would not remedy that problem. And while the result of the debate may be to trim or amend existing affirmative action programmes, it is unlikely that the result will be to eliminate all forms of race-conscious policies. On the contrary, it may well be that the alternatives which replace or supplement affirmative action will be equally group-specific in their focus—e.g. support for black colleges, or state-sponsored mentoring programmes for promising black students. That is, one form of multiculturalism policy will be replaced, amended, or supplemented with another form of multiculturalism policy.

Indeed, we can generalize this point. Since mainstream institutions privilege the majority's culture and identity in so many ways, and since people's interests in culture and identity are so important, the question we face is not whether to adopt multiculturalism, but rather which *kind* of multiculturalism to adopt. Once we jettison the idea that group-specific rights are wrong in principle, and instead get down to brass tacks and examine particular institutions, then the question becomes which sort of multiculturalism is most fair and effective, and how best to combine group-specific multiculturalism policies with difference-blind common rights. It is in this sense, as Nathan Glazer put it recently, that 'we are all multiculturalists now' (Glazer, 1997), even though we profoundly disagree over the merits of particular multiculturalism policies.

To my mind, Shachar's chapter is an excellent illustration of this new type of debate. Her focus is on multicultural accommodations in the area of family law, and on the potential injustices these multiculturalism policies can create. She convincingly argues that particular forms of multiculturalism in family law can impose unfair burdens on women members of the group. As she puts it, women often 'bear disproportionate costs for preserving their group's nomos' (p. 91).

But she is not arguing against multiculturalism in general, or defending the principle that justice requires a common family lay which is blind to group differences. While she occasionally talks about 'the perils of multicultural accommodation',[6] she is not in fact denying that we should adopt a multicultural conception of family law. On the contrary, she takes for granted that justice requires the explicit recognition and accommodation of group differences in family law. She is simply insisting that we rethink or 'reshape' multiculturalism, so as to protect the vulnerable members within identity groups (p. 108 n. 73). In short, like Glazer, she accepts that we are all multiculturalists now, and the only question is what kind of multiculturalists we will be.

As I noted earlier, I agree with the central claim of Shachar's chapter—namely, that we must look carefully at intragroup inequalities, and specifically at gender-inequalities, when examining the justice of minority group rights. Justice *within* ethnocultural groups is as important as justice *between* different ethnocultural groups. Group rights can help promote justice if they remedy inequalities between ethnocultural groups, but are unjust if they create or exacerbate gender inequalities within the group. The benefits and burdens of multiculturalism must be fairly distributed, both between groups and within groups.

I have tried to emphasize this point by distinguishing between two kinds of 'group rights'. Sometimes an ethnocultural group claims rights against its own members—in particular, the right to restrict individual choice in the name of cultural 'tradition' or cultural 'integrity'. I call such group rights 'internal restrictions', since their aim is to restrict the ability of individuals within the group (particularly women) to question, revise, or abandon traditional cultural roles and practices. A liberal theory of minority group rights, I have argued, will view such internal restrictions as unjust, since they violate the autonomy of individuals, and create inequalities within the group.

However, liberals can endorse a second sort of group rights—namely, rights which are claimed by a minority group against the larger society in order to reduce its vulnerability to the economic or political power of the larger society. Such rights, which I call 'external protections', can take the form of language rights, guaranteed political representation, funding of ethnic media, land claims, compensation for historical injustice, or the regional devolution of power. All of these can help to promote justice between ethnocultural groups by ensuring that members of the minority have the same effective capacity to promote their interests as the majority.

At various points, Shachar expresses doubts about this distinction (e.g. 102 n. 23), but I don't fully understand her objections. It still think that the basic distinction is sound, and indeed provides a potential framework for Shachar's own conception of a 'reshaped' multiculturalism. It seems to me that what she means by a reshaped multiculturalism is precisely one which provides external protections to groups, so as to reduce inequalities between groups, but which ensures that all group members are able to exercise their basic rights, including their right to question and revise the group's cultural traditions.[7]

I also agree with many of the other claims in Shachar's paper—e.g. that the idea of non-intervention by the state in family matters is a myth, since political authorities set the background rules for family organization; that any acceptable form of multiculturalism must recognize the reality of people's multiple identities, so that no one group identity or membership is assumed to automatically trump or subsume all others; and that the right of exit is not a sufficient safeguard to protect against the oppression of individuals. On all of these points, Shachar's analysis is persuasive.

Where we *may* differ, however, is on the question of state intervention, or rather, the question of *which* state has the rightful authority to intervene in cases where the decisions of self-governing identity groups are unjust. Or put another way, we may disagree, not about the relevant standards of *justice*, but about the issue of *jurisdiction*.

Shachar talks throughout the chapter about 'the state' or 'the political community', as one of the three elements in her 'trichotomy' (along with individuals and identity groups). Talking about 'the' political community in this way, in the singular, implies that all citizens belong to just one political community. When Shachar claims that 'the state' should intervene in identity groups to protect the basic rights of women members, she takes it for granted that there is just one state which is in a position to do so, and that we all know and agree which state this is. And reading between the lines—since she never explicitly states or defends this assumption—it seems clear that Shachar thinks that the relevant political community is the *nation-state*.

I think we need to question this. People belong to various political communities, operating at various levels, and it is not at all clear (to me, at least) which level of polity should have the rightful authority to intervene in cases where identity groups act unjustly towards their own members. In contexts where there are two or more levels of government exercising jurisdiction over particular individuals and territories, it may well be that the best defender of individual rights is a level of government which is below the level of the nation-state (e.g. a subunit of a federation), or one which is above the level of the nation-state (e.g. international human rights tribunals).

This is particularly important when thinking about indigenous peoples. Shachar discusses the case of Indian tribes in the United States, and argues that we shouldn't give *carte blanche* to tribal leaders to determine the family status of Indian women. But in defending the need for state intervention, she takes for granted, without any discussion, that the relevant state which should intervene is the American federal government.

This is a common assumption, particularly amongst people trained in American jurisprudence. American liberals often assume that to have a 'right' means not only that legislators should respect one's claim when passing legislation, but also that there should be some system of judicial review to make sure that the legislature respects one's claim. Moreover, this judicial review should occur at a country-wide level. That is, in addition to the various state and tribal courts which review the laws of state and tribal governments, there should also be a Supreme Court to which all governments within the country are answerable. Indeed, many American liberals often talk as if it is part of the very meaning of 'rights' that there should be a single court in each country with the authority to review the decisions of all governments within that country, to ensure that they respect liberal rights.

This is a very particularistic understanding of rights. In some liberal countries (e.g. Britain), there is a strong tradition of respecting individual rights, but there is no constitutional bill of rights, and no basis for courts to overturn parliamentary decisions which violate individual rights. (The same was true in Canada until 1982.) In other countries, there is judicial review, but it is decentralized—that is, political subunits have their own systems of judicial review, but there is no single constitutional bill of rights, and no single court, to which all levels of government are answerable. Indeed, this was true in the United States for a considerable period of time. Until the passage of the Fourteenth Amendment, state legislatures were answerable to state courts for the way they respected state constitutions, but were not answerable to the federal Supreme Court for respecting the federal Bill of Rights.

It's easy to see why American liberals are committed to giving the Supreme Court authority over the actions of state governments. Historically, this sort of federal judicial review, backed up by federal troops, was required to overturn the racist legislation of Southern states, which state courts had upheld. Given the central role federal courts have played in the struggle against racism, American liberals have developed a deep commitment to the principle of centralized judicial review, according to which a single body should have the authority to review and overturn the actions of all levels of government within each country, on the basis of a single bill of rights. So when the question is raised about applying centralized judicial review to self-governing indigenous groups, many liberals automatically support it, even though indigenous peoples were historically exempt from such review.

But we need to tread carefully here. There is overwhelming evidence that most Indians oppose having their self-governing decisions overturned by American courts interpreting an American Bill of Rights. And I think this opposition to federal intervention is perfectly understandable. The American Supreme Court is the court of the conquerors. It is a court which has historically legitimated the dispossession of Indian lands and the forcible resettlement of Indian peoples. It is a court which has denied both the individual rights and treaty rights of Indians on the basis of racist and ethnocentric assumptions, and which has generally played the role of providing legal and moral justifications for conquest. To automatically assume that the federal court has jurisdiction over Indian peoples is, therefore, highly problematic.

This doesn't mean we should give *carte blanche* to tribal leaders to restrict the rights of their members. Rather, it means we need to think creatively about new or alternative mechanisms for protecting rights.[8] For example, we can push for the development and strengthening of international mechanisms for protecting human rights. Some Indian tribes have expressed a willingness to abide by international declarations of human rights, and to answer to international tribunals for complaints of rights violations within their communities. They accept the idea that their governments, like all governments, should be accountable to international norms. Indeed, they have shown greater willingness to accept this kind of international review than many nation-states, which jealously guard their sovereignty in domestic affairs. Most Indian tribes do not oppose all forms of external review. What they object to is being subject to the constitution of their conquerors, which they had no role in drafting, and being answerable to federal courts, composed solely of non-Indian justices.

This shows, I think, that Shachar's assumption that the national court within each country should be the ultimate defender of individual rights seems doubly mistaken, at least in the case of indigenous peoples. History has shown the value of holding governments accountable for respecting human rights, and family law should not be immune from this accountability. But the appropriate forums for reviewing the actions of self-governing indigenous peoples may skip the federal level, as it were. Many indigenous groups would endorse a system in which their self-governing decisions are reviewed in the first instance by their own courts, and then by an international court. Federal courts, dominated by the majority, would have little or have no authority to review and overturn these decisions.

These international mechanisms could arise at the regional as well as global level. European countries have agreed to establish their own multilateral human rights tribunals. Perhaps North American governments and Indian tribes could agree to establish a similar multilateral human rights tribunal, on which both sides are fairly represented.

My aim here is not to defend any particular proposal for a regional or international body, or to defend any particular criteria for intervention, domestically or internationally. My goal, rather, is to question Shachar's oversimplified picture of the trichotomy between individuals, identity groups, and the state. Shachar is certainly right that political communities are not external to identity groups, and that any defensible model of multiculturalism must account for the ways that political communities structure identity groups. But in addition to examining the relationship between identity groups and the political community, we also need to examine the relationship between different political communities within a state. In particular, we need to think seriously about the relationship between conquered/colonized indigenous groups and the courts of the larger society.

In questioning the legitimacy of federal intervention in the self-governing decisions of indigenous peoples, I am not disputing the prevalence or seriousness of rights-violations within many identity groups. On the contrary, it is precisely because individual rights are so important that we need to think creatively about finding new mechanisms for protecting the rights of vulnerable individuals—mechanisms which do not rely on unacceptable colonial assumptions.

This raises an important point which remains undertheorized in debates about the justice of particular multiculturalism policies. It is one question to evaluate whether a particular multicultural accommodation would promote or hinder justice; it is quite another to determine which level of government has the rightful authority to implement or eliminate these accommodations. As I noted earlier, we need to think not only about the *justice* of multiculturalism policies, but also about *jurisdiction* over multiculturalism policies. In today's world, where the powers of the nation-state are slowly being devolved downwards to subnational governments, and upwards to suprastate institutions, the question of who should have the power to decide on the adoption of multiculturalism policies is not an easy one. Earlier debates took for granted that the nation-state was the ultimate arbiter of the justice of multiculturalism, but that assumption is increasingly in need of rethinking.

2. *Eroding citizenship*

So far, I have focused on critics who question the justice of particular multiculturalism policies. The shift towards a more context-sensitive evaluation of policies is a good one, and has led to a more fruitful debate. But as I noted earlier, the more we examine particular cases, the more difficult it is to sustain a blanket critique of multiculturalism as such. Indeed, the typical result of such a shift is that we are no longer debating whether to become multiculturalists, but rather what kind of multiculturalists we should be.

However, there are still those who wish to make a more broad-ranging critique of multiculturalism. Since it is no longer plausible to argue that all forms of multiculturalism are inherently unjust, critics have had to find another basis on which to condemn the very idea of multiculturalism. And the most common argument is one which focuses on *stability* rather than justice.

This focus on stability represents, I think, the opening of a second front in the multiculturalism wars. Many critics claim that multicultural accommodations are misguided, not because they are unjust in themselves, but rather because they are corrosive of long-term political unity and social stability. They may promote justice in principle, but in practice they are dangerous.

Why are multiculturalism policies seen as destabilizing? Different authors offer different answers, but the underlying worry is that multiculturalism involves the 'politicization of ethnicity', and that any measures which heighten the salience of ethnicity in public life are divisive. Over time they create a spiral of competition, mistrust, and antagonism between ethnic groups. Policies which increase the salience of ethnic identities are said to act 'like a corrosive on metal, eating away at the ties of connectedness that bind us together as a nation'.[9] On this view, liberal democracies must prevent ethnic identities from becoming politicized by rejecting any multiculturalism policies which involve the explicit public recognition of ethnic groups.

The extreme version of this critique treats multiculturalism as the first step on the road to Yugoslavia-style civil war. The idea that multiculturalism within Western democracies could lead to civil war is almost too silly to be worth discussing. But there is a more modest version of this criticism which is worth considering, and which is often phrased in the language of *citizenship*.

Multiculturalism, on this view, may not lead to civil war, but it will erode the ability of citizens to fulfil their responsibilities as democratic citizens— e.g. it will erode their ability to communicate, trust, and feel solidarity across group differences. And so even if a particular multiculturalism policy is not itself unjust, examined in isolation, the trend towards the increased salience of ethnicity will erode the norms and practices of responsible citizenship, and so reduce the overall functioning of the state.

Critics of multiculturalism worry that if groups are encouraged to turn inward and focus on their 'difference', then as Glazer put it in the American context, 'the hope of a larger fraternity of all Americans will have to be abandoned' (Glazer, 1983: 227). Citizenship cannot perform its vital integrative function if it is group-differentiated—it ceases to be 'a device to cultivate a sense of community and a common sense of purpose' (Heater, 1990: 295). Nothing will bind the various groups in society together, and prevent the spread of mutual mistrust or conflict. If citizenship is differentiated, it no longer provides a shared experience or common status. Citizenship would be yet another force for disunity, rather than a way of cultivating unity in the face of increasing social diversity. Citizenship should be a forum where people transcend their differences, and think about the common good of all citizens.

This is a serious concern. It is clear that the health and stability of a modern democracy depends, not only on the justice of its basic institutions, but also on the qualities and attitudes of its citizens—e.g. their sense of identity, and how they view potentially competing forms of national, regional, ethnic, or religious identities; their ability to tolerate and work together with others who are different from themselves; their desire to participate in the political process in order to promote the public good and hold political authorities accountable; their willingness to show self-restraint and exercise personal responsibility in their economic demands, and in personal choices which affect their health and the environment; and their sense of justice and commitment to a fair distribution of resources. Without citizens who possess these qualities, 'the ability of liberal societies to function successfully progressively diminishes' (Glaston, 1991: 220).[10]

There is growing fear that the public-spiritedness of citizens of liberal democracies may be in serious decline. And if group-based claims would further erode the sense of shared civic purpose and solidarity, then that would be a powerful reason not to adopt multiculturalism policies.

While I agree that this is an important issue that needs to be investigated, I also suspect that many of these claims about the erosion of citizenship are not entirely in good faith. It's interesting to note that many of the same people who used to argue vehemently that multiculturalism was unjust in principle, now argue with equal vehemence that while multiculturalism policies may be just in principle, they are dangerous in practice. It sometimes appears as if critics of multiculturalism, no longer confident about claims of justice, are casting around for another argument to use, and citizenship happened to be the most convenient. This suspicion is strengthened, I think, by the fact that so many critics raise this objection without providing any evidence for it.

Still, we cannot ignore this worry that multiculturalism will erode the norms and practices of responsible democratic citizenship. What we can do, however, is to insist that people provide reasoned arguments and empirical evidence, not just armchair speculation. And this is what is strikingly lacking in many of the discussions to date.

Fortunately, this is just the gap which Spinner-Halev is helping to fill, both in his chapter and in his earlier book (Spinner, 1994). His chapter provides the sort of fine-grained and context-sensitive exploration of the impact of multiculturalism on citizenship that we need.

What I particularly like about his work is that he has a firm commitment to both the accommodation of diversity and the need for a robust conception of responsible citizenship, and does not seek to defend the one by denigrating the other. Too often, proponents of responsible citizenship jump to the conclusion that multiculturalism is a threat to citizenship, and so seek to trivialize the importance of accommodating cultural diversity. Conversely, some proponents of multicultural accommodations defend their position by downplaying the importance of citizenship. But Spinner-Halev argues that we need both, and so takes seriously the question of how they are related.

I agree with the basic claims in Spinner-Halev's chapter. In particular, I agree that most forms of multiculturalism sought by immigrant groups in North America are about *inclusion*, and that such claims pose no threat to citizenship.[11] As he puts it, multicultural accommodations aimed at accommodating immigrant diversity within inclusive institutions may be difficult, but 'will not, however, harm citizenship. It will allow more people to be first-class citizens while adhering to their particular practices and beliefs' (p. 70).

Spinner-Halev is entirely right, I think, to reject the common assumption that immigrant multiculturalism is promoting 'separatism'. As he notes, North American multiculturalism policies are intended to make immigrant groups feel more comfortable within *common* institutions. This is true, for example, of demands that the curriculum in public schools be revised so as to provide greater recognition for the historical contributions of immigrant groups; or of demands that public institutions recognize the religious holidays of immigrant groups (e.g. recognizing Muslim and Jewish as well as Christian holidays); or of demands that official dress-codes for schools, workplaces, and police forces be amended so that Sikh men can wear turbans, or Jewish men can wear skullcaps, or Muslim women can wear the hijab; or of demands that schools and workplaces provide a welcoming environment for people of all races and religions by prohibiting hate speech; or of demands that the media avoid ethnic stereotyping, and give visible representation to society's diversity in their programming; or of demands that professionals in the police, social work, or health care be familiar with the distinctive cultural needs and practices of the people in their care.

Critics of these policies typically focus entirely on the fact that they involve public affirmation and recognition of immigrants' ethnic identity —a process which is said to be inherently separatist. But they ignore the fact that this affirmation and recognition occurs *within common institutions*. There is no sense in which any of these policies encourages either an Amish-like withdrawal from the institutions of mainstream society, or a nationalist struggle to create and maintain separate public institutions. On the contrary, these policies are flatly in contradiction with both ethnic marginalization and ethnonationalism, since they encourage integration into mainstream institutions. They encourage more immigrants to participate within existing academic, economic, and political institutions, and modify these institutions to make immigrants more welcome within them.

Some critics might think that even this modest form of giving recognition to ethnic differences will harm citizenship, and that any form of politicizing ethnicity is dangerous. But Spinner-Halev gives us good reasons for thinking that such a fear is misplaced. And indeed the evidence from Canada and Australia—the two countries which first adopted official multiculturalism policies for immigrants—is unambiguous on this. There is no evidence in either country that multiculturalism has promoted ethnic separatism, political apathy, or instability, or the mutual hostility of ethnic groups. On the contrary, these two countries in fact do a better job integrating immigrants into common civic and political institutions than any other country in the world. On any relevant statistical measure, multiculturalism in these two countries has succeeded in helping to ensure that those people who wish to express their ethnic identity are respected and accommodated, while simultaneously increasing the ability of immigrants to integrate into the larger society.[12]

I also agree with Spinner-Halev that this sort of inclusive immigrant multiculturalism is very different from the sort of isolationist separatism desired by ethnoreligious sects, like the Amish or Hutterites. Their demands are in many ways the reverse of immigrant groups. Their aim is not to gain greater participation and recognition within common institutions, but rather to avoid all contact with the institutions of larger society, which they see as irredeemably corrupt.

Spinner-Halev's description of these sects as 'partial citizens' is, I think, a very apt one, and is an important conceptual innovation (p. 71). As he puts it, these groups have struck a kind of 'bargain' in which they forgo most of their citizenship rights in return for exemption from most of their civic responsibilities (p. 72). I also agree that these groups pose no threat *at present* to the health and stability of citizenship, since there are only a few such groups, each of which is small in numbers and politically inactive.

However, and this is my one question about Spinner-Halev's argument, one could imagine circumstances in which the threat to citizenship from such 'partial citizens' grew larger. In particular, how should liberal states think about religious groups which have not yet formed? To date, we have a fixed number of well-established isolationist ethnoreligious sects, all of which have been around for a while, and all of whom are more or less peacefully accommodated. But imagine that, for some unexplained reason (the end of the millennium?), there is a sudden upsurge in new religions, some of which might develop in illiberal directions, and so seek similar accommodations as these historical isolationist sects.

How should the liberal state respond to such a situation? In his chapter, Spinner-Halev tends to treat state policy and religious beliefs as wholly independent factors. He writes as if state policy must respond (one way or another) to pre-existing religious beliefs. But state policy also influences how religious belief develops. This is clear enough in the case of mainstream Catholics and Jews in America. Many of the original Catholic and Jewish immigrants were illiberal, and they initially expressed hostility to the norms of liberal citizenship. But once it became clear that the state was firm in its expectations of liberal citizenship, they adapted. Of course, some conservative Catholic and Jewish groups have not adapted. But they are the minority. Faced with a firm liberal state, the majority within these religions adapted their beliefs to fit the expectations of the state. Historically, then, religious belief has been an endogenous factor, not exogenous. Religious belief responds to pre-existing state policy, just as much as state policy must respond to pre-existing religious beliefs.

Faced with the possibility that new religious groups will emerge in the future, the state must decide whether it will stand firm in its expectations of liberal citizenship, or whether it will grant accommodations to any group which demands them. We can reliably predict that if the state offers accommodations, many groups will accept them rather than adapt to conform to liberal norms. As Spinner-Halev notes, exemptions from the norms of liberal citizenship make is easier for religious groups to maintain themselves over time (p. 107). In the absence of explicit state pressure, therefore, we can expect many religious groups will seek such exemptions, and will come to view such exemptions as necessary to their 'way of life'. This is the path of least resistance for new religious groups.

This is not a happy prospect for liberal states. The liberal state has an interest, I think, in discouraging new religious groups from adopting the view that their way of life is inherently in conflict with norms of liberal citizenship. Unfortunately, unless the state gives new religious groups a powerful incentive to avoid a doctrinal conflict with liberal citizenship, they are unlikely to do so of their own accord.

It might be desirable, then, from a liberal point of view, to draw a sharp distinction between the claims of older established religious groups, and the claims of newly emerging religious groups. It might be prudent and wise to accommodate the former, but equally prudent and wise to stand firm *vis-à-vis* the latter. And indeed I think this is the practice which we see in North America. Accommodations which were offered to the Hutterites and Amish at the turn of the century are not offered to newly emerging religious sects or cults.

Of course such a policy would only be justified if we had a particular view of the justification for accommodation. If the moral argument for accommodation is that toleration is an inherent moral value, on a par with freedom and equality, then presumably it would be unjustified to distinguish between the claims of older and newer religions. If there is some sort of inherent argument of justice or right why isolationist religious groups should be accommodated, then it would seem indefensible to give justice to older groups but not to newer groups.

However, it is not clear to me that Spinner-Halev thinks that isolationist religious sects have a claim of *justice* to the accommodation of their illiberal practices. Instead, it often seems as if his argument for accommodation is more prudential and contingent, resting for example on the claim that intervention to impose liberal norms on well-established isolationist sects might simply backfire and worsen the situation; or on appeals to the existence of specific historical agreements which guarantee certain exemptions to particular groups.

In my view, the most plausible argument in favour of exemptions for the Amish is indeed rooted in historical agreements. One could argue that the Amish have a stronger claim to accommodation than newly emerging isolationist religious groups because, as the Supreme Court put it, the Amish were implicitly *promised* that they would be accommodated. If they hadn't received this promise, they would have emigrated elsewhere. Moreover, the fact that these groups have been granted certain exemptions for generations now, and have been able to build up a wide range of institutions based upon this accommodation, arguably gives rise to a legitimate expectation that this accommodation will continue.

But these accommodations could be seen as one-off exceptions which arose before the state had a clear conception of, or policy on, norms of liberal citizenship. As Spinner-Halev rightly notes, the state today is more intimately involved in social life, and this has greatly increased the demands of liberal citizenship. Norms of non-discrimination which used to apply only to public institutions now apply to institutions of civil society, and this requires more from liberal citizens (p. 102). It is understandable and appropriate, therefore, that as the demands of citizenship have increased, the state has become less willing to grant such exemptions or accommodations. Justice may require fulfilling solemn historical agreements, even if we now regret them, but it does not require allowing new groups to gain access to the same exemptions which were historically granted.

I do not know whether Spinner-Halev would agree with this history-based argument for allowing the Amish to retain the status of 'partial citizens', or whether he thinks that this status should be made available to any ethnic or religious group which would like to adopt it. If the latter, then it seems to me that he is perhaps underestimating the danger which partial citizens could raise for liberal citizenship. To date, partial citizens pose little threat to the functioning of liberal democracies because only a few small groups have been offered this status. Newly emerging groups have not been offered the 'bargain' of forgoing their citizenship rights in return for exemption from their civic responsibilities. If, however, the status of partial citizenship is seen not as a historical exception, but rather as a status which any group can rightfully claim if it accords with their beliefs and doctrines, then one could imagine a more serious impact over time on the practice of democratic citizenship.

3. CONCLUSION

These two chapters are indicative, I think, that the debate over multicultur-alism is making progress. We are moving beyond the sterile debate about whether it is inherently right or wrong for public policies and public institu-tions to be group-specific rather than difference-blind, and instead are look-ing at the concrete benefits and burdens of particular policies. This is a much more fruitful debate.

I also think that it is important, when assessing these burdens and benefits, to consider the long-term impact of multiculturalism policies on political stability, and on the norms and practices of democratic citizenship. This too is a useful development in the debate.

However, I also worry about this new preoccupation with civic virtues. It seems, at times, to be displacing the older concern with justice. Rawls famously argued that 'justice is the first virtue of social institutions', and I think he was right to do so. Justice is an intrinsic value, and the most basic obligation of the State. Civic virtue, by contrast, is only an instrumental value. Indeed, the main reason to be concerned about the erosion of civic virtue is that it may over time diminish the ability of the State to secure justice.

It would be a profound mistake, therefore, to privilege the promotion of civic virtue over the remedying of injustice. If particular multiculturalism policies help remedy disadvantages that minorities face, then we have a powerful reason to adopt such policies, and we should not refrain from doing so simply on the basis of armchair speculation about the harmful impact of multiculturalism on citizenship. Policies which remedy injustices should be adopted unless we have evidence that they pose a 'clear and present danger' to political order. Like Spinner-Halev, I believe that many forms of multiculturalism promote both justice and citizenship. But even if remedying injustices through multiculturalism policies might create small or speculative decreases in the level of civic virtue, this is no reason to reject multiculturalism policies. It is important to study the connection between multiculturalism and democratic citizenship, but it is equally important to keep our priorities clear. Justice is the first virtue of public institutions, and civic virtue is one means to help achieve justice. To sacrifice justice in the name of promoting civic virtue is to put the cart before the horse.

NOTES

1. I will use the term 'multiculturalism' to refer to all such claims, whether made by immigrant groups, indigenous peoples, national minorities, racial groups, or ethnoreligious sects. Other authors use other terms, e.g. 'differentiated citizenship' or 'group-differentiated rights'. All of these terms have their drawbacks, but for the purposes of this chapter, I will follow Shachar and Spinner-Halev in using 'multiculturalism' as an umbrella term.
2. See Minow (1990); Young (1990); Parekh (1991); Taylor (1992); Phillips (1993); Spinner (1994); Tully (1995).
3. For more detailed discussion, see Kymlicka (1997). This is one area where the debate over multiculturalism has had important ramifications for broader issues about the nature of the liberal-democratic state.
4. Margalit and Raz (1990); Taylor (1992); Tamir (1993); Nickel (1995).
5. Any plausible examination of this issue will show, I think, that affirmative action has worked well in some contexts, and less well in others. For an example of where it has been strikingly successful (the Army), see Moskos (1996).
6. This is the title of Shachar (1998).
7. Shachar says that she disagrees with my presumption that 'the external and internal aspects of group accommodation can or should be considered separately' (p. 102 n. 23). But my claim is not that they can be 'considered separately'. It's clear that the capacity to impose internal restrictions is inextricably bound up with the acquisition of external protections, and so we need to analyse them together. However, my claim is that the goal, from a liberal point of view, is (a) to ensure that groups have the external protections they need, while (b) creating the institutional safeguards which prevent groups from imposing internal restrictions. If Shachar thinks this is impossible to achieve, then I disagree.
8. For a more detailed discussion, see Kymlicka (1996).

9. Ward (1991: 598); cf. Lind (1995); Schlesinger (1992).
10. Galston (1991: 215–17, 244); Macedo (1990: 138–9). For a more detailed discussion of this renewed focus on citizenship within contemporary political philosophy, see Kymlicka and Norman (1994).
11. Spinner-Halev doesn't make explicit that he is talking specifically about multiculturalism in the context of immigrant groups to North America, but I think this is clearly his reference point. As he himself notes elsewhere, the situation is very different for non-immigrant national minorities or indigenous groups (Spinner, 1994).
12. For the statistical evidence, see Kymlicka (1998: ch. 2).

REFERENCES

Galston, William (1991), *Liberal Purposes: Goods, Virtues, and Duties in the Liberal State* (Cambridge: Cambridge University Press).
Glazer, Nathan (1983), *Ethnic Dilemmas: 1964–1982* (Cambridge, Mass.: Harvard University Press).
—— (1997), *We Are All Multiculturalists Now* (Cambridge, Mass.: Harvard University Press).
Heater, Derek (1990), *Citizenship: The Civic Ideal in World History, Politics and Education* (London: Longman).
Kymlicka, W. (1996), 'Minority Group Rights: The Good, The Bad and the Intolerable', *Dissent*, Summer 1996: 22–30.
—— (1997), 'The New Debate over Minority Rights', Working Paper, Robert Harney Professorship Publications, University of Toronto.
—— (1998), *Finding Our Way: Rethinking Ethnocultural Relations in Canada* (Toronto: Oxford University Press).
Kymlicka, W. and Norman, Wayne (1994) 'Return of the Citizen: A Survey of Recent Work on Citizenship Theory', *Ethics*, 104/2: 352–81.
Lind, Michael (1995), *The Next American Nation* (New York: Free Press).
Macedo, Stephen (1990), *Liberal Virtues: Citizenship, Virtue and Community* (Oxford: Oxford University Press).
Margalit, Avishai, and Joseph Raz (1990), 'National Self-Determination', *Journal of Philosophy*, 87/9: 439–61.
Minow, Martha (1990), *Making all the Difference: Inclusion, Exclusion and American Law* (Ithaca, NY: Cornell University Press).
Moskos, Charles (1996), *All That We Can Be* (New York: Basic Books).
Nickel, James (1995), 'The Value of Cultural Belonging', *Dialogue*, 33/4: 635–42.
Parekh, Bhikhu (1991), 'British Citizenship and Cultural Difference', in Geoff Andrews (ed.) *Citizenship* (London: Lawrence & Wishart): 183–204.
Phillips, Anne (1993), *Democracy and Difference* (University Park: Pennsylvania State University Press).
Schlesinger, Arthur M., Jr. (1992), *The Disuniting of America* (New York: Norton).
Shachar, Ayelet (1998), 'Group Identity and Women's Rights in Family Law: The Perils of Multicultural Accommodation', *Journal of Political Philosophy*, 6/3: 285–305.

Spinner, Jeff (1994), *The Boundaries of Citizenship: Race, Ethnicity and Nationality in the Liberal State* (Baltimore: Johns Hopkins University Press).

Tamir, Yael (1993), *Liberal Nationalism* (Princeton: Princeton University Press).

Taylor, Charles (1992), 'The Politics of Recognition', in Amy Gutmann (ed.), *Multiculturalism and the 'Politics of Recognition'* (Princeton: Princeton University Press): 25–73.

Tully, James (1995), *Strange Multiplicity: Constitutionalism in an Age of Diversity* (Cambridge: Cambridge University Press).

Ward, Cynthia (1991), 'The Limits of "Liberal Republicanism": Why Group-Based Remedies and Republican Citizenship Don't Mix', *Columbia Law Review*, 91/3: 581–607.

Young, Iris Marion (1990), *Justice and the Politics of Difference* (Princeton: Princeton University Press).

III

Do Minorities Require Group Rights?

7

Liberal Justifications for Ethnic Group Rights

RAINER BAUBÖCK

---

1. INTRODUCTION

In this essay I want to discuss four arguments which support claims of ethnic and national groups to specific group rights. The path towards such a positive defence of ethnic group rights is mined with various kinds of objections
raised by liberal theorists.

A first barrier which has to be overcome is the rejection of all group
rights as incompatible with principles of equality or individual liberty. In
this essay I will not elaborate on the purely theoretical question whether it
is conceptually possible to conceive of social groups as the bearers of rights
and, if it is, what type of arguments would be needed to justify group rights
within a broadly liberal philosophy of rights.[1] Instead I will go on the
counter-offensive by describing three strategies of opponents of group rights
and attempting to show why they are unattractive, uninteresting, or counter-
productive.

A second type of objection accepts the existence and potential legitimacy
of group rights but argues against specific rights for ethnic groups. Some authors
object against special privileges for ethnic compared to other groups and want
to extend the liberal principle of treating all individuals as equals to groups.
They want to make sure that liberal group rights are neither partial between
various groups of the same kind, e.g. by favouring a national majority over
ethnic minorities,[2] nor partial between different kinds of groups, e.g. by giving stronger rights to ethnic groups compared to groups characterized by a
common religion, gender, or lifestyle.[3] Others are more worried about ethnic
group rights than about those of other kinds of groups because they believe
that ethnic groups are more likely to use such rights for suppressing individual liberties.[4] One way of arguing for strictly equal group rights is to derive
all such rights from voluntary association. In this view, any group can enjoy
rights if its members freely adhere to it and can freely leave it and all such
group rights ought to be constrained by the same requirements that they should
neither restrict their members' liberty nor impose unfair external costs on non-
members. Ascriptive groups then can enjoy rights insofar as they are able to
organize their members in voluntary associations. By doing this, they will

also overcome the problems of effective agency and clear identity which are obstacles for attributing rights to informal groups.[5]

I will address these critiques only indirectly by arguing that positive justifications for ethnic group rights refer to special characteristics of such groups and can therefore not be easily generalized for other kinds of groups. A theory of group rights must pay attention to the impact of group differences on the allocation of those social goods that John Rawls has called primary ones: liberty and opportunity, income and wealth, and the social bases of self-respect (Rawls, 1971: 62) and must consider whether affiliation to certain cultural groups should itself be regarded as a primary good (Kymlicka, 1989: 178). The lesson of this exercise is that strong group rights must always be justified contextually. If national and ethnic minorities enjoy stronger group rights than, say, chess-players or green-eyed persons it is because in the context of our societies and states ethnic membership represents a much stronger value for individuals and has a much more pervasive effect on their opportunities. And although I want to affirm that ethnic membership shouldn't be seen as entirely beyond individual control, most reasons for ethnic group rights do not conceive of the group as a voluntary association.

In this discussion I will use the term group rights as comprising two different categories: group-differentiated rights and collective rights.[6] The former refer to a differentiation of individual rights according to membership in groups, the latter to those rights where the group itself is the bearer of the right. There are two reasons why prima facie the liberal hostility towards group rights is hard to understand. First, rights of both kinds exist in every liberal democracy and not merely for cultural groups. Voting rights are group-differentiated by age; social welfare is differentiated for the able-bodied and disabled citizens; wage negotiations involve collective bargaining rights for the members of unions; local and provincial self-government establishes collective rights for the inhabitants of municipalities and territorial units of federal states. Second, there is neither a clear dividing line between individual and collective rights[7] nor is it true that rights are more disputed the closer they are to the purely collective pole.[8] Group-specific exemptions for Amish parents with regard to the schooling of their children[9] have certainly aroused more debate than the collective rights of provincial self-government. These initial objections against any wholesale rejection of collective rights become stronger once we consider the implications of arguments that all rights should be purely individual ones.

2. THREE LIBERAL STRATEGIES AGAINST COLLECTIVE RIGHTS

Liberals who proclaim their opposition to group rights may pursue three different strategies towards existing arrangements. They may deny their legitimacy, they may deny the collective nature of the rights involved, or they may accept the collective nature of some arrangements but deny that these involve rights. Let me call these the strategies of rejecting, reducing, and renaming.

The existing panoply of group rights can be most consistently rejected within a libertarian framework which derives all rights from individual self-owner-ship and property entitlements. On the one hand, such rights ought to be strictly equal. Social inequality that emerges from voluntary transactions among holders of equal rights is by definition just (Nozick, 1974). A differentiation of entitlements which takes into account structural disadvantage of groups is therefore at best a temporary measure to compensate individuals for past injustice, but more likely it is a mere pretext for redistributive policies which increase state power and infringe on individual liberty. The libertarian rejection of collective rights properly speaking is less straightforward. If they want to distinguish themselves from anarchists, even libertarians have to admit one quintessential collective right, the state monopoly of legitimate violence, as a necessary safeguard for securing individual liberties in society (ibid. 88–119). They will also tend to accept quite strong rights of voluntary asso-ciations constrained only by the individual freedom of exit (ibid. 320–5) and will view cultural groups as associations of just this sort (Kukathas, 1992, 1997). Libertarians may suggest that rights of states and associations are reducible to individual ones in the sense that they originate in rights of indi-viduals to form a state (which is a territorial political association) or other kinds of unions (Steiner, 1994: 265, n. 61). However, such an assumed *ori-gin* in individual liberties does not prove that the *resulting* rights are not col-lective ones which can be held independently from, and in some cases even against, individuals. In order to deny this possibility, one would have to make the further claim that individual rights always trump collective ones. In the case of collective rights of states individuals subjected to a political auth-ority would fully retain not only their right to emigrate, but also to dissolve the association itself by secession.[10] Libertarians may succeed in developing a strictly individualistic theory of political legitimacy on such grounds. What they normally do not accept and can consistently reject within their theoretical approach is when a state grants special benefits and protection to groups within society or when it arrogates further rights for itself (such as a monopoly in school education) which infringe on the liberties of both individuals and vol-untary associations (to organize themselves the education of their children as they wish).

Egalitarian liberals who defend some existing welfare-state policies against libertarian attacks will have to choose a different strategy. They may say that what appear to be collective rights are really individual ones in disguise. The most difficult challenge for this strategy is how to account for democratic self-government. Liberals will of course defend the view that ultimately democracy is meant to protect the fundamental interests of all individual members of the polity. However, if there are any collective rights, this must be one. First, the idea of popular sovereignty which is fundamental for a democratic order implies that the bearer of this right is a political *community*. Second, in contrast with markets, democratic government provides *public* goods and is itself a public good which is produced and consumed cooperatively.[11] Third, the right attaches to a collectivity membership in which is basically *ascriptive* rather than voluntarily chosen. Citizenship is attributed at birth. The voluntary character of affiliation is only affirmed negatively by optional expatriation after emigration or opportunities of naturalization after immigration.[12]

Yael Tamir's claim that national self-determination can be understood as an individual right attempts to circumvent the challenge of accounting for self-government. She argues that even isolated individuals separated from their group by emigration can exercise this right by declaring themselves members of their nation of origin and retaining its language and culture.[13] For Tamir, what is commonly perceived as a collective right of self-determination, is nothing else but the accumulated *benefits* of the individual right that result from living in the same territory. Yet this confuses two very different senses of 'self-determination'. One is the liberty of individuals to determine themselves their membership. This right is, for example, exercised when people are free to state, or to refuse to state, their ethnic origin in a census questionnaire. The other is the political powers of a group to govern itself. There is no way that the latter could be derived from the former. Members of a national minority may be allowed to declare themselves as such and be granted complete freedom to use their language, but still be denied self-government rights which would, for example, allow them to make their language the medium of instruction in regional public schools. Language rights provide thus another illustration for the irreducible difference between individual and collective rights. The right to speak a language in private life, to teach it to one's children, and to publicly promote it via voluntary associations and private media is an individual liberty. The right to use a language in court or parliament will be generally group-differentiated because it requires public institutions to enable all parties involved to communicate in this language. Establishing a language as the general language of public life and of instruction in public education is a collective right of majorities in a given territory. Again, there seems to be no simple way that the latter could be derived from the former. And a libertarian strategy of abolishing the latter for the sake of maximizing the former would hurt minorities who have a dual interest to preserve their native language and to be able to communicate in the wider society, more than it would hurt majorities who would anyway remain dominant in a market place of private languages.

These are just two examples where reductionism seems to fail. I do not want to generalize that it is logically impossible to reduce collective rights to individual ones. I only want to point out that if this exercise were to succeed it would considerably aggravate the political problems these liberals are concerned about. Claiming that all existing collective rights can be reduced to individual ones seems to provide a wholesale justification for their promotion and proliferation. It will then become rather difficult to argue for a general priority of individual liberties or for other constraints on such rights. Only if we accept that collective rights exist and are different from individual ones can we insist that the former set limits for the latter. As an alternative strategy, liberals might distinguish between reducible collective rights and irreducible ones and deny that the latter can ever be justified. However, this leaves some of the most contested group-differentiated rights like affirmative action quota in the justifiable category, while putting some rather uncontroversial rights, such as legislative powers of federal provinces, into the unjustifiable group.

A third strategy seems more promising. The idea is that, unlike individual rights, group rights should be seen as a matter of policy. In order to avoid the strong implications of a liberal view of rights as trumps we ought to speak of institutional arrangements and collective provisions rather than of collective or group rights.[14] Such arrangements fall into the range of the politically permissible, not the prescribed or obligatory. States may, for prudential reasons, adopt such schemes, but they should not publicly proclaim them as rights or entrench them in their constitutions. The hope is that group rights will thereby become less rigid and less controversial. However, this strategy may fail in most cases. First, such renaming will alienate minorities by distorting the nature of their claims for group rights. They do not see their demands as a begging for privileges which a state is free to grant or withhold. Moreover, this strategy strengthens the legitimacy of collective arrangements working in favour of national majorities and against minorities. If policies in these matters are not constrained by minority rights, why should a dominant group not use its majority of voters and deputies to institutionalize collective arrangements that will serve their interests (e.g. by declaring a majority language the only official one)? In states where minorities are small, dispersed, and powerless they will need external protection in order to block majority preferences[15] and this is why such collective arrangements should be recognized as rights. Second, where there is a rough balance of power between groups in societies deeply divided along religious or ethnic lines consociational forms of democracy will normally be the only viable ones (Lijphart 1991/1995). In schemes of institutionalized power-sharing each group has a vested interest in introducing collective arrangements that make group membership a precondition for access to public services and goods. If they fall within the sphere of simple legislation which is normatively and constitutionally unconstrained by rights, such arrangements will tend to proliferate. These provisions often leave out those who do not belong to any of the constitutive groups and they may also weaken individual rights of the members of these groups as citizens of the common state. Acknowledging that some of the underlying claims are in fact demands for rights makes it easier to establish more stringent criteria for their validity and compatibility than would be applied to collective policies and arrangements.

Affirming the existence and potential justifiability of collective rights is thus not necessarily a plea for their proliferation but may, on the contrary, provide better arguments for constraints on such rights within an overall framework of equal individual citizenship. However, we should first be clear how we conceive of the tension between individual and collective rights. I would like to argue that this is not like a zero-sum game where the former are diminished to the same degree that the latter expand. In order to make this plausible imagine three systems of rights, a Lockian state of nature with equal individual rights only, something like an Ottoman millet system with purely collective rights, and a mixed system like those liberal democracies we are familiar with. My claim is that from the perspective of individual autonomy or well-being the total value of a system of rights is greatest in the mixed one. If this is true, individual and group rights must at least potentially complement each other.

3. FOUR ARGUMENTS FOR ETHNIC GROUP RIGHTS

At the level of abstract moral philosophy we cannot do more than defend the possibility of collective rights. If we want to provide justifications for particular rights of particular kinds of groups, we have to turn to applied normative political theory. The basic structure defended by liberalism in this area is one of equal individual citizenship within each state and universal human rights at the global level of the international political system. Quite obviously, a collective can neither be a citizen nor the subject of a human right. However, collective rights need not conflict with this basic structure when they emerge from a free choice of affiliation, when all can equally share in their benefits, and when they do not constrain the liberties of citizens. Collective rights of voluntary associations or of the liberal state itself can be broadly defended on such grounds. What is prima facie difficult to justify is when the rights of citizens are conditional upon their membership in ascriptive social groups that have to be named in the law.

In this section I will only consider arguments for rights of ethnic groups. These are a special case within the broader category of cultural groups. Ethnic groups are characterized by an imagined common descent more than by shared beliefs and practices. Different from cultural lifestyle groups, ethnic ones always imagine themselves as intergenerational communities. In contrast with 'racial' categories members of ethnic groups inherit a shared culture rather than phenotypic markers. In this sense, ethnic membership involves the kind of affirmation and the possibility of discarding it characteristic for cultural groups. While religious groups are held together by specific beliefs and practices, ethnic ones only need to 'believe' in the commonality that defines the group. They are defined by their boundaries more than by any specific cultural difference (Barth, 1969). In the following discussion I will sometimes refer to ethnic and sometimes to national groups. How could these two categories be distinguished? Often, national and ethnic groups refer to a territory as their homeland or speak a language or dialect of their own but these are accidental rather than constitutive elements for both kinds of groups. The former are characterized by their striving for, or asserting of, collective political autonomy. Ethnic groups can transform themselves into national ones and national communities may define their identity in terms of common ethnic origins. However, this broad area where ethnicity and nationhood overlap does not make the two phenomena identical. National unity need not refer to common descent and ethnic groups need not understand themselves as separate political communities within the wider society.

Ethnic membership involves choice only marginally and mostly indirectly. Normally it is acquired at birth and retained passively throughout one's life. It is neither chosen nor can it be simply abandoned at will. However, it can be changed by voluntary or coerced assimilation into another culture. This is more difficult than changing a religious affiliation or a language, but it can certainly be done. If I want to be seen as a full member of an ethnic group different from the one into which I have been born, and if the members of this group accept me as an equal member, then the circumstances of my birth do no longer matter for my current group and I have changed my membership. The special difficulty of changing an ethnic membership is that it requires more than an effort on behalf of the individual who wants to join another group. The criterion for successful assimilation is always whether the group fully recognizes the new member without stigmatizing his/her descent. Individuals may feel to be multiple members of various ethnic groups when they are of mixed descent, when they have married outside the group, or when they migrate and assimilate into a new host culture. However, multiple membership will often become a predicament rather than an asset when the groups involved do not respect each other and cannot imagine themselves as overlapping.

A differentiation of rights along ethnic boundaries raises concerns about equality as well as liberty. First, individuals belonging to different groups might be treated unequally in a way that violates standards of equal citizenship; and, second such rights may involve pressure either to deny individuals their inherited membership or to force them to stay within a group they want to leave. Any liberal defence of differentiated and collective rights for ethnic groups has to answer to these two concerns.

I will examine four arguments for special rights of ethnocultural groups which should be combined in a comprehensive theory. I call these the arguments of historical boundaries, compensation for collective disadvantage, the value of membership, and the value of diversity.

3.1. Historical boundaries

The argument about historical boundaries addresses two contrasting cases of state formation: the rare one of voluntary federation and the more common one of coercive inclusion.[16] For the former, the case for collective rights is simple and straightforward. When two or more previously separate political communities agree to join their territories to form a single federal state, a contract about the union may give each part a certain autonomy, including the ultimate right to leave the union if it feels seriously disadvantaged. Such precautions will rarely be taken if the populations joining together already have a long common national history and do not differ in their national language (as was the case in the unification of the two German states in 1990). However, if populations are clearly different in their linguistic or religious make-up, as well as in size and economic strength, the representatives of the smaller parts will normally insist on some constitutional provisions for collective rights and territorial autonomy which allow them to maintain their formerly independent polity as a distinct community within the larger state. The common state would in this case be conceived from the start as a federated polity of polities. A national majority originating from one of the former separate states acts unjustly and in breach of an ongoing contract when it abuses its legislative power to eliminate such collective rights of a minority from the constitution—not because such constitutional arrangements can never be changed, but because they should never be changed unilaterally. In such a federation, the consent of all constituent parts of the union to the constitutional framework is a constraint on majority decisions which adds to the more general constraint of protecting equal individual liberties against majority preferences. Imagine that in a federal state consisting of various national groups a majority representing overwhelmingly only one of the groups decides in a state-wide plebiscite to abolish all institutions of self-government of an autonomous national province or decides to change the borders of the province in such a way that the national minority concentrated there will also become a minority in its own province. Would we say that no one's rights have been violated as long as all individual rights of members of the minority as citizens of the federal state are fully retained? This seems to be the conclusion we ought to adopt if we think that there cannot be any collective rights in a liberal democracy or that all such rights should rather be called political arrangements.

I have already pointed out that there is almost no historical case that can be interpreted as a truly voluntary federation of political communities which have not shared common national aspirations long before unification. However, the model is still highly relevant where a pluralistic federation has emerged from a less-than-voluntary process of state formation. In the Western world, the cases of Canada, Belgium, Spain, and the United

Kingdom can be read in this way. Where culturally distinct minorities have succeeded, against historical odds, in keeping alive their language or their distinct political and legal traditions, liberal principles suggest that one should now ask the question: what kind of constitutional arrangement would have been acceptable to national minorities had they ever been invited to join a federation voluntarily?[17] Because historical processes cannot be undone, the answer to this question does not necessarily yield the arrangement that should be adopted now. We have to take into account that a framework of common liberal citizenship would have changed some cultural characteristics and preferences of the minority with regard to the initial arrangement. Nevertheless, the thought experiment about a fair initial agreement is useful to warn present liberal democracies against a mindless continuation of past coercive assimilation.[18]

Ethnic groups which have been completely assimilated cannot be reinvented.[19] Yet some groups have remained distinct not because they were strong enough to resist assimilation, but because they were exposed to coercive segregation. The history of the indigenous First Nations in the US is instructive in this regard because it mixes policies of coercive assimilation and segregation. In the nineteenth century sham autonomy in their native reserves turned into a pretext for driving them from their original lands and their recognition as distinct nations became an excuse for denying them US citizenship.[20] Yet, ironically the results of this particularly violent process of extermination and coercive inclusion serves as a starting point for a defence of their collective rights today. On the one hand, a fair agreement on liberal grounds has to make good for the ongoing effects of territorial relocation, deprivation of economic subsistence, and second-class citizenship. These effects are so pervasive that equal individual rights are clearly insufficient. Group-differentiated programmes of community development and affirmative action are needed to overcome them. On the other hand, equal citizenship for all native Indians ought to be combined with cultural and territorial autonomy for communities living in tribal reserves. Even though these reserves emerged from policies of exclusion and extermination they have today become the terrain for reasserting collective political rights which had been abolished step by step since Andrew Jackson's presidency.

Historical boundaries may also serve to justify group rights for a third category of groups who are no longer able to claim self-government within an autonomous province or territory. Coercively assimilated linguistic minorities which do no longer form regional majorities, like Austria's indigenous Slovenes, Croats, and Hungarians, may still demand bilingual public education for all children in their historical homeland areas or some special political representation at provincial and federal levels. Although the collective rights they require are fairly weak ones, they articulate a strong demand for symbolic recognition: the Austrian nation should be considered as a multilingual one so that these minority groups can see themselves as building blocks of this nation.

3.2. Collective disadvantage

The argument about historical boundaries applies only in a limited number of cases. For many minorities it makes little sense to reconstruct their claims starting from the question of what would have been a fair contract of federation. By and large, we can only apply this to national minorities whose historic continuity, territorial concentration, and cultural distinctness support their claim to be political communities without a state, or to ethnic ones which form historical communities within a larger polity. Yet there are other kinds of ethnic minorities which have been territorially dispersed and half-assimilated into a dominant culture, or which have emerged from migration. These are often set apart from national majorities in social, economic, and cultural dimensions but not as (potentially) separate polities within the state. A more general argument for group-differentiated and collective rights of ethnic minorities calls for compensatory justice. The idea is that both the formation of nation-states and their internal dynamic create inevitable disadvantages for ethnic and cultural minorities. Liberal justice does not require to undo these historical processes which cannot be undone, but it suggests that such groups have rights to remedial and compensatory policies if these disadvantages seriously diminish the value of their members' citizenship.

The arbitrary results of state formation which have favoured some ethnic and cultural groups over others are reinforced by the economic, social, and political dynamics of a liberal society. A modern industrial economy and a modern public administration require the socialization of the general population in standardized cultures (Gellner, 1983). Free movement within the territory and the lowering of social barriers for intermarriage lead to a mix of populations. Within a mobile society of mixed origins dominant languages become the most useful ones for communication in public settings where anonymous citizens meet. These structural advantages for majority cultures are reinforced by normative reasons for promoting them in state policies. Public education in liberal states must prepare their citizens for the widest possible opportunities in their society and for democratic participation in their polity. This does not exclude the possibility of a limited linguistic pluralism, but no great number of different languages and ethnic cultures can be promoted as official ones. All these circumstances create powerful forces of assimilation of smaller and dispersed ethnic minorities.

If this were the end of the story, there would be little reason to defend differentiated and collective rights for ethnic groups who are bound to disappear anyway and whose members can acquire full and equal citizenship by assimilating into a mainstream culture. Yet there are also countervailing tendencies. Ethnic diversity is perpetuated through discrimination as well as through political mobilization. First, the economic and political institutions of liberal democracies have often reinforced ethnic and cultural discrimination in labour and housing markets, public education, or systems of political representation. Discrimination has created specific concentrations of minorities in occupations and residential areas which heighten their cultural distinctness in the eyes of the national majority. When social segregation reduces inter-ethnic contact, structural disadvantages and unequal opportunities are no longer necessarily the effect of direct and intentional discrimination. State intervention against overt social discrimination is already quite constrained in liberal societies with their extensive economic and political liberties and the separation of public and private spheres. The effects of structural disadvantage are even harder to overcome. For many groups cultural assimilation is simply no way out if ethnic origin has become a marker of social disadvantage. Second, these same liberties have also been used by minorities to form their own migratory networks, residential strongholds, economic niches, associations, educational institutions, and political movements. Liberal democracy offers ethnic minorities opportunities for voluntary segregation and these may be used to affirm even outcomes of discrimination as a positive element of a group's collective identity. In the period after World War II ethnonationalist and republican ideologies defending the assimilation of ethnic minorities in the name of national unity have also become less dominant and this has stimulated a public articulation of previously suppressed ethnicity in Western democracies among some old and many new minorities.

National majorities enjoy an advantage because their culture is sponsored by the state and distributed throughout society as a public good. Minorities mostly suffer a dual disadvantage. On the one hand, national majorities often consider minority cultures as inferior and prefer their own group in economic, social, and political interactions. On the other hand, minority members have to invest and pool their private resources in order to maintain and develop their group's culture as a communal good (see Kymlicka, 1989: 188–9).[21] Because the public culture of the wider society is not a neutral context for minorities their situation differs from that of voluntary associations whose members pursue some shared activity or goal. Liberal equality requires therefore more than the mere freedom to maintain a minority culture in domestic life and associations of civil society. First, protection against ethnic discrimination is needed. If there is strong evidence that pervasive prejudice among national majorities leads to structural disadvantage that seriously diminishes a minority's economic opportunities and political representation, affirmative action which identifies the group as entitled to special concern may be justified. Second, if states cannot be redesigned to become truly neutral with regard to the different cultural affiliations of their citizens, then disadvantaged minorities have to be compensated in order to regain the full value of their citizenship. This will support politics of cultural recognition, for example by changing the curricula of public schools so that ethnic minorities are offered additional tuition in their native languages and all children are taught about the history of the various ethnic groups in their society.

3.3. The value of membership

The collective disadvantage argument is explicitly about justice for minorities. It accepts as given a political framework which tends to disadvantage ethnic minorities and asks for rights which redraw a balance of resources and powers so that membership in a minority does not diminish the value of individual citizenship. This still allows for two objections against accepting ethnic group rights as a permanent feature of liberal democracies.

One such view equates ethnic differences with 'racial' ones. Affirmative action to compensate for racist discrimination is indeed meant to be temporary. When there is no more evidence for persistent disadvantage the justification for the policy expires as well. If ethnic group rights are necessary to restore equal citizenship, then we may think that they are merely a result of past wrongs and present imperfections of Western states and will become ultimately redundant in a more perfect liberal democracy. The argument about collective disadvantage points out that such a solution may be a very remote one, but it does not discard it in principle. Cultural group rights appear to be only instrumentally necessary in order to achieve equal citizenship which is regarded as intrinsically valuable. Of course racial distinctions are inherently vicious and therefore a liberal state should try to make them socially irrelevant as far as possible. Ethnic distinctions may be regarded less unfavourably, but they could still be seen as merely a reaction to state nationalism to be eventually overcome in a post-national society.[22]

Another objection equates ethnic identity with religious membership. Marxism had seen religion much as many contemporary liberals regard ethnicity, i.e. as a product of alienation and oppression, a false consciousness which divides groups of common interests and blocks emancipatory movements, and a phenomenon which will ultimately vanish in a truly free society because there is no more human need to which it answers. Liberalism rejects this view of religion. Although few liberal theorists after John Locke have themselves been strongly religious, many among them have supported the view that religious affiliations of citizens have a positive impact on their sense of civic duties as long as there is a clear separation between political power and religious authority and as long as religious groups share an attitude of mutual toleration.[23] Moreover, liberals have valued religion not only instrumentally insofar as it promotes social integration. Most of them have acknowledged that religious beliefs may be a strong and legitimate source of moral guidance for those who hold them and that they answer to a fundamental, although by no means universally shared, human need which is not likely to pass away in a more liberal type of society. In short, liberals have tended to recognize that membership in a religious community has intrinsic value for strong believers and that liberal states should honour this. Voluntary religious affiliation is a manifestation of what John Rawls has called the moral capacity to form and to revise a conception of the good (Rawls, 1993: 19–20). This background conviction distinguishes the liberal motivation for religious toleration from, say, the toleration of pornography or of the use of soft drugs.

Liberals should accept that ethnic membership has some similarities with religious affiliation. It may be voluntarily affirmed even if it is originally acquired at birth, it teaches individuals virtues of solidarity within a larger group, it provides people with social status and recognition by others and, most importantly, it offers them a rich culture that helps to interpret and evaluate different options how to lead their lives.[24] Such parallels should convince liberals to see ethnic groups in a more favourable light. They could welcome a multicultural society where groups cultivate their ethnic ways of life. However, this is not yet sufficient to endorse an argument for special group rights. Liberalism started with rejecting the political privileges states granted to established churches. The analogy with religion will also support demands for strict state neutrality in cultural matters. To those who point out that the modern state is inextricably involved in protecting, reproducing, and favouring specific national cultures liberals may respond that it must also have been very difficult to imagine a secular state during the European medieval period. They may agree that special group rights for ethnic minorities are justified as long as we live in the dark age of nationalism but can insist that this is a temporary concession to a grossly imperfect world.

Yet this does not grasp the full force of the political argument that citizenship in a modern state requires access to a public culture which cannot be reproduced autonomously in the domestic sphere or by associations of civil society. When we combine this with the recognition that cultural membership is an intrinsic value for citizens in a liberal society we arrive at the conclusion that liberal states have a positive obligation to maintain a public culture which is accessible to all citizens.

The different implications for liberal policies of the three kinds of ascriptive distinctions can be best illustrated in public education. Schools should actively fight 'racial' segregation. They ought to teach children to work in mixed groups, to be aware of and resist discrimination, but to disregard 'racial' difference in their own contact with others. In contrast, public schools must teach children to respect the others' religion but they can leave the business of religious instruction to parents and churches. However, schools have to teach children languages, history, music, and arts. Ethnic and national cultures cannot be kept out of schools, their reproduction is what schools are all about. While public education can or should be colour-blind and faith-blind in the way I have specified, there is no such thing as a culture-blind school. Teaching culture is a 'functional requirement' of the institutions of public education, and at the same time an affirmation of an intrinsically valuable form of membership for individuals. This is why ethnic minorities have a basic claim that their cultures be not only tolerated, but also represented in public education.

The previous arguments from historical agreement and collective disadvantage did not lend any *moral* support to majority dominance. In contrast, the combined arguments for the intrinsic value of ethnic membership and for the public task of cultural reproduction do not only apply to minorities. They also support the claims of national or regional majorities to use the resources offered by a modern public administration for shaping the public culture of their societies. There is no clear threshold for what kind of support liberal states may give to the development of a national culture. If they run public schools where the national language is the dominant language of instruction, why should they not also use taxpayers' money to sponsor theatres and cultural festivals? Everybody may be better off in a society with a rich public culture sustained by government support compared to a society where only wealthy citizens have access to many cultural activities. Even for most minorities full participation in a national culture may be no less important than the public recognition of their particular ethnic languages and traditions.

In contrast with pluri-national states based on historical agreement multi-ethnic ones need therefore not strive for symmetry in intercultural relations. Often the asymmetry is seen as a unilateral obligation of immigrants and other dispersed ethnic minorities to adapt to the dominant national culture. I suggest that, on the contrary, minorities may claim public resources to preserve and develop their cultural heritage for their own members, while the representatives of a national majority are obliged to include the minorities into the common public culture. The dividing line between nationalism and liberalism in this regard is that the former is concerned about preserving the purity of a dominant culture from the impact of ethnic diversity, while for the latter the culture which dominates public life must be as open and inclusive as possible for the various ethnic affiliations and practices of all citizens. There is thus a double asymmetry: on the one hand, territorial majorities are privileged with regard to the power of establishing their cultural traditions and languages in public life, but this obliges them to grant support to minority efforts for maintaining their own cultures; on the other hand, insofar as the majority culture dominates public spheres, it is under a stronger obligation to transform itself so that it does not exclude minorities from access to public spheres and institutions, whereas minorities need not provide majority members with free access to their culture.[25]

3.4. The value of diversity

The demand that dominant cultures should be open for ethnic diversity already goes a step beyond the argument of the intrinsic value of cultural membership for each individual. It requires that members of national majorities learn to cherish not just their own cultural traditions but also those of minorities within the society. Popular advocacy of multiculturalism often argues that dominant cultures would be enriched by including minority traditions. Assimilation is said to deprive not only minorities of their cultural membership but also majorities of cross-cultural experiences which would widen their intellectual horizons and refine their tastes. This argument is no longer about the value of cultural affiliation for the members of the group, but about an external value a culture has for those who are not its members.

One manifestation of such external valuation is what we may call 'philo-ethnicism'. It picks out a specific group or culture to which some superior value is attributed that one's own group is seen to lack. Not all such attitudes are irrational. Why should Germans not have a special preference for French or Italian food? A more disturbing phenomenon is when the external valuation is simply the reversal of some deep-seated and often racist stereotype which it confirms indirectly. Thus anti-Semites and philo-Semites may both think that Jews are intellectually superior, which gives the former a reason to fear and hate what the latter pretend to admire. Much the same is true for stereotypes about African Americans' special capabilities in sports and music which are a thinly disguised way of asserting their intellectual inferiority. No matter how it has come about, it is obvious that no such external preference (Dworkin, 1977) among a majority for other groups ought to be taken into account in public policies and in the allocation of specific rights.[26]

A more interesting argument says that what should be added to the individual value of each culture for its own members is not the value of other cultures taken separately, but the value of diversity, i.e. the fact that cultures are different and coexist at a societal or global level. Liberals cherish diversity for three reasons: because it provides a potential for collective experimentation, for individual choice, and for self-reflection. The first reason operates at the level of collective benefits, whereas the second one defends individual liberty, and the third one applies simultaneously to collective and individual identities.

Let me first illustrate these reasons with regard to the less controversial example of democratic diversity. There is a great variety of democracies within the international system. Democratic states are separated from each other by national borders and democratic constitutions are very different with regard to their procedures of representing citizens or of dividing political powers. Why should this state of affairs be preferred to a global democratic state with a single constitution? The first reason is that there is no plausible theory about which constitutional arrangement is the best or the most democratic one. At the level of humanity democratic diversity is like a huge experiment with different forms of democracy. Optimists may hope that cooperation and peaceful competition between democratic states will give an 'evolutionary advantage' to the better arrangements so that experimentation also makes for improvement over time. Global fusion or internal assimilation of all democracies towards one supposedly best model would destroy this very motor for improvement. For pessimists it may be enough to emphasize that preserving diversity helps to prevent an unlimited accumulation of power and to keep spontaneous deterioration reversible. The second reason is that a diversity of regimes allows for individual choice by way of exit, whereas one could not exit from a global state. The freedom of exit is, on the one hand, a necessary condition for justifying subjection to collectively binding laws. On the other hand, it is also one mechanism for internal improvement in response to dissatisfaction.[27] The third reason is that diversity is necessary for a democratic polity in order to understand better its own institutions, traditions, and political culture, i.e. in order to develop a self-reflective political identity. In this perspective other democratic states are not seen as competitors or potential destinations for dissatisfied emigrants, but as a necessary mirror for any rational affirmation of loyalty. Only by learning about other systems and even looking at ours from their different perspectives can we assert the value of our own membership and replace unreflective affiliation with critical loyalty.

Not all of these reasons apply equally to every kind of cultural difference. Those who believe in a revealed religious truth will necessarily reject the value of experimentation. For gender and racial difference the choice argument will generally be of only marginal significance. Let me therefore examine how these reasons might apply to national and ethnic diversity.

Multinational diversity within a state may, for example, be supported by the first reason as a background condition for political liberty or as a motor for social development. The political argument was stated by Lord Acton who claimed that 'liberty provokes diversity, and diversity preserves liberty by supplying the means of organisation' (Acton, 1907: 289). He concluded from this that the 'coexistence of several nations under the same state is a test, as well as the best security of its freedom' (ibid. 290). This view is diametrically opposed to John Stuart Mill's dictum that '[f]ree institutions are next to impossible in a country made up of different nationalities' (Mill, 1972: 392). While Mill emphasized that solidarity among citizens requires a common language and history, Acton thought that a multiplicity of nationalities would have similar effects as the separation of church and state. Diversity constrains the accumulation of political power at the centre and teaches citizens to distinguish between the political loyalties of patriotism and narrower, but still legitimate, group interests. We can find similar controversies about the effects of ethnic diversity on social and economic development. Who is right or wrong will depend both on empirical evidence and on further specifications of the underlying normative concepts such as liberty or development. In any case, what is at stake here is not an intrinsic but an instrumental value of ethnonational diversity.

This should raise suspicions which are independent of the presumed beneficial effects of diversity. A first suspicion is that the value of diversity is not only itself instrumental but provides a pretext for instrumentalizing others. External preferences may enter once more indirectly, not as blatant favouritism for a specific foreign culture, but in the disguise of a special duty of minorities to preserve their culture in order to maintain diversity for everybody's benefit even when their members wish to change or to abandon it. If a modern liberal society has the kind of assimilationist dynamic I have discussed above, it is quite likely that many individuals and some groups would want to get rid of their cultural baggage. A state may for example encourage indigenous minorities which have become a tourist attraction to stay in their native territories and to preserve their traditional practices when most of them wish to move to the cities and to adopt modern ways of life. Even less exploitative reasons for valuing diversity over spontaneous assimilation come into conflict with liberal principles. Cultural anthropologists may sincerely believe that the vanishing of an ancient culture is an irretrievable loss for humanity. Benevolent paternalists may tell minority members that assimilation is bad for their own well-being. Both may be right but their arguments should not carry any political weight because they do not respect minority members as morally autonomous individuals and equal citizens.

A second suspicion is that the value of diversity is shallower than the value of membership. This can be illustrated by comparing ethnicity once again to religion. What could convince a true believer that it is better for her to live in a society together with people of other faiths, agnostics, and atheists rather than in one where her religion is shared by all? While agnostic liberals will prefer religious diversity to uniformity, the faithful ones will at best accept Locke's argument that politically coerced belief is an absurdity which cannot please God (Locke, 1956: 129). Yet even this may be a specifically Protestant attitude which cannot be easily generalized for, say, all catholics or Muslims. We may build a broader case for religious toleration on the assumption that even those who do not endorse the separation of church and state for theological reasons may well support it for political ones. They may genuinely value to be citizens of a liberal democracy which grants them the same freedom as others and protects them also from an arbitrary exercise of political power by their own religious authorities. But demanding that religious citizens not only tolerate other religions but should positively value diversity would be asking too much. Liberals have to respect profound religious convictions that one's own faith is the true one and that the world would be a better place if it were adopted by everybody. Does valuing ethnic diversity not presuppose a similar detachment from one's own group of origin? Maybe the values of membership and of diversity are substitutive rather than additive, so that we cannot appreciate the one without abandoning the other? And perhaps the value of diversity is only another name for promoting a superficial relativism which does not grasp the full strength of the unchosen ties that relate individuals to their ethnic groups?

Still, I think that a case can be made for the value of ethnic diversity which relies on the other two reasons listed above and avoids these traps. The first move is to abandon the holistic image of culture which underlies much of the arguments I have discussed so far. At the level of concepts culture understood as a system of ideas, symbols, codes of communication, values, practices, and habits does not match in any simple way with the notion of ethnic group. While such groups are assumed to be clearly demarcated, cultural exchange may always take place across ethnic boundaries. Ethnic groups use cultural markers to define their boundaries, but their culture is never enclosed within these boundaries in the same sense as their land or settlements are. Cross-cultural communication occurs in every human society and it establishes a wider cultural field within which group boundaries are negotiated. Within modern societies, such boundaries often acquire a new fluidity. They shift and overlap more often than in agrarian societies where cultural markers divided groups by local origin and social rank in such a way that communication between them was minimal.[28] Geographical and social mobility has produced an increasing fragmentation of local and ethnic cultures while the newly created national cultures have provided broader umbrellas of standardized high cultures. Under the impact of globalization in the contemporary world even these boundaries of national cultures have become increasingly uncertain and unstable. Some groups are faced with previously unimaginable opportunities to choose cultural and ethnic identities they had not acquired at birth. For others, social segregation along lines of ethnicity, class, and 'race' creates new kinds of cultural stigma and deprivation.

In this world, diversity will become an important value for individuals; not in the sense of mere difference, but of a more general accessibility of cultures associated with other groups and origins than one's own. Only small religious sects who voluntarily withdraw from the wider society will find that their community provides them with a full range of all options they need for their lives. For most others a sufficiently wide range of meaningful opportunities can only be provided by a diverse cultural background. Even long-established national cultures fail to be sufficiently comprehensive in this regard. And even the decision to affirm a minority identity acquired at birth is no longer a natural attitude but turns into an act of choice against a background of accessible alternatives. As I have argued above, changing an ethnic identity by shedding it is possible but difficult and does not only depend on indiviual effort. Although the negative aspect of choice by exit might therefore not fully apply to ethnic groups, the positive aspects may very well be relevant in the sense that an identity ascribed at birth will be later on enriched with additional layers resulting from encounters with different cultures. In contrast with monotheistic religious faith this process can be additive rather than subtractive. Paradoxically, the unchosen and ascriptive nature of our original ethnic affiliation makes it not only more difficult to exit from it, but makes it also easier to combine it with other chosen affiliations of a similar kind. In this regard, ethnicity is more like language, where the language of origin will always retain a special emotional significance but does not prevent us from learning other languages. In the context of modern societies most people have therefore positive reasons to value ethnic diversity.[29]

The third argument for diversity as a necessary background for self-reflective identities is even broader in scope. It applies also to minorities (or to political theorists) who do not value choice in matters of culture. For Bhikhu Parekh 'cultures are not options' (Parekh, 1995: 208).[30] We should cherish cultural diversity as a public good not because it enables us to choose, but because access to other cultures allows us 'to appreciate the singularity as well as the strengths and limitations of our own' (ibid.) and because 'no way of life, however rich it might be, can ever express the full range of human potentiality' (ibid. 203). I do think that mobility and migration in contemporary societies confront more and more people with tough choices about their cultural belonging and that the possibility of combining various affiliations, instead of having to choose one at the expense of others, is one eminently desirable feature of liberal diversity. Parekh gives us no good reason to dismiss the value of diversity derived from cultural fragmentation and choice. However, he does suggest a more general argument why there need not be any incompatibility between the internal value of culture for its members and the external value of diversity for the wider society. The value of membership will be increased by the reflexivity that results from experiencing other cultures and, conversely, only those cultural practices that are intrinsically valued by the group's members will contribute to the diversity of a public culture. Diversity is thus a public good which is jointly produced and enjoyed by all groups.

Taken together, these arguments for diversity can dispel the suspicions we have encountered before. First, the fragmented character of most ethnic and national cultures explains the difference with religion. Apart from a few remaining pre-modern ways of life, self-enclosed ethnic cultures have indeed become shallower than sincere religious belief. Only by opening up for the experiences of other cultural groups, which coexist with ours at the societal or global level, can we hope to restore to some extent the richness of our own. Second, what is valuable about diversity is not just difference, but the fact that it provides opportunities for communication between reflectively affirmed ways of life. There is thus no justification for imposing diversity by segregating groups and encouraging them to preserve traditional cultural practices. Accessible diversity is an opposite of both uniformity through assimilation and of difference through segregation. And the liberal conceptions of equal citizenship and a shared public culture are incompatible with both negations of diversity. Obviously, it would be naïve to assume that such liberal diversity will prevent the outbreak of ethnic conflicts. However, the dream of a society without group conflict is anyway an anti-political utopia. A pluralistic conception of liberal democracy with institutionalized group rights offers the best hope for resolving such conflicts by political means rather than by force.

4. CONCLUSIONS

Let me conclude by considering in which way the four arguments support the plea for ethnic group rights.

The argument from historical boundaries provides the strongest case for rights which are group-differentiated as well as collective. It suggests that constitutions should name specific ethnic and national communities and give them rights to set up their own regional legislation, to run their own local governments or courts, to be exempted from, or to have the power of nullifying or vetoing national legislation which affects their vital interests, and to enjoy special representation in political institutions at the national or federal level. Of course such far-reaching collective powers should be tamed by constitutional guarantees for basic individual liberties, but this caveat applies to fully sovereign states in an even stronger way than to autonomous communities within a state. It gives us no reason to deny the legitimacy of collective autonomy for national minorities. Among the four arguments this is also the only one that applies exclusively to national minorities and in a weaker sense to some ethnic groups.

The argument about collective disadvantage applies to many more groups (not only ethnic ones but also those defined by 'race', gender, sexual orientation, and economic class) and to virtually every contemporary liberal society. It supports a broad range of group-differentiated rights and some collective ones, but rarely a combination of both. The rights dispersed or immigrant ethnic minorities need in order to regain the full value of their citizenship do not support claims to establish autonomous political communities within a state.

The argument about the value of cultural membership has an even broader scope but also weaker implications in terms of group rights. It applies not just to ethnic minorities but equally to national majorities.[31] Majorities are entitled to use the powerful resources of the modern state for maintaining and developing their national culture. However, in a liberal state their right to do so will be constrained by an obligation to create a shared public culture which includes all ethnic minorities.

Finally, the argument for diversity has the broadest possible scope. It applies at the national, the transnational, and the global level and is not only a plea for institutionalizing rights in a national or international legal order, but also for norms of behaviour to guide interactions of individuals and groups. Maintaining diversity and intercultural dialogue is not only, and maybe not even primarily, a task for government, but also for groups, associations, and citizens in civil society. Liberal diversity does not so much depend on specific legal rights for ethnic groups. What is required is a full guarantee for the common liberties of speech, association, and religious worship. Only the discarded version of diversity as involuntary segregation requires a clear-cut differentiation among groups. Once the group rights derived from historical boundaries or collective advantage have been granted, there is no need to extend these rights to others in order to increase diversity. Moreover, it is not at all obvious that group rights would always promote greater diversity. Collective autonomy has probably more often been used by ethnic minorities for modernizing traditional economic, social, and political practices than for preserving them. And affirmative action has done much to assimilate an African-American middle class into the mainstream of American culture. Group rights for ethnic minorities are a necessary precondition for liberal diversity, but not the ultimate goal. Realizing Acton's virtuous circle is what liberal politics should aim for: equal individual liberty which provokes diversity, and diversity which helps to sustain liberty.

I have therefore not argued in this chapter that special rights for ethnic groups are in every case justified, that they should not be constrained, or that they do not conflict with individual rights and with each other. Analysing such conflicts between rights and how they can be made compatible with equal individual citizenship is a task beyond the scope of this chapter.[32] We will only be able to address it once we abandon the misguided liberal hostility to group rights on grounds of principle.

NOTES

1. I have tried to briefly address these question in Bauböck (1997).
2. A critique of this claim will emerge from my discussion of the inevitable asymmetries between cultural rights of territorial majorities and minorities in Sect. 3.3 below.

3. This latter concern has been cogently stated by Thomas Pogge: 'differential treatment of groups must never be based on their difference in type' (Pogge, 1997: 188).
4. See also Tamir in this volume.
5. See Nickel (1997).
6. See Kymlicka (1995a: 35, 45).
7. Thomas Pogge (1997: 192) has suggested to further distinguish a third category of group-statistical rights, which is a mixed one. It applies to rights where individuals are the sole beneficiaries but either only up to a maximum point which defines the extent to which their group is entitled to special treatment (as in affirmative action quotas) or only if their number reaches a minimum threshold (as in native language classes for immigrant children). One can easily introduce further distinctions which break down the dichotomy into a continuum of individual and collective rights (see Bauböck, 1996).
8. Kymlicka and Shapiro (1997: 5).
9. Wisconsin V. Yoder, 406 U.S. 205 (1972).
10. Some liberal theorists defend a right to secession which would maximize the number of citizens who live in a state of their choice. See e.g. Beran (1984), Gauthier (1995), Pogge (1997). For a critique of choice theories of secession see Buchanan (1997), Chwaszcza (1998), and Bauböck (1998).
11. See the discussion in Raz (1986: 207–9), Bauböck (1997).
12. See Bauböck (1994).
13. Tamir (1993: 73–4) and in this volume.
14. See Tamir in this volume.
15. Kymlicka (1995a: 35–44).
16. Both cases figure prominently in Will Kymlicka's argument for minority rights (1989, 1995a).
17. See Norman (1994).
18. A multinational federation may come about in two ways: by bringing together different self-governing groups in a single state or by transforming a unitary state into a multinational one through devolution. An alternative way of thinking about fair terms of federation argues that such devolution is required in all unitary states composed of territorially concentrated national groups with long-standing aspirations to partial autonomy. This would even apply to minorities which had never been self-governing in their history but had only become national ones through resistance to imposed assimilation or segregation. I explore these various arguments for multinational federation in Bauböck (1998a).
19. In contrast, languages may be reinvented as national ones even after complete assimilation of the group which originally spoke them. The reintroduction of Hebrew in Israel and Gaelic in Ireland illustrate different scopes and degrees of success of such national policies. Nationalists may see restoring cultural practices which have already been fully abandoned as an obligation towards past generations. For liberals, it is clearly a matter of policy, not of justice.
20. Collective goods can be split into two categories: public goods are non-exclusive whereas communal goods are accessible only to members of a particular group. In modern nation-states dominant cultures tend to become public goods for all members of society, whereas most minority cultures remain communal goods for

the group only. (Seen from a global perspective the exclusive rights of citizens are again communal rather than public goods.) Like many other authors, Tamir (in this volume) fails to make this distinction. If all collective goods were non-exclusive, it would indeed make no difference who is the bearer of a right to these goods. But this does not apply to goods whose value is specific for a certain group.

21. By classifying them as 'domestic dependent nations' the Supreme Court also denied Indian tribes the right to address complaints against breaches of treaties or forced resettlement to the highest judicial authority (Cherokee Nation v. Georgia, 30 U.S. 1, 1831).

22. Claus Offe, for example, ties the justification for ethnic group rights to perceived oppression: 'But the minority, in order to make a plausible moral claim to special rights, must also be seen as an (unjustly) "oppressed" group' (Offe, 1998: 126).

23. For a contemporary statement see Galston (1990: 257–89).

24. See Kymlicka (1989: 165), Buchanan (1991: 53), and Raz and Margalit (1990/ 1995). The argument that ethnic and national membership has intrinsic value for individuals may be stated in different ways. Kymlicka's emphasis on cultural membership as a primary good for individual autonomy has been criticized by a number of authors who point out that this makes it difficult to account for the value of membership in traditional and non-liberal cultures which do not cherish their members' autonomy (Tomasi, 1995: 599–603; Tamir, 1995; Weinstock, 1998). I cannot enter this important debate here.

25. National minorities in a multinational federation are simultaneously exposed to both sides of this double asymmetry: as minority at the federal level they can demand special recognition and support for their culture, but as majorities at provincial or state levels they have to ensure that their locally dominant culture does not exclude members of the federal majority or other minority groups.

26. See also Tamir in this volume.

27. See Hirschman (1970).

28. See Gellner (1983, ch. 2).

29. Cultural fragmentation and overlap in modern societies is a condition which makes individuals aware of the particularity of their own cultural affiliations. It does not necessarily mean that they have to conceive of their own cultural identities as being similarly fractured and multiple. This latter assumption seems to me the basic error in Jeremy Waldron's 'many fragments' model of multiculturalism (Waldron, 1992, 1996). While nearly every individual is in some way exposed to various cultural fragments in her social environment, only some will self-consciously embrace this experience. Our arguments about the general value of cultural membership and the specific processes of cultural identity formation in socially disadvantaged groups help to explain, and also to ratify, cultural choices which highlight a particular identity at the expense of others. The choice argument values a diverse cultural background, but cannot commit everybody to choose a cosmopolitan cultural *mélange* for herself. Even less can this argument serve to release liberal states from their obligation to support a general public culture and to compensate specifically disadvantaged minority cultures.

30. Parekh explicitly defends the external value of culture and criticizes that 'Kymlicka sees cultures only from the standpoint of their members and not that of the society at large' (Parekh, 1994, n. 5: 220).
31. It applies obviously also to religious groups in secular states.
32. I have addressed some of these questions in Bauböck (1996).

REFERENCES

Acton, John Emerich Edward Dalberg (1907), 'Nationality', in *The History of Freedom and Other Essays* (London: Macmillan): 270–300.
Barth, Fredrik (ed.) (1969), *Ethnic Groups and Boundaries. The Social Organization of Cultural Difference*, Universitetsførlaget, Oslo.
Bauböck, Rainer (1994), *Transnational Citizenship* (Aldershot: Elgar).
—— (1996), 'Cultural Minority Rights for Immigrants', *International Migration Review*, 30/1: 203–50.
—— (1997), 'Can Liberalism Support Collective Rights?', in P. Koller and K. Puhl (eds.), *Current Issues in Political Philosophy: Justice in Society and World Order* (Vienna: Hölder-Pichler): 227–35.
—— (1998), 'Why Stay Together? A Pluralist Approach to Secession and Federation', Vienna Working Papers in Legal Theory, Political Philosophy, and Applied Ethics, No.1, at: http://www.univie.ac.at/juiridicum/
Beran, Harry (1984), 'A Liberal Theory of Secession', *Political Studies*, 32: 21–31.
Buchanan, Allen (1991), *Secession. The Morality of Political Divorce from Fort Sumter to Lithuania and Quebec* (Boulder, Colo.: Westview Press).
—— (1997), 'Theories of Secession', *Philosophy and Public Affairs*, 26/1: 31–61.
Chwaszcza, Christine (1998), 'Selbstbestimmung, Sezession und Souveränität. Überlegungen zur normativen Bedeutung politischer Grenzen', in Wolfgang Kersting and Christine Chwaszcza (eds.), *Philosophie der Internationalen Beziehungen* (Frankfurt am Main: Suhrkamp).
Dworkin, Ronald (1977), *Taking Rights Seriously* (Cambridge, Mass.: Harvard University Press).
Galston, William (1990), *Liberal Purposes. Goods, Virtues, and Diversity in the Liberal State* (Cambridge, Mass.: Cambridge University Press).
Gauthier, David (1995), 'Breaking Up: An Essay on Secession', *Canadian Journal of Philosophy*, 24/3: 357–72.
Gellner, Ernest (1983), *Nations and Nationalism* (Oxford: Blackwell).
Hirschman, Albert O. (1970), *Exit, Voice, and Loyalty* (Cambridge, Mass.: Harvard University Press).
Kukathas, Chandran (1992), 'Are There Any Cultural Rights?', *Political Theory*, 20: 105–33.
—— (1997) 'Cultural Toleration', in W. Kymlicka and I. Shapiro (eds.), *Ethnicity and Group Rights*, Nomos 39 (New York: New York University Press): 69–104.
Kymlicka, Will (1989), *Liberalism, Community, and Culture* (Oxford: Clarendon Press).
—— (1995a), *Multicultural Citizenship* (Oxford: Oxford University Press).

—— (ed.) (1995*b*) *The Rights of Minority Cultures* (Oxford: Oxford University Press).

—— and Shapiro, Ian (1997), Introduction in W. Kymlicka and I. Shapiro (eds.) (1997) *Ethnicity and Group Rights*, Nomos 39 (New York: New York University Press): 3–21.

Lijphart, Arendt (1991/1995), 'Self-Determination versus Pre-Determination of Ethnic Minorities in Power-Sharing Systems', repr. in Will Kymlicka (1995*b*): 275–87.

Locke, John (1956), 'A Letter Concerning Toleration', in *The Second Treatise of Government and A Letter Concerning Toleration*, ed. with an Introduction by J. W. Gough (New York: Macmillan).

Mill, John Stuart (1972), 'Considerations On Representative Government', in *Utilitarianism, Liberty, Representative Government*, ed. by H. B. Acton (London: Everyman's Library).

Nickel, James W. (1997), 'Group Agency and Group Rights', in W. Kymlicka and I. Shapiro (eds.), *Ethnicity and Group Rights*, Nomos 39 (New York: New York University Press): 235–55.

Norman, Wayne (1994), 'Towards a Philosophy of Federalism', in Judith Baker (ed.), *Group Rights* (Toronto: University of Toronto Press): 79–100.

Nozick, Robert (1974), *Anarchy, State, and Utopia* (Oxford: Blackwell).

Offe, Claus (1998), ' "Homogeneity" and Constitutional Democracy: Coping with Identity Conflicts through Group Rights', *Journal of Political Philosophy*, 6/1: 113–41.

Parekh, Bhikhu (1995), 'Cultural Diversity and Liberal Democracy', in David Beetham (ed.), *Defining and Measuring Democracy* (London: Sage): 199–221.

Pogge, Thomas (1997), Group Rights and Ethnicity, in W. Kymlicka and I. Shapiro (eds.), *Ethnicity and Group Rights*, Nomos 39 (New York: New York University Press): 187–221.

Rawls, John (1971), *A Theory of Justice* (Cambridge, Mass.: Harvard University Press).

—— (1993), *Political Liberalism* (New York: Columbia University Press).

Raz, Joseph (1986), *The Morality of Freedom* (Oxford: Clarendon Press).

—— and Margalit, Avishai (1990/1995), 'National Self-Determination', repr. in Will Kymlicka (1995*b*: 79–92).

Steiner, Hillel (1994), *An Essay on Rights* (Oxford: Blackwell).

Tamir, Yael (1993), *Liberal Nationalism* (Princeton: Princeton University Press).

—— (1995), 'Two concepts of multiculturalism', in Yael Tamir (ed.), *Democratic Education in a Multicultural State* (Oxford: Blackwell).

Tomasi, John (1995), 'Kymlicka, Liberalism, and Respect for Cultural Minorities', *Ethics* 105 (April 1995): 580–603.

Waldron, Jeremy (1992), 'Minority Cultures and the Cosmopolitan Alternative', *University of Michigan Journal of Law Reform*, 25: 751–93.

—— (1996), 'Multiculturalism and Melange', in R. K. Fullinwider (ed.), *Public Education in a Multicultural Society* (Cambridge: Cambridge University Press): 90–118.

Weinstock, Daniel (1998), 'How Can Collective Rights and Liberalism be Reconciled?' in R. Bauböck and J. Rundell (eds.), *Blurred Boundaries. Migration, Ethnicity, Citizenship* (Aldershot: Avebury).

8

Against Collective Rights

YAEL TAMIR

In recent years, the notion of collective rights has been gathering considerable support.[1] Collective rights, it is argued, are necessary to protect and
promote the interests of members of minority groups. This latter claim is
supported by theoretical and political arguments. The former suggest that unless
bestowed upon a collective, the existence of some rights cannot be justified,
the latter assert that unless granted to a collective, some rights cannot be protected. I will take issue with both claims and argue that one can, and should,
justify all rights in terms of individual rights. This does not imply that all the
rights referred to as 'collective rights' can be reduced to individual rights. The
'missing rights' are institutional arrangements that shouldn't have been justified by using rights discourse.

Not all just and desirable political arrangements could be, or should be,
defined in terms of rights. Rights language should delineate basic liberties,
powers, and immunities; it should not specify the particular political arrangements that must be installed in order to realize and protect these rights. For example, while individuals have a right to be protected, they do not have a right
to a particular kind of protection; while they have a right to be represented
in the public sphere, they do not have a right to a particular system of representation, and so on.

It is important, then, to distinguish between rights and the political
arrangements that ought to be put in place in order to defend and promote
rights: the former ought to reflect the nature of moral and political agents;
the latter must take into account contingent limitations embedded in particular social and political circumstances. Expending the language of rights so
that it will cover all desirable social policies weakens rights claims. It places
a wide range of social demands on an equal footing, disallowing us to distinguish between demands which are worthy of special protection and those
which do not merit such treatment.

SOME SOCIOLOGICAL OBSERVATIONS

Demands for collective rights commonly arise when the walls of traditional
communities start crumbling down unveiling the external world. Exposure to

alternative ways of life threatens social cohesion and cultural continuity and forces the community to seek ways of securing its existence. It is in these moments of transition that we ought to decide whether to side with the community or with its individual members (especially with those who wish to dissent from the traditional way of life).[2] Those who endorse the notion of collective rights side, intentionally or unintentionally, with the former.

Supporters of collective rights may find this claim objectionable and argue that they do not side with the community against its members; their aim is to support those individuals members who wish to retain the communal identity. These individuals must be helped in their struggles against trends of assimilation, conversion, language transformation, as well as against moves to reform the communal tradition resulting from pressures exerted by the dominate culture(s). Collective rights are offered as a way of countering these pressures. This may indeed be a noble goal. And yet, attempts to protect individuals from external influences by legal means which expropriate their rights and prevent them from following their preferences open the door for dangerous paternalism, and violations of basic human rights. This is the main political danger embodied in collective rights.

Why are these dangers so commonly ignored? The answer seems to be of a sociological nature: those who favour collective rights come from two entirely different backgrounds. The first group, which dominates the academic world and produces most of the relevant literature, consists of liberal social thinkers who observe with horror the social, political, and cultural disintegration of their society and wish to re-establish communal life as a means of confronting loneliness, alienation, and apathy. Their fears are reflected in essays such as Putnam's 'Bowling Alone', and Walzer's 'Multiculturalism and Individualism'. Rates of disengagement from communal associations for the sake of the private pursuit of the happiness (or desperate search for economic survival) are so high these days, Walzer observes with deep concern, 'that all groups worry all the time about how to hold the periphery and ensure their own future.'[3] Authors belonging to the first group feel they live in an atomized society which could benefit form the strengthening of communal life, and are ready to lend a hand to those who strive to pursue this goal.

The second group is comprised, mainly, of leaders of traditional communities who see and fear the destruction of their own communities. These include, among others, leading members of the Native-American nations, of the Amish community, of ultra-orthodox Jewish communities and fundamentalist Muslim communities. Members of this group seek to assure the stability, continuity, and often the economic prosperity of their communities. For that purpose they are ready to overlook the interests of some dissenting individuals whose personal choices contradict communal interests.

What are the social and political implications of collective rights? Are they used to reinvigorate communal life or to prevent members of marginalized subgroups—women in traditional societies, liberal Jews in Israel, converts to

Christianity among Indian tribes—from dissenting from the traditional way of life? Unfortunately all too often they are used for the latter purpose.

This chapter is, then, a word of caution, calling upon liberal political theorists, and liberal political activists to acknowledge the fact that rights can rarely help to rebuild a community but can easily be used to strengthen dominant subgroups, privilege conservative interpretations of culture over reforms, and disadvantage all those who wish to diverge from accepted social norms and question the traditional role of social institutions. Liberals should then be aware of the price embedded in bestowing rights on groups and be more cautious in their support of such rights.

COMMUNAL SURVIVAL AND VIOLATIONS OF INDIVIDUAL RIGHTS

In those cases in which the welfare or the interests of the community are at stake rights should be granted to the community rather than to its individual members or else the community is left defenceless and might face destruction. This is the main argument adduced in support of group rights.

Risks to the community increase, McDonald argues, if individuals may, on their own, without prior community agreement, exercise rights. 'This expresses a slide from *ours* to *mine* that should be resisted. In particular on a conservative notion of community as a union of past, present, and future generations. I would argue that the claimant's role in collective rights is one of stewardship, and this is best played by the present generation which is mindful of its history and its future.'[4]

What are the implications of McDonald's argument for the ability of individuals to exercise their rights? An example may clarify the issue: in the political debate over a possible withdrawal of Israel from the territories it occupied in the 1967 War, some opponents of withdrawal put forward a claim very similar to the one professed by McDonald. The territories in question, they argued, were promised by God to the Jewish people as a whole—past, present, and future generations included. The present generation cannot, without the approval of all other generations, surrender rights grounded in this divine promise. As such an approval cannot possibly be achieved, no withdrawal can ever be morally justified.

In fact, even if members of all past generations as well as members of the present one prefer a withdrawal, it will not be justified, as it is impossible to know the preferences of future generations. The present generation, if it is no more than a steward of a transgenerational whole whose will cannot be confirmed, is therefore deprived of its ability to reinterpret, amend, or waive its rights. Collective rights thus turn into individual duties. Duties which may be imposed on individuals not only by their own community but also by the State against which the community claims rights.

Note that if collective rights exist, those from whom the rights are claimed
—usually state institutions—acquire correlative duties, the most important
of which is the obligation to preserve the collectives whose existence is a
necessary condition for the protection of the rights. One way of fulfilling this
obligation is to impose on individuals duties to act in ways which would
guarantee the continued existence of the collective.[5] Consequently, the idea
of rights as trumps which could be used by individuals to defend themselves
against the community becomes meaningless, and with it collapses one of the
most important distinctions between theories of rights and utilitarianism.[6]

Van Dyke also grounds collective rights in arguments which undermine
the power of individual rights. Many individual rights, he argues, should be
seen as derivative from communal rights, especially from the community's
right to self-preservation.

For example, individual freedom of expression can often be interpreted in terms of
the right of a linguistic community to preserve its language. But taking individual
rights as exhaustive of all rights would not allow us to defend the interests of communities, and particularly their interest of self-determination.[7]

Like McDonald, Van Dyke gives priority to the interests of the community over the rights of individuals. One should examine the implications of
this argument especially when it is entangled with the notion of survival. Even
those who are suspicious of collective rights often claim that when the very
existence of a collective is endangered, collective rights must prevail over individual ones. It is important to distinguish in this context between two very
different meanings of the term 'survival': the first refers to cases in which the
survival of the community is endangered irrespective of the will of its members;
the second to cases in which the survival of a community is endangered as
a result of its members' will. Obviously there are good reasons to protect the
community in the first kind of cases; one may wonder, however, whether it is
legitimate to protect 'a community' against its own members. More precisely,
is it just, or desirable, to allow those who aspire to preserve the community—
often members of the dominant and privileged élite—to force others to preserve a way of life to which they have grown indifferent or even hostile?

The dangers embodied in adopting the second interpretation are clearly exemplified by the case of the Pueblo Indians. In this case members of a
dominant group within the tribe use powers granted to them by collective
rights to persecute dissenters. Svensson provides us with the testimony of one
of these dissenters, Delfino Concha. Mr Concha claims he was subject to a cruel
injustice as he was exposed to 'intimidation, and isolation from social affairs
enjoyed by the community simply because I did not conform to the religious
function.'[8] Svensson's response to this testimony is sympathy not with the
persecuted individual, but with the persecutors. The tribe's reaction to religious dissent is more understandable, he writes,

when it is remembered that in tribal societies, and even more particularly in one which is a theocracy, religion is an integral part of the community's life which cannot be detached from other aspects of the community. Violation of religious norms is viewed as literally *threatening the survival* of the entire community.[9]

The term *survival* seems to be doing most of the justificatory work here; when the freedom of an individual is contrasted with the survival of the community, the latter seems to have much more weight. This, however, would not have been the case if the dissenter's interests were weighed against those of other individuals, especially if they were weighed against the external preferences of others concerning the behaviour of the dissenter.[10]

How should we interpret the term 'survival' as used in this context? Taylor's use of the term sheds light on this question:

It is axiomatic for Quebec government that the *survival* and flourishing of French culture in Quebec is a good . . . It is not just a matter of having the French language available for those who might *choose* it . . . Policies aimed at *survival* actively seek to *create* members of the community, for instance, in their assuring that future generations continue to identify as French speakers.[11]

In the Canadian case, as in many others, the term *survival* refers not to the actual survival of the community or its members but to the survival of the traditional way of life. Is there a reason to defend a particular way of life from undergoing change? Should one protect a community against cultural revisions or reforms, even radical ones, if these are accepted by its members?[12]

Note that in discussing matters regarding social-cultural changes in terms of a threat to the survival of the community one serves orthodox voices within the community which seek to justify taking extreme measures, including disregard for individual rights and forceful suspension of internal criticism, for the sake of preventing change.

As this discussion exemplifies, in periods of social and cultural transition, when collective rights are most needed to protect a community from external pressures, they are especially dangerous to social reformers. If rights are granted to the group as a whole then feminists, religious reformers like liberal Jews or Muslims, social activists like the opponents of the Indian cast system, etc. are deprived of their rights. This cannot happen if rights are granted to individuals. It thus makes a considerable difference who is the bearer of rights. Kymlicka disagrees with this claim: theoretical debates concerning the distinction between collective rights and individual rights are sterile, he argues, 'because the question whether the right is (or is not) collective is morally unimportant'.[13] Is Kymlicka right? In order to answer this question we should examine his own arguments in some details. Kymlicka draws a distinction between community rights understood as the rights of a group against its own members, and community rights as rights against the larger society. He rejects the former and endorses the latter kind of rights which he terms *group-differentiated rights.*[14] Group-differentiated rights, he argues, could be 'accorded to individual members of a group, or to the group as a whole, or to a federal state/province in which the group forms a majority.'[15]

Is it really the case that the question of how rights are allocated bears no moral significance? Kymlicka himself acknowledges that the language of differentiated citizenship rights may be abused. This was the case with laws supporting racial segregation and ethnic discrimination in South Africa (before the abolition of Apartheid), the USA, and Israel. They may also be abused in some of the cases Kymlicka himself endorses. A by-product of granting land rights to Indian tribes as a collective, Kymlicka argues, is that individual members lose control over their property which they cannot use in order to borrow money or to sell if they wish to leave the community.[16] As hunting rights are given to Indian tribes as collectives rather than to their individual members 'an Indian whose hunting is restricted by her council cannot claim that this is a denial of her rights, because Indian hunting rights are not accorded to individuals.'[17] Unfortunately, Kymlicka concludes, this 'seems to be a natural by-product' of protecting the rights of minority cultures.

One may wonder, however, how natural or unavoidable this 'by-product' is. Note that if the above rights had been granted to individuals rather than to groups, these individuals could have used these rights to protect themselves against the group. The language of collective rights deprives them of this possibility. This is true even if the justifications offered in defence of these rights are liberal ones.

This chapter then sends a warning and calls upon liberal political theorists, and liberal political activists to acknowledge that group rights strengthen dominant subgroups within each culture and privilege conservative interpretations of culture over reformative and innovative ones. Women rarely belong to the more powerful groups in society, and protectors of women's rights do not affiliate themselves with conservative segments. It follows then that women, and those who strive to protect their rights and equal status, are among the first to be harmed by group rights. Their plight, however, is not unique. It is shared by all those who wish to diverge from accepted social norms and question the traditional role of social institutions.

As Okin argued there is an inherent conflict between feminism and group rights 'which persists even when the latter are claimed on liberal grounds, and are limited to some extent by being so grounded.'[18] Her claims can be extended to cover a large number of cases in which collective rights come into conflict with the rights of other powerless groups: dissenters, reformers, converts, and the like.

The conflict is not restricted to matters concerning the interpretation of certain rights but also raises the more crucial question of who can claim or waive a right. When individuals are unable to waive their rights, these rights turn into duties, restricting personal autonomy rather than protecting it.

Individuals who are deprived of their ability to decide which rights to demand and which to waive, who cannot determine for themselves whether to retain their communal tradition, strive to bring about a change, or assimilate, or who cannot decide in which language to educate their children and what to teach them are deprived of their most basic liberties.

The more one consults actual case studies the more one comes to the conclusion that the category of collective rights which are harmless to individual members, is (for all practical purposes) an empty one. It thus seems that the debate between defenders of collective and supporters of individual rights is not a vacuous semantic controversy but a crucial debate which bears significant theoretical and practical consequences.

Moreover, terminological questions are, in themselves, not unimportant. It is nowadays a commonplace to claim that language not only expresses reality, but also shapes it. The language of rights one uses has educational and political implications which shouldn't be overlooked. One of the few social and political tools we can use in order to raise consciousness among oppressed individuals of their rights is to teach them to think of these rights as individual rights, as trumps that can be used against communal oppression and discrimination. The language of collective rights might prevent us from conveying this message. We should then be wary of using it.

COLLECTIVES AND ASSOCIATIONS

Before we continue the discussion, the concept *collective rights* needs to be clarified. In the recent literature this term has been used to describe a wide range of rights. Van Dyke sees collective rights as corporate rights: this view 'is suggested by the idea of a corporation, which has rights and liabilities distinct from those of the persons composing it.'[19] Kymlicka rejects this interpretation and prefers the term 'minority rights', as it focuses attention on 'the claims of "natural" groupings, rather than the rights of voluntary or contractual associations such as unions and corporations.'[20] Others, like Raz and Margalit, favour the term *group rights*.[21]

I do not attempt to settle this terminological dispute. Let me however clarify my own terms. The notion *collective* as used in conjunction with *rights* can be understood in two distinct ways: as the rights of a collective, or of individuals who are members of a certain collective. While the latter term refers to different kinds of individual rights, the former refers to rights granted to a particular kind of agent—a collective one.

In order to analyse the notion of a collective's right it is imperative to distinguish between two kinds of collectives: unorganized, informal collectives and organized ones which constitute legal personalities.[22] My main criticism focuses on bestowing rights to informal collectives like national, religious, ethnic, or gender groups. I shall therefore refrain from addressing issues concerning the nature of obligations or rights granted to legal personalities.[23] I take it for granted that in order to claim that states, corporations, or associations are entitled to some legal rights and could be burdened with some legal duties, one need not introduce collectivist concepts. Such rights and obligations are deeply embedded in the legal system of most states and international organizations. The notion of *collective rights* is of theoretical and political value only if it succeeds in enlarging the scope of the existing rights discourse by applying it to a new type of agents.

One should however note that the distinction between formal and informal associations is not as straightforward as it may seem. In the USA, Young argues, 'civic groups, more often than not, are organized along the lines of gender, race, religion, ethnicity or sexual orientation, even when they have not explicitly aimed to do so.'[24] And most of these groups are neither purely voluntary nor purely ascriptive; many of them have a loose formal structure and a set of unwritten norms and practices.[25] No wonder, then, that in the literature the discussion swings back and forth between groups, communities, and civic associations. Despite these difficulties, I shall concentrate on the rights of informal collectives.[26]

CAN COLLECTIVES BE RIGHTS-HOLDERS?

When rights theories were born, the range of rights-holders was fairly narrow: it included white males who were property owners. In the last two centuries it has been expanded first to non-property holders, then to women, blacks, and members of minority groups. Should we now expand it to include collectives? Note that the traditional description of a rights-holder could be easily extended to include members of the above-mentioned groups. It could, in fact, be claimed that in these cases the social-political applicability of theories of rights was expanded while their theoretical scope remained constant. This, however, is not the case with collective rights.

Can collectives be *rights-holders*? Unfortunately this question is rarely discussed.[27] Let's look at this issue from the point of view of the two dominant theories of rights: the choice theory and the interest theory. The choice theory is described by H. L. A. Hart. Hart interprets the claim 'P has a right to X' as: P has a right to do X if he so chooses. If P has a right to X, others require special justifications for limiting P's freedom in pursuing X, while P has a justification for limiting the freedom of others in the course of his pursuit of X.[28] The role of a right then, is to secure a realm of choice in which rights-holders are free to act without external intervention.

Who can qualify as a rights-holder? According to Hart, a rights-holder is 'an adult human being able of choice', whose activities depend on his ability to make rational decisions.[29] For the choice theory, then, rationality and autonomy are indispensable features of rights-holders. This description makes it particularly hard to apply the choice theory to collectives, as it would demand that collectives be seen not only as active, intentional agents but also as rational and autonomous ones.

The interest theory of rights may offer better support for group rights. According to this theory, 'X has a right if and only if X can have rights and, other things being equal, an aspect of X's well-being (his interest) is a sufficient reason for holding some other person(s) under duty.'[30] This is a purely formal view which needs to be supplemented by a specification of the kind of agents that can have rights and the kinds of interests that can produce sufficient reasons for holding others under duty.

According to Raz, an agent is entitled to have rights 'if either his well-being is of ultimate value or he is an artificial person (e.g. a corporation)'[31]. The collectives discussed here fall under neither of these definitions. Are they the kind of agents whose interests, or parts thereof, can be seen as sufficient grounds for holding others under duty?

Raz obviously believes they are. Belief in the existence of rights, he claims, 'does not commit one to individualism. States, corporations and groups might be rights-holders. Banks have legal and moral rights. Nations are commonly believed to have the right of self-determination, and so on.'[32]

He restates his assumption that groups can have rights in his discussion of the right to national self-determination (together with Margalit), which the following question raises: 'Assuming that self-determination is enjoyed by groups, what groups qualify?'[33] This question presupposes that groups, some groups, could qualify as rights-bearers.

Margalit and Raz ground their justifications for national self-determination in the importance of membership in encompassing communities for the self-identification and prosperity of individual members. These arguments are used to explain why membership in such communities is an individual interest worthy of protection. But how can arguments grounded in the interests of individuals be used to support a *'collective's right'*?

In order to answer this question we have to take a closer look at Raz's definition of collective rights. According to Raz a collective right exists when the following three conditions are met: First, there exists an aspect of the interest of human beings that justifies holding some person(s) under duty; second, the interest(s) in question are interests in a public good and the right is a right to that public good; and lastly, the interest of no single member of that group in the public good is sufficient, by itself, to justify holding others under duty.[34]

The first condition is strictly individualistic; it depends on the existence of an individual interest which justifies holding some person(s) under duty. The second condition brings in a communal dimension which relates to the nature of the interest—an interest in a public good. The third condition brings in consequential considerations. A right is a collective one if its realization imposes far-reaching duties on others. As the interest of no single individual can justify imposing such duties no individual can be a bearer of this right. This latter condition is stated by Raz in the following form:

If B's interest does not justify holding A to be under a duty to do X then B has no right that A shall do X even if A has a duty to do X based on the fact that the action will serve the interests of a class of individuals of whom B is one. Thus a government may have a duty to try and improve the standard of living of all its inhabitants even though no single inhabitant has a right that the government shall try to improve his standard of living.[35]

This definition embodies a cost-benefit analysis. The nature of rights is then to be defined in a two-step procedure: the first identifies the kind of individual interests that could, in principle, give rise to a right, the second evaluates the burdens imposed by rights defending these interests and weighs them against the benefits of their protection. Only if the result of the weighing process is of a certain kind (unspecified by Raz) can we claim that there is a sufficient reason to impose the relevant duties on others.[36]

The precise nature of both steps is unclear. As I cannot develop here a full-fledged criticism of Raz's approach, let me concentrate on one issue only. Can this theory be applied to the kind of collective agents in which I am interested here? A theory that places interests at its core must have an underlying theory of agency which will allow one to identify the kinds of interests worthy of protection. In Raz's writings such a theory is implied (though never fully stated) by the relations between X's ability to be the bearer of rights and the fact that X's well-being is of ultimate value. It is unlikely that this kind of theory—which seems to be a derivative of Kant's kingdom of ends—could be extended to corporations, associations, social groups, or collectives. The existence of collectives may indeed be of value and their preservation could impose certain duties, but unless one is ready to claim that collectives are the kind of agents whose existence is of ultimate value, the Razian definition collapses.

And yet, Raz's theory demands that collectives will be granted rights lest a whole set of rights will go unrecognized. This phenomenon results from the fact that according to Raz's definition the very existence of a right depends on it being a sufficient reason for holding other(s) under duty. In those cases in which the realization of a certain right imposes too heavy a burden on others, such a right can be defended only if it is enjoyed by a large enough number of individuals whose accumulated benefit justifies the imposition of duties. Consequently, no single individual could be the bearer of this right.

There are two problems with this account: first, while it makes the very existence of a right dependent on a cost-benefit analysis, it does not specify what should be placed on both sides of the scale. In determining the nature of rights, should we make a general a priori estimate as to what the cost-benefit analysis might be under normal circumstances, or should we look for actual particular cases in which the right is about to be implemented? If we take the latter route, we will not be able to make decontextualized, a priori, judgements about rights—not even about basic rights. All we would be able to say is that under certain circumstances X has a right to freedom of speech whereas under some other circumstances he does not. But this will rule out rights discourse as an educational, corrective, or guiding tool. Moreover, instead of promoting justice this interpretation of Raz's theory would motivate individuals and institutions to hinder justice.

A real-life example might clarify this point: In the thirty years since Israel has occupied the West Bank, it has settled hundreds of thousands of individuals in the occupied territories. The settlers have established a life for themselves and their children in these territories, and developed expectations to continue living in their houses, working their fields, and sustaining their communal life. All these activities have raised the costs of an Israeli withdrawal from the West Bank. According to Raz's theory, raising costs has two effects: first, in order to justify the duties imposed on Israelis the number of Palestinians who enjoy the right to national self-determination must constantly be on the rise, and second, there might be a point at which the costs will be so high that the right will disappear altogether. In this latter case the right will not be violated, or overridden, but will cease to exist.

The ability to cause a right to vanish must motivate those who oppose it to raise the costs of its implementation. This is not an unknown procedure. Consider the following example: suppose that in a certain community there will be enough anti-abortion fanatics who will attempt to kill a member of the personnel of an abortion clinic every time an abortion is being performed. Under these circumstances the price of protecting women's rights to perform abortions might be exceedingly high. If we accept the interpretation of Raz's theory offered so far, we might have to conclude that under these circumstances women's right to control their bodies has been expunged. It follows that in such cases women's inability to gain control over their bodies does not constitute a violation of their rights.

One could, however, argue that Raz does not endorse the above interpretation, rather he sees the qualification 'other things being equal' as referring to some hypothetical set of 'normal' circumstances. How can we evaluate the burdens imposed by the interest of women in having control over their bodies under such 'normal' circumstances? We may start by assuming that the term *normal* ought to refer only to those actions which are morally justified. The costs imposed by immoral acts should not be taken into account. This would imply that women's right to their bodies is a right immoral acts cannot negate.

Collective rights, then, are the kind of rights the realization of which, under normal circumstances, is too costly if only one person can benefit from them (provided that the costs calculated are solely moral and normal ones). Which rights fall under this description? The answer depends on an account of the nature of 'normal' circumstances and the costs involved in the implementation of a right under such circumstances. What would the costs of freedom of speech, or of the right to national self-determination be under normal circumstances? The answer depends on the scope of the right. If freedom of speech demands that individuals should be able to speak on any topic, at any time, in any place, in any volume, then the social costs of such a right might be unreasonably high (for example, if the right includes the right of secret agents to disclose, at times of war, national secrets). Similarly, if the right to self-determination demands that each individual would be given a state of her own, the costs might indeed be exceedingly high. However, the fact that realizing one's right in the most satisfactory and expanded form would impose far too heavy burdens on others should not imply that a more modest and restrained realization of this right should not be defended. No right ought to be realized regardless of its costs, but no right should be eliminated just because it is impossible to implement it in the most extended form.

As all rights could be realized at different points along a continuum, how can we define the point along this continuum in which we should situate ourselves in order to evaluate the costs of each right? Raz seems to use different standards for evaluating individual and collective rights. In the case of the former he takes the more modest forms of realization to be the standard for the implementation of the right, while in the case of the latter he takes the more extreme version to be the standard. This leads to the conclusion that collective rights are the kind of rights that cannot exist at all, when applied to individuals. This leaves Raz with a real worry. How could some rights, which have moral and political importance, come into being? His answer is given in terms of collective rights.

One must remember that this conclusion is valid if, and only if, we endorse Raz's theory. If, however, we accept the claim that cost-benefit analysis should not enter into the definition of basic rights, or argue that theories of rights must take into account the fact that each right can be implemented in different forms, then the theoretical vacuum created by Raz's theory disappears and with it the need to turn to collective rights.

The claim that cost-benefit analysis should not play a role in determining the rights we have concurs with the view that the nature of a right should be defined by its justifications rather than by its modes of implementation. Namely, that rights which are justified by making reference to individual interests are individual rights even if, most commonly, they cannot be implemented by single individuals. We should then distinguish between matters of principle and matters of policy. As a matter of principle, rights which are meant to

protect the interests of individuals are individual rights; as a matter of policy, a decision to protect individuals in exercising these rights might be justified only if there is a certain threshold number of beneficiaries. Hence, the
size of the group deriving benefits from a particular right might influence
the prospects of its realization: the larger the number of beneficiaries, the
stronger the justification to burden others with the relevant costs.

Another way of understanding Raz's notion of collective rights is to merge
his interest theory of rights—according to which a right is seen as an interest-
based reason for imposing some duty(ies) on others—with the claim that
groups have interests which are non-reducible to those of individuals, thus
claiming that groups should be seen as independent rights-bearers. But in order
to do so, the argument must start not with the well-being and interests of
individuals but with that of groups. Yet Raz supports the importance of collective rights by making reference to the importance of group membership
for individuals and dedicates little space to the more crucial question of group
interests. Do such interests exist at all? Margalit and Raz claim they do, and
that due to their relative independence of individual interests there is no a
priori way of correlating the former with the latter. Their arguments seem
unconvincing. But suppose, for the sake of argument, that some interests could
best be described as group interests; does it follow that groups should be seen
as bearers of rights defending these interests?

According to Kukathas, the claim that groups have independent interests
is insufficient to establish that groups can be rights-holders, as the particular
nature of group interests excludes the possibility of seeing such interests as
grounds for rights. Group interests, he argues, 'exist or take their particular
shape, only because of certain historical circumstances or because political
institutions prevail and not because they are part of some natural order.'[37] But
surely Kukathas does not think that individuals' interests are part of some
natural order or that they are formed free of all historical circumstances or
social influences. The reason to respect individual rather than group interests
cannot possibly be the fact that the former are natural while the latter are not.

Moreover, Kukathas's argument invites an unnecessary discussion concerning the origin of individual interests. Yet, the debate between supporters and
opponents of collective rights is not grounded in different views of the origins
of individual interests, preferences, or motivations. It would be misleading
to claim that supporters of moral individualism see individuals as essentially
atomized, autonomous, self-creating agents, while communitarians see individuals as totally encumbered by their communal setting. The real debate
concerns the following question: how should the facts, recognized by both
supporters and adversaries of collective rights, that individuals are contex-
tualized, that they find meaning and pleasure in communal affiliations, and
that their interests are structured (at least partly) by membership in various
collectives, influence our theory of rights?

Note that liberalism, even in its more traditional forms, is committed to protecting personal autonomy, yet it is not committed to defending only those interests and preferences which are autonomously formed. It is quite obvious that many of the basic liberties liberalism defends, are, by definition, community-bound, including religious and political rights. The claim that ethical individualism fails to respect persons bound by duties derived from sources other than themselves is, therefore, unfounded.

The reason we should respect the interests of individuals and not of groups derives from the nature of the agents who have these interests, and not from the nature or the origins of the interests themselves. Here we can find support in Raz's own definition of rights bearers. An individual is capable of having rights, he argues, 'if and only if, either his well-being is of ultimate value or he is an "artificial person" (e.g. a corporation).'[38] If we apply this definition to Raz and Margalit's own argument, a disturbing inconsistency emerges. Their argument in support of the right of groups to self-determination is grounded in the claim that the prosperity of encompassing groups is 'vital for the prosperity of their members'.[39] This line of argument suggests that group interests should be protected because groups are *instrumental* to the interests of individuals, not because their own well-being is of ultimate value. Hence, on its own grounds Raz's argument fails to establish the status of groups (which do not constitute themselves as artificial persons) as potential rights-holders.

Consequently, asking which collectives qualify as rights-holders is asking the wrong question. And yet this question has attracted much attention. Supporters of collective rights like Kymlicka, Van Dyke, Margalit, Raz, and Svensson, as well as opponents of collective rights like Kukathas and Reaume devote lengthy discussions to establishing distinctions between different kinds of collectives. Supporters of collective rights attempt to find 'the right kind of collectives', which are entitled to be rights bearers—according to Van Dyke these include ethnic communities, nations, the populations of political dependencies and sovereign states and trade unions, and exclude 'chance aggregates and even social and economic classes, [which] may have group interests, but not group rights'.[40] According to Raz and Margalit the collectives that qualify as rights bearers are encompassing groups, while Kymlicka attributes collective rights to national minorities and indigenous peoples.

Opponents both search for deficiencies in the particular defenses offered by supporters of collective rights, and argue that in general the concept 'collective' is too vague to describe a right bearer. The chief concerns about according rights to groups are an interrelated set of problems of indeterminacy, Reaume argues: 'First, there may be indeterminacy concerning the group's boundaries, which in turn threatens to give rise to indeterminacy *vis-à-vis* its interests. Second, it may be difficult to identify group actions and decisions of the sort normally associated with exercising and waiving rights.'[41]

This unnecessary debate results from the fact that efforts to define the characteristics of those collectives that are entitled to enjoy collective rights are made prior to discussions of the much more fundamental question: can any collectivity qualify as a rights-bearer? If the answer to this preliminary question is negative, as I have argued, the rest of the debate is vacuous.

Nevertheless, some may insist that despite the objections raised so far, the language of collective rights cannot be surrendered, as the language of individual rights simply does not make sense in certain cases. In what follows I shall challenge these claims.

ARE COLLECTIVE RIGHTS INDISPENSABLE?

Is the notion of collective rights indispensable? I shall answer this question by raising, and answering, four possible objections to my own position, all of which make a similar claim: no matter how convincing arguments against collective rights are, if we are to defend certain kinds of interests we simply cannot do without them. The first two objections take individual interests as their starting point but claim that these interests would be best served by granting rights to collectives rather than individuals. The last two draw on the notion of collective goods, and claim that rights protecting the pursuit of such goods must be collective ones.

Objection a: Collective rights are the kind of rights that could be realized only within a collective framework. It makes no sense, it is argued, to grant an individual a right to pursue a communal practice. Is this claim well founded? Let us look at one of the most common examples of a collective right, that of national self-determination. At the heart of this right lies an interest to preserve and express one's communal identity and culture. Does it make sense to grant such a right to an isolated individual? The answer depends on the different ways the right can be realized. It is quite clear that one can declare oneself Israeli, Palestinian, Basque, or French even when alone, and that some features of the national culture and tradition can be retained in complete solitude; reading to oneself in one's own language, reciting poems, practising some traditional ceremonies, etc. The ability to enjoy these benefits in solitude is indeed restricted; it grows with the size of the group, and reaches full expression in the presence of a community.

The fact that a certain right can be realized in its fullest form only within the framework of a community does not imply that it is worthless to isolated individuals. Modern technology opens up new opportunities that allow individuals to communicate with distant communities: they can read daily newspapers on the Internet, listen to radio programmes or watch TV shows, talk on the phone to their relatives, fax them written material, and fly back home for a visit. Such individuals can remain in touch with their community of origins even when they reside miles away from home, and may wish to preserve the communal traditions and way of life to the best of their ability.

Acknowledging the full spectrum of possible expressions of identity and culture is of utmost importance in an age of massive immigration in which individuals struggle to retain their identity even when detached from their homeland. For such individuals, being granted rights which allow them to preserve their identity—in the restricted form dictated by the lack of a community—is the only barrier against pressures of assimilation and feelings of uprootedness.[42]

There are, however, some rights one can enjoy only within the framework of a group. For example rights which are dependent on the existence of a certain institutional setting such as the right to be elected, the right to due process, or the right to enjoy a fair system of criminal justice. As no isolated individual can form her own set of institutions these rights seem to be dependent on the existence of a group. Are these rights to be seen as collective rights? Hartney rejects the claim that rights which are grounded in a social setting only a group can establish are group rights. This erroneous conclusion, he maintains, leads to the following implausible consequences: 'since a fair system of criminal justice is something only a group, and not an individual, can have, it would follow that individuals cannot have any right to a fair system of criminal justice, and that no individual's right would be violated if the system is not fair.'[43] One can conclude then, that the fact that a right cannot be enjoyed outside the existence of a socio-political system, and that no isolated individual can construct such a system on his own, is no evidence that the rights the system protects are collective ones.

Objection b: Some interests can best be served by allocating the relevant right to a group. The apparent plausibility of this objection is grounded in a confusion between two claims: that some interests can be better saved within a collective framework, and that some interests will be better served if granted to the community rather than to its individual members. There is a world of difference between these two claims. The first is commonplace, and poses no threat to an individualistic conception of rights. After all, the desire to secure for oneself the most individualistic right of all—the right to self-preservation—leads individuals to contract and form political frameworks, as they believe that this right will be best served within such frameworks. It would be ludicrous to claim that for that reason we should see this right as a collective right.

The second claim is not only more problematic but embodies an actual threat to individual rights and liberties. Its plausibility depends on a particular interpretation of the term *individual interests*, which presupposes that all members of a collective have at least some identical interests and that the collective would use the rights granted to it to defend these interests and these interests only. There is, however, no reason to accept either of these claims.

Collectives are not undifferentiated wholes, and their members may entertain radically different, even conflicting, interests. Granting the right to 'the collective' in order to protect 'its interests', forces 'the collective' to define a uniform set of interests—a process which is likely to provoke among members of the dominant subgroup(s) the motivation to repress dissenting or marginalized individuals, and the power to do so. An interesting example comes out of Svensson's discussion of the case of the Pueblo Indians. Difficulties had arisen, he argues, 'when a few individuals among the Indians, under various types of pressures and influences, particularly conversion to Protestant Christianity, chose to withdraw from certain communal functions while at the same time demanding their "share" in the community and its resources.' Svensson's wording reflects the way dissidents are portrayed; they are seen as weak-willed individuals who, under pressure, betray the group. Those who conform to the norms of the group, on the other hand, are viewed as authentic, loyal, and virtuous individuals. These images place social, religious, and cultural reformistist and dissenters at a clear disadvantage. They are often excluded from the centres of power, and are deprived of their ability to pursue their own interpretation of the collective's norms, traditions, and way of life.

This is well exemplified by an analysis of the difficulties reform and liberal Jews face in Israel. In Israel, religious rights are granted to religious communities rather than to individuals. The chief rabbinical authorities thus determine for all Jews the acceptable ways of practice. Consequently, reform and conservative Jews who disagree with the orthodox interpretation of Judaism are deprived of their religious rights; they do not get a fair share of the state's support of religious practice, they are unable to get land for burial, the marriages and conversion they perform are not recognized by the state, they are never invited to perform official ceremonies and the like. No surprise then that these movements have failed to establish a strong hold in Israel. In the USA, on the other hand, where religious rights are granted to individuals, each Jew can decide to which of the existing Jewish congregations he/she will adhere. All American Jews thus enjoy equal religious rights, and use them to form institutional settings in which they can follow the practices of the community of their choice. As a result, the reform and conservative movements flourish in the USA.

One can summarize this section by claiming that functionalist attempts to defend collective rights by making reference to the interests of individuals fail. Indeed many rights cannot be realized outside of a community, but this is no evidence that these rights belong to the community. There are many enabling arrangements without which rights are meaningless, but these arrangements, in themselves, need not be the bearers of rights.

One could still claim that as some goods cannot be given to individuals they must be the subject of collective rights. The next two objections refer then to the nature of the good the rights serve to protect and argue that there could be no individual right to a collective good.

Objection c: According to Waldron the justification of a right depends on the good it promotes. Those rights which protect the pursuit of a collective good cannot be a matter of individual right, as the value of a collective good can only be appreciated with reference to its benefit to the group as a whole. A claim of right does two things, Waldron argues: 'it specifies a good, and it specifies a person—a beneficiary, a right-bearer—for whom, or for whose sake, the good is to be brought about.'[44] As no account of the worth of common goods to any particular individual can be given except by concentrating on what they are worth to all,

the duty to realize such goods must be grounded in an adequate characterization of their desirability, and that is their worth to members of the group considered together not as individual recipients of benefit . . . So since no adequate account of its desirability can be pinned down to either X or Y or Z, there can be no *point* in saying it ought to be pursued as X's or Y's or Z's right.[45]

Waldron suggests that the worth of communal goods cannot be measured for each individual. The worth of culture, solidarity, or shared language is larger than its cumulative worth to each individual. These experiences are unintelligible without reference to the mutual experiences of the participants. I certainly agree that the full worth of culture can be appreciated only if we take into account the importance of interpersonal exchanges; nevertheless I argue that the worth of culture to individuals can be measured and should be the only criterion for the allocation of cultural rights.

The claim that cultural rights should be grounded only in the value of culture to its individual members has far-reaching implications, as non-members may also favour the preservation and flourishing of a certain culture. Suppose a small community of Latin speakers exists on some remote island. Members of this community may believe they would be better off, for both financial and cultural reasons, if they gave up their original language and assimilated into the English-speaking community that surrounds them. Yet, others who are not members of this community may think that keeping Latin alive is of great cultural value and that members of the community should continue to preserve and develop the Latin language. As the community of Latin speakers is very small and the number of non-members who are interested in the survival of the language is very large, taking external preferences into account might justify forcing members of the community to preserve their culture.[46] To call such an oppressive attitude a right is absurd.

I therefore agree with Dworkin's claim that external preferences should not count and cannot provide a justification for a right. Rights ought to be justified only with reference to their internal value to individuals even if this justification will fail to capture the full worth of the good in question.

Objection d: As collective goods are non-exclusive it make no difference who is their bearer. Indeed collective goods are provided in ways which makes exclusion almost impossible. Nevertheless it does make a difference whether they are granted to individual members or to the collective as a whole. Granting the right to individuals protects their freedom and promotes pluralism within groups as well as among them. It makes a difference whether I have a right to language which I can use or waive at will, or whether the community has a right to language which I cannot waive, or demand on my own. In the first case I am recognized as an independent agent who can determine her life plan and pursue it, in the second I am but an organ of a whole I cannot control. We are then back to the claims that opened our discussion, regarding the political importance of the ability to demand and waive rights and the educational importance of the kind of rights language that is being used.

CONCLUSIONS

Some may argue, that despite the reservations raised so far, the language of group rights should be preserved, as it has symbolic importance; it signifies the role groups ought to play in social life. The decision whether to adopt the language of individual rights or of group rights, Glazer argues, is of great importance, as it reflects the model of social life a state endorses:

If the state sets before itself a model that group membership is purely private, a shifting matter of individual choice and degree, something that may be weakened and dissolved in times as other identities take over, then to place an emphasis on group rights is to hamper this development . . . If, on the other hand, the model a society has for itself, today and in the future, is of a confederation of groups, with group membership as central and permanent, and with divisions among groups making it unrealistic or unjust to envisage these group identities weakening in time to be replaced by common citizenship, then it must take the path of determining what the rights of each group shall be.[47]

The debate between supporters of individual rights and group rights is thus portrayed as a debate between two camps. One camp consists of those who believe that members of ethnic and national groups should be protected against discrimination and prejudice, and should be free to maintain whatever part of their ethnic heritage or identity they wish to maintain, but believe that these 'efforts are purely private, and it is not the place of public agencies to attach legal identities or disabilities to cultural membership in ethnic groups'.[48] The other comprises those who think that ethnicity should be displayed in the public sphere and that the state should support public measures aimed at protecting or promoting an ethnocultural identity.

This may have been an adequate portrayal of the state of the debate in the 1970s when Glazer wrote the above passage, but in recent years the debate has shifted elsewhere: it is no longer a debate between liberals who claim that pluralism is a historically contingent fact of social life which societies ought to overcome and communitarians who see it as an enduring feature of modern societies.[49] Instead it is a debate which takes the fact of pluralism as its starting point and asks what is the best way to assure to individuals, rooted in their own cultural, linguistic, and religious communities, their rights.

It is from this point of view that I have analysed the distinction between rights granted to collectives and rights granted to individual members of collectives and endorsed the notion of individual rights. Granting rights to collectives rather than to individuals, I have argued, too often leads to the violation of basic individual rights.

The fact that collectives cannot be the bearers of rights does not mean that policies adopted in order to protect members of disempowered groups, to promote social justice, or to remedy injustice are undesirable: but it seems advisable to avoid defining such arrangements in terms of collective rights, as individuals do not have a right to any particular political arrangement, but only to a just one. Nor does my argument imply that there is no room in the public sphere for any other association but the state. Individuals have a right to form associations or corporations, which allow them to pursue their rights collectively. But in order to deal with these agencies there is no need to turn to the language of collective rights. For all these reasons the language of collective rights should be abandoned.

NOTES

This chapter has a long (and tormented) history. I started writing it while I was a visiting scholar at the Center for Human Values at Princeton University, and returned to it while I was a visiting scholar at the Program in Ethics and the Profession, at Harvard University. I am grateful to Lea Brilmayer and the participants of the International Jurisprudence Colloquium at NYU, and to Susan Dwyer, Robert Fullinwider, Ken Greenawalt, Richard Fallon, Judith Licthemberg, Nancy Rosenblum, Dennis Thompson, Sue Uniacke, and Noam Zohar for their for many instructive comments, good advice and productive discussions. Special thanks to Tamar Meisels for her many helpful comments.

1. As it will become clear when the discussion unfolds, this chapter examines the theoretical and political implications of rights which are bestowed on a collective as a *whole* rather than on individual members of the collective. The adequate term to use was *collective's right*. In this paper I use the more common, but misleading term *collective rights* in order to be able to relate to the literature I'm criticizing without confusing the reader.

2. In periods when communities can shut themselves off and shelter their members from external influences there is little practical difference between granting cultural,

religious, or linguistic rights to individual members or to the community as a whole.

3. M. Walzer, 'Multiculturalism and Individualism', in *Dissent* (Spring 1994): 188.
4. M. McDonald, 'Should Communities Have Rights? Reflections on Liberal Individualism', in *Canadian Journal of Law and Jurisprudence*, 4/2 (1991): 232.
5. I am grateful to Sue Dwyer for her helpful discussion on this issue.
6. See Rawls's discussion of utilitarianism. Classical utilitarianism, he argues, 'fails to take seriously the distinction between persons. The principle of rational choice for one man is taken as the principle of social choice as well', *Theory of Justice* (Harvard: Harvard University Press, 1972): 187.
7. V. Van Dyke, 'Collective Entities and Moral Rights: Problems in Liberal Thought', *Journal of Politics*, 44 (1982): 29.
8. F. Svensson, 'Liberal Democracy and Group Rights: The Legacy of Individualism and its Impact on American Indian Tribes', *World Politics*, 29 (1977): 432.
9. Ibid. 433.
10. See R. Dworkin's discussion of external preferences in *Taking Rights Seriously* (London: Duckworth, 1978): 234.
11. C. Taylor, 'The Politics of Recognition', in A. Gutmann (ed.), *Multiculturalism* (Princeton: Princeton University Press, 1994): 58–9 (my emphasis).
12. One can claim that individuals have no choice but to accept the change if they want to enjoy the benefits offered by the surrounding society. This may indeed be true yet accepting this claim may eventually lead to dangerous paternalism.
13. W. Kymlicka, *Multicultural Citizenship* (Oxford: Clarendon Press, 1995): 45.
14. W. Kymlicka, 'Individual and Community Rights', in J. Baker (ed.), *Group Rights* (University of Toronto Press, 1994): 18.
15. Kymlicka, *Multicultural Citizenship*: 45.
16. Ibid. 43.
17. Ibid.
18. S. Okin, 'Feminism or Multiculturalism', *Boston Review of Books*, Oct. 1997.
19. V. Van Dyke, 'The Individual, the State, and Ethnic Communities in Political Theory', repr. in W. Kymlicka (ed.), *The Rights of Minority Cultures* (Oxford: Oxford University Press, 1995): 33.
20. W. Kymlicka, *Multicultural Citizenship*: 33.
21. J. Raz and A. Margalit, 'The Right to National Self-Determination', *Journal of Philosophy* (1990).
22. In the legal sense a corporation can own property, make contracts, or commit torts, but 'it is not a group: it is a single fictitious-person, distinct from all the members of the group and from the group itself' (see M. Hartney, 'Some Confusion concerning Collective Rights', in W. Kymlicka (ed.), *The Rights of Minority Cultures* (Oxford: Oxford University Press, 1995): 214.
23. I follow here May's distinction between unorganized collectives which he calls *mobs* and organized collectives which he calls *corporations*. Yet I will not follow his terminology. As the term *mob* often carries pejorative connotations I will use the terms *collectives* or *groups*, terms that will be used interchangeably. (See L. May, *The Morality of Groups: Collective Responsibility, Group-Based Harm, and Corporate Rights* (Notre Dame Ind., University of Notre Dome Press, 1987)).

24. I. Young, 'Social Groups in Associative Democracy', in E. O. White (ed.), *Associations and Democracy* (London: Verso Press, 1995): 209.
25. I must stress then that while I argue against the notion of *collective rights* and claim that it is theoretically inconsistent and politically dangerous, I endorse the notions of *associational* and *corporate rights*. The purpose of this chapter is, in fact, to urge liberal political theorists to surrender the language of collective rights not only in favour of individual rights, but also to examine the kinds of rights that legal entities—be they states, associations, or corporations—are entitled to.
26. I shall not enter here into a discussion concerning the rights of associations. Nevertheless, let me make one brief remark in order to prevent misunderstandings: I do not adopt a libertarian line according to which as long as the right to exist is protected associations are allowed to adopt any policy they wish even if these violate the basic rights of their members. Associations and corporations possess rights, for instance the right to determine the rights and duties of their members. But liberal societies acknowledge the existence of certain fundamental rights that all individuals must possess and cannot be lost through corporate membership. Hence, while in reference to a large range of interests, members of associations may be legally invisible to the government, membership ought not render them wholly invisible. A liberal-democratic government must be ready to protect the basic rights of its citizens against incursion. For example, unions are granted rights in order to protect the interests of their members. Consequently, the interests of those who deviate from the union's line could be harmed. For example, those who feel they are better off bargaining on their own are unable to do so. Under a regime of collective bargaining and closed shop, individual workers become legally invisible to the courts, and even to their own employers, with respect to a vast range of economic interests. Their interests are mediated by the union, which becomes their spokesperson and agent. Their rights and duties are defined by the union's bylaws and by the agreements that the unions exact from the industry. Yet, union bargaining is legitimate only when as it does not violate the basic rights of its members. If the union will accept an agreement which will force Jews to work on a Saturday, women to be paid less than men, or blacks to do only manual works, then there will be good reason to overrule that agreement. If, on the other hand, the agreement reached by the union disallows some individuals from earning more than they could have earned if they had bargained individually, then no basic rights have been violated as no individual has a right to earn more than his fellow workers.
27. One could, at this stage of the debate, turn to international legal documents in which the rights of peoples are recognized; but these documents are notoriously ambiguous both in their definition of rights bearers and in the definition of the rights that could be attributed to them. I therefore choose not to base my argument on these documents but to seek an independent justification.
28. H. L. A. Hart, 'Are There Any Natural Rights?', in J. Waldron (ed.), *Theories of Rights* (Oxford: Oxford University Press, 1984).
29. Ibid. 77.
30. J. Raz, *The Morality of Freedom* (Oxford: Oxford University Press, 1986): 166.
31. Ibid.
32. Ibid. 166.

33. Raz and Margalit, 'The Right to Self-Determination': 442.
34. Raz, *The Morality of Freedom*: 208.
35. Ibid. 182 n. 1.
36. I am grateful to Tamar Meisels for discussing this issue with me.
37. C. Kukathas, 'Are There Any Cultural Rights?', *Political Theory*, 20 (1992): 111 (my emphasis).
38. Raz, 166.
39. Raz and Margalit, 449.
40. Van Dyke, 'The Individual and the State': 33.
41. D. Reaume, 'The Group Right to Linguistic Security; Whose Rights? What Duties?', in J. Baker (ed.), *Group Rights* (Toronto University Press, 1994): 124.
42. Telecommunication can also allow for a form of electronic immigration in which the emigrant need not abandon his/her culture to reside in another.
43. Hartney, 'Some Confusion concerning Collective Rights': 218.
44. J. Waldron, 'Can Communal Good be Human Rights?' in J. Waldron, *Liberal Rights* (Cambridge: Cambridge University Press, 1993): 355.
45. Ibid. 359.
46. Similarly, taking into account external preferences might justify refusing members of some other community a right to preserve their language or tradition on the grounds that non-members consider this language and tradition to be of inferior value, or even dangerous.
47. N. Glazer, 'Individuals' Rights against Groups' Rights', in W. Kymlicka (ed.), *The Rights of Minority Cultures*: 134.
48. W. Kymlicka, introduction, *The Rights of Minority Cultures*: 9.
49. See J. Rawls's discussion of the fact of pluralism in *Political Liberalism* (New York: Columbia University Press, 1995).

IV

What Can Europe Learn from North America?

IV

What Can We Learn from Latin America?

9

Multiculturalism and American Exceptionalism

NATHAN GLAZER

A few years ago, I noted with interest that the term 'multiculturalism', whose use in the United States had exploded, was also beginning to appear in European countries. We had enough difficulty in the United States deciding what multiculturalism meant, and what it portended for the United States. The term 'multiculturalism', which appeared in only forty articles (as reported in the database covering leading American newspapers and periodicals, Nexis) in 1981, appeared in 2,000 in 1992.[1] Its use had spread from education, higher and lower, still the primary venue for its appearance, to cover disputes over the handling of racial stories in newspapers, seminars to sensitize public and private employees to the nuances of word usage affecting racial and minority groups, conflicts over how to celebrate—if at all—the 500th anniversary of Columbus's voyage (now no longer called a 'discovery'), and endless other matters in public and private life in the United States.

These disputes seem so characteristically American that one wonders what multiculturalism could possibly mean in European countries, with neither a history of deep racial division, nor of immigration as a central theme of identity. These are the central features characterizing the rise of multiculturalism in the United States. It is true that the situation regarding ethnic diversity in Western European countries is similar to what we find in the United States, which would seem to undermine any notion of American exceptionalism[2] in either the presence of or response to multiculturalism. Thus, the proportion of the foreign-born in the populations of the countries of Western Europe and the United States is quite similar. The 1990 census shows 9 per cent of the population of the United States was born abroad, and is thus technically 'immigrant', a figure not very different from what we find in France, Germany, and some other West European countries. Even Sweden has the same percentage of foreign-born as the United States. In both the United States and Western Europe we also find a similar commitment to civil and human rights, which outlaws any crude efforts at either mass expulsion or forced assimilation. This of course does not preclude the presence of widespread prejudice and discrimination, some violent racist episodes, anti-immigrant movements, and some prominent national figures who do not share the generally liberal public atmosphere of the economically advanced democracies. And one can find other

similarities that link Western Europe and the United States, despite significant historical and constitutional differences.

Nevertheless, the differences are also profound, in particular the long existence of a deep and historically significant racial division in the United States,
and the prominent place of immigration in shaping the American conception
of the nation. They do justify the extension of that elastic term 'American
exceptionalism', which has been used to explain so many things in the United
States, from the absence of socialism to the high rates of social disorder, to
the pattern of ethnic and racial diversity in the United States.

Whether there is anything that Europe can learn from the United States is
another question. We in the United States keep on looking at other nations
that seem to manage some part of their economy or society better, but generally conclude, if we know enough, that the differences in our histories make
it very difficult to adopt the practices of other nations. We wish our society
had as little crime as Japan, that our social policy provided as extensive benefits
as those of the advanced democracies of Europe, that our educational system
was as rigorous as those of Europe and Japan, but we generally regretfully
conclude that our social characteristics, our economy, our educational system,
our polity, are distinctive not because of ignorance of other and better practices but because of our distinctive history, and that we cannot easily remove
one element in our practices, as if it were a defective piece of machinery,
and insert an improved replacement.

We do believe however—or many of us do—that at least in the area of
race and ethnic relations we can teach others: so the First Lady, Hillary Rodham
Clinton, in her visit to American troops in Bosnia in March, 1996, was quoted
as saying:

There is no better example in the world of what a multiethnic, multiracial, multicultural team means than the United States military. You look around at the men and
women in this room. By your example, you are saying to the people of Bosnia, Croatia,
Serbia, Europe, the world, 'Yes, people can get along with each other. . . . There is
another way. Look at America!'[3]

This may be an example of American arrogance as well as American exceptionalism. One doubts that the stay of American troops in Bosnia will have any
such effect, but this may be too pessimistic a view as to the possibility of
social learning. In any case, if we are to learn from one another, the first step
is to properly characterize just what the situation is in each of our countries.

II

Two things characterize American racial and ethnic diversity, compared to
that of the Western European countries, and therefore make multiculturalism in the United States different from multiculturalism in Western Europe,

and more important for us. The first is a deep racial divide that has little to do with immigration and its effect in increasing American diversity, but is instead native to the United States, a constituent element of American society (to use the term in its narrower meaning, as referring to the people of the United States) from its very origins. I do not think there is an equivalent in the major West European countries. There may have been such deep racial or caste-like divisions in the distant past (Saxons and Normans in England, Franks and Celts in France?), but these ancient divisions are lost in the mists of time and have no present relevance to life in most Western European countries. We do find serious and long-lasting divisions of language and nationality in Spain, as in the case of the Basques and the Catalans, but these are not divisions by race, and do not exhibit a caste-like character, which divide the presumed high from the low, which is the most distinctive characteristic of the racial divide in the United States.

The second is that immigration plays a completely different role in the United States from what it plays in Western Europe. In Western Europe immigration has been driven by the practicalities of the need for labour, or of family reunification, or by international commitments in regard to refugees and asylum-seekers, and is sharply limited by public policy when alarm rises over numbers or difference. The same is of course true in the United States. But in addition, in the United States immigration is driven by ideological considerations which go to the heart of the common understanding of the nature of American society and the American nation. Presidents, Republican and Democratic alike, celebrate immigration and immigrants as one of the distinctive glories of the United States. The Statue of Liberty has become an icon welcoming immigrants. The museum celebrating immigration on Ellis Island is probably the most visited museum of American history in the nation. Our public school curricula celebrate immigration and the diversity of the United States. These developments may be recent, and have fully established themselves only in the past few decades, but are now so solidly established that it is inconceivable that they will change.[4] These two characteristics together mean that multiculturalism in the United States must also be different from what it is in Europe. It must be more important, and it must be more divisive.

No differences are absolute, and even in laying out these two major characteristics of American exceptionalism—the long-lasting racial divide and the distinctive role of immigration in shaping the nation and the national self-image—one can think of parallels that have a good deal of similarity in various European countries. How different is the racial divide in the United States from some deep regional and ethnic divisions in Western European countries, for example? Certainly there are similarities. I will not try to establish a metric by which we can determine the scale of difference and similarity. I will rather characterize what I see as distinctive in the United States, and consider to what extent any lessons can be drawn from American experience as Europe, too, becomes more diverse.

One distinction between the United States and Europe in the use of the term 'multiculturalism' directs us to one important difference. In the United States, when we speak of multiculturalism, or diversity, we commonly have in mind the culture of 'minorities', and these are conceived of as native to the United States. Multiculturalism in the United States is something for minorities. It is also thought of secondarily as something for immigrants, but its use is restricted to immigrants who are considered part of an American minority. So multiculturalism is primarily for blacks, but also for Puerto Ricans (who are technically not immigrants, since Puerto Rico is part of the United States) or Mexicans, for the Chinese and Koreans, but not for the Irish or Russians. In Europe, I believe, multiculturalism is considered something for immigrants or foreigners. (For those born abroad, we use the term 'immigrants' in the United States; in Europe I note the term commonly in use is 'foreigners'. There is a significance in the difference that I will discuss later.) In the United States, it is minority leaders who demand multiculturalism. They argue for it because of the value they claim for the culture they carry, because they believe it will improve the self-image and educational achievement of minority children, and because they hope it will improve the attitude of the majority towards minorities, by teaching them respect and appreciation for minorities.

The term 'minority' says nothing about whether the minority is native or foreign, and indeed minorities in current American usage are assumed to be native and citizen groups entitled to the same rights all other Americans have. The essential definition of minority in current American usage is a racial or ethnic group, whether native or immigrant, that has been subjected to prejudice and discrimination. While Jews and Irish and Italians and perhaps other European groups were in the past subjected to prejudice and discrimination, and were once considered minorities, they are not considered minorities today. The term is reserved for groups that are racially different. The minorities thus are African-Americans, Latinos (who are not formally considered racially different, but who are, because of the large admixture of American Indians, considered a quasi-race), Native Americans, and Asians. The names of all these groups steadily undergoes change, and if I were writing thirty years ago, I might have called them Blacks, Hispanics, Indians, or Orientals.

It is a matter of some significance that the category 'minorities', which encompasses the specific groups who are highlighted in multicultural programmes in schools and for whose benefit they are presumably implemented, indiscriminately combines natives with immigrants. The issue of multiculturalism in the United States is one that affects major native groups of the population, who are more active in promoting it than recent immigrant groups. The latter remain outside the discussion unless they are also considered part of an American 'minority'. One of these affected minority groups, American Indian, is entirely native, and the largest of them, African-American, is overwhelmingly native. Some parts of the Hispanic population precede even the English in the date of their earliest settlement on what is now the soil of the United States. Only Asian-Americans are dominantly of recent immigrant origin. Despite the prominence and intensity of the debate over immigration today in the United States, the distinction between immigrant and native simply does not play much role in American consciousness. The great majority of those living in the United States who were born abroad are citizens or permanent residents, and the others are expected to become citizens soon. Otherwise, the ordinary American asks, why would they come? The distinction between 'citizen' and 'non-citizen' is more meaningful to the American than the distinction between the foreign-born immigrant and the native.

The term 'foreigner' in common American usage is reserved for the temporary visitor, the person who does not expect to become a permanent part of the United States, and these are relatively few compared to immigrants. The immigrant may be called a 'foreigner', but rarely is. This term, if applied to the American who was born abroad, would be considered invidious and pejorative. The immigrant, whatever his own attitude towards the country of his origin, is expected to become a citizen speedily enough, at which point there is almost no legal difference between the foreign-born and the native-born citizen. Henry Kissinger and his equivalents number in many millions, and while they are technically immigrants, they would never be called foreigners. A deeper dividing line for American consciousness than that between the immigrant or the foreigner and the native, and the one to which multiculturalism points, is the racial or ethnic dividing line, and it operates independently of whether the members of a racial or ethnic group are native or foreign: multiculturalism is for minorities.

The term 'minority' has itself an odd history, which alerts us to the greater salience of the racial division compared to the native–foreign division. Up until the late 1960s, one could find in wide use textbooks for courses in American race relations and minority studies which included among the minority groups to be studied the major European immigrant groups. Indeed, Jews and anti-Semitism were central subjects in minority studies in the 1940s and 1950s, and Jews played a prominent role in these texts along with Italians, Poles, and other European immigrant groups.

All groups of European origin have for some time been excluded as suitable subjects for minority studies. They are also not considered to be minorities for any public purpose. In the late 1960s, minority status became a legal category, owing to the implementation of government affirmative action—that is, preferential treatment or positive discrimination—to raise the economic and educational level of Blacks, as they were then called. In an obscure decision with major consequences, government agencies decided to include other racial groups which had been subject to prejudice and discrimination, even if of a lesser order than that which afflicted blacks, in the categories to be benefited by affirmative action. American Indians, Asians, and Hispanic groups (who were in earlier stages of American history considered a 'racial' group, but who are now placed ambiguously by the census and official records between race and ethnic group, occupying a special and unique category) were included in the affirmative action categories, as minorities who needed the special protection of affirmative action. (They of course already had protection against discrimination on grounds of race and national origin, under Civil Rights laws and constitutional interpretations which cover every American.) These groups have never been removed from government regulations as groups protected by affirmative action.[5]

European groups were not included as minority groups who would receive the special benefit of affirmative action. This meant, for example, that employers and colleges and universities did not have to report on the numbers in these ethnic groups they employed, as they were required to do for the officially listed minority groups. It would have been in any case difficult to do so, since there is a great deal of intermarriage among European ethnic groups, and so many of European origin now have two, three, or more ethnicities among their forebears. Further, there exists only a very inadequate census count of European ethnic groups in the form of a question on 'ancestry', and thus there are no good baseline figures against which one could rate an employer's record in employment of such groups. In contrast, the census does make a count of all non-white races, and all Hispanics or Latinos. There were a few suggestions and demands at the time affirmative action was being developed that some European groups, Eastern and Southern Europeans, be considered 'minorities', but such proposals were soon abandoned. It was clear that European ethnic groups were already in the late 1960s 'assimilated' to the majority. They may have once been minorities in the sense of common American usage: they were such no longer.

Divisions which had once been important had thus faded away, while the one great division in American society that had marked it from its origins remained. In a country with a history of successful assimilation—successful that is for European and Middle Eastern groups—the groups considered in some ways disadvantaged had changed over time. Catholics were once considered for example a 'minority'. They were so considered because they faced discrimination and prejudice, because they were composed largely of recent immigrants, because they were economically not as well off as Protestants, because they were different in religion at a time when religious differences were important. In terms of numbers, Catholics of course are still a minority. But numbers are the least significant part of the meaning of minority. In consciousness, their own and others, Catholics are now part of the 'majority'—that is, if they are of European origin. Jews are certainly a minority in numbers, and so consider themselves, not only because of their numbers, but also because of their history, and occasional incidents of anti-Semitism, but in the minds of everyone else—including writers of textbooks on minority and race relations—they are now part of the 'majority'.

If this pattern of assimilation was universal, affecting all groups in the United States similarly (it was near to universal for immigrants until the 1970s, while they were dominantly European in origin), multiculturalism would pose no great problem. It would be considered a transitional adjustment to make matters more comfortable for groups on the way to assimilation. Indeed, something like multiculturalism was proposed for European ethnic groups in World War I in opposition to the prevailing patriotic or chauvinistic assimilatory culture. Had it been implemented it is most unlikely it would have done anything to stem the assimilation of European ethnic groups into the majority. A mild multiculturalism was modestly implemented in American schools during World War II and the years after, and did nothing to stem the assimilatory process.[6]

What makes multiculturalism so agitating and disturbing today is that there is one large group that does not become part of the prevailing assimilatory process, a group which, while presently being increased substantially by immigration, does not find its origin in the history of free immigration. The essential point is that troubling ethnic and racial divisiveness in the United States is only in part, and in lesser part, created by immigration. We expect that the kind of diversity we experience because of immigration will be overcome with time. Just as immigrant minorities of the past are now part of the majority, so we believe the immigrant minorities of the present will become part of the majority—certainly if they are of European or Middle Eastern origin, very likely if they are of Asian origin, but most doubtfully if they are African or Caribbean black.

This expectation, fulfilled for the European immigrants of the past and expected for the European immigrants (few as they are) of today, was not unlimited and did not cover all groups during most of American history, despite the universalizing rhetoric of the Declaration of Independence. The definition of what groups were suitable to enter into the assimilatory process and become fully accepted Americans has been steadily extended over time. Jews and Italians and Greeks and Poles, once considered of a different race difficult to assimilate, are now part of the majority. Hardly anyone doubts today that Asian minorities, considered unassimilable in the past, will be assimilated as rapidly as most European immigrants of the past were. There may be more doubt about some Latino groups, who trail the Asians in education and income, but even there assimilation is a reasonable expectation. Cubans today are considered no more different from the 'majority' than European ethnic groups. We still find in the public mind a spectrum defining the ease and speed of assimilation for different groups. At one end are the English-speaking immigrants from Canada or England or Ireland, for whom the term 'assimilation' is almost meaningless, for they are never called 'foreigners' or 'minorities', and are considered part of majority America from their arrival. As we move towards the other end of the spectrum, and add groups of different language, race, religion, the assimilatory process is expected to be slower.

So minorities can expect in time to stop being minorities, because they change in their culture and economic and social status, and there is a concurrent change in how others, part of the pre-existing 'majority', view them. The minorities become like the majority, are seen to be like the majority, and the distinctions which once made them minorities lose importance. And so, the Irish, Catholics in general, Jews, Italians, Greeks, Slavs, and all those ethnic Europeans once considered of different and inferior race, were in time no longer considered to be of a different race at all, and lost their minority status.

III

The immigrant minority does not stay a minority for more than two or three generations. The power of assimilation, operating through a common American culture, through intermingled residence and schooling, through intermarriage, is such that the ethnic identity, whatever it is, becomes in time only a vague and partial identity, put on or taken off depending on circumstances.[7] There is one major exception to this pattern of assimilation: African-Americans. Overwhelmingly native, their numbers have been increased by substantial immigration from the Caribbean and more recently Africa. But it is not this that makes them an exception to the overall pattern of assimilation. Americans in general do not make distinctions among natives and immigrants of African origins. These distinctions, important as they are, because different groups of African origin will fare very differently in achieving higher education, or better economic status, are not taken much account of by non-African-Americans, and in any case seem to fade in the consciousness of the individuals of these various groups by the second or third generation, as all of African origin are merged into a single group. The differences among African-origin Americans is great, in religion, language, original nationality, and culture. In the American context, they all become one group, more sharply separated from the majority, however conceived, than any other major group. (I leave aside for this comparison Indians on reservations, and some small religious groups, such as the Amish and Hasidic Jews, who also maintain apartness and difference from the majority on the basis of religion.)

Thus multiculturalism has two very different roots in the United States. One has nothing to do with American immigration, past or current. It stems from the great racial divide that has fissured American life since its origins. The second does stem from American diversity as created by immigration.

But the first is more important and serious than the second. The first kind of multiculturalism, if established, threatens to become permanent and divisive, as permanent and divisive as the racial division itself. The second we can expect will be transitory, owing to the power of American assimilation. Were it not for the condition of African-Americans, I doubt that there would be any great concern about multiculturalism in the United States at all.

I have made a rather sharp distinction that advocates of multiculturalism in general do not, that between African-Americans and all the others, white or non-white, immigrant or non-immigrant, European or non-European. The significance of this distinction will certainly be disputed. Multicultural advocates in the United States insist on ranging on one side all the 'people of colour', some of whom are predominantly of recent immigrant origin. They claim all people of colour are equally oppressed by the majority whites, all have had their cultures denigrated, all must receive recognition and respect. But the amalgam, or the 'rainbow coalition', does not hold, except on college and university campuses, where ideology tends to submerge key differences in interest and outlook and condition. These differences divide Asians from all the others, owing to their generally higher education and occupational status. (Twice as many Asians as whites are college graduates.) They divide blacks from Latinos, because these two largest 'minority' groups increasingly compete with each other, politically and economically, in the central cities where they both are found in large number, and because one cannot expect blacks to have the same attitude towards immigration as Latinos, since immigration can scarcely benefit African-Americans, and probably harms them.

The distinctiveness of African-Americans is what gives bite to the issue of multiculturalism. It is the African-American version of multiculturalism —'Afrocentrism'—that has made the cover pages of *Time* and *Newsweek*, that is denounced in books by major American intellectuals, that is seen as most dangerous, and that simultaneously is most widely established in urban school districts. African-Americans have simply not participated to the same degree in the process of assimilation to a majority and common culture that all European ethnic groups have now undergone (leaving aside some small resistant minorities), that Asian-Americans can expect to participate in, that is already realized for some Hispanic origin groups (such as the Cuban), and may be expected, if at a slower rate, for others.

Recent research—on residential separation and on intermarriage—points to the distinctive position of African-Americans. Thirty years after the Civil Rights revolution and the revolutionary changes in American attitudes and law that made discrimination illegal as well as socially unacceptable, African-Americans still show a degree of residential separation from others—not whites alone—that has no parallel. This is not explained by recency of immigration (the great majority of blacks are of course not recent immigrants), not found among the other two large 'minority' groupings, Asians and Hispanics, it is only modestly affected by higher income and education, and it changes remarkably slowly.[8]

Intermarriage, that most decisive marker of assimilation, sharply separates blacks from others. Groups with large percentages of recent immigrants, such as the Asian-American and Hispanic groups, show much higher rates of out marriage than one finds for blacks, despite the reasonable expectation, owing to language and cultural differences, of a greater degree of social isolation.[9] School desegregation, despite great efforts, is all but abandoned in the large cities, and a pattern of separation of the two races in public schools in large cities, based on their residential separation, is generally accepted. Language use among large parts of the African-American population shows a distinctive pattern which maintains itself—and indeed may be increasing its hold—over generations, when in contrast non-English speaking immigrant groups lose all evidence of linguistic distinctiveness in two generations.[10] In December 1996, a major national controversy erupted when the school board of Oakland, California, a predominantly black city, decided that teachers should take account of lower-class black English in their teaching and treat it as a separate language, 'Ebonics' (a word made up of 'ebony' and 'phonics'), derived from African languages. This decision was widely denounced, by black leaders and others, but it did point to the remarkable degree of separation in language between inner-city blacks and the rest of the English-speaking population.

This separation, along with the ideological trends in the African community that both reflect it and in some measure foster it (though it is clear the primary source of the separation historically is to be found in white attitudes towards blacks), finds reflection in the institution that was considered most important in integrating immigrants into a common American culture, the American public school (once called the 'common school'). This separation is what gives power and weight to multicultural trends in the United States, and raises fears that American assimilation, or if we prefer a milder term, American integration, is failing. I believe it is not failing as regards immigrant groups and immigration: it is failing only where, throughout American history, it has failed, when it comes to American blacks. Despite a great Civil War, constitutional amendments, the civil rights struggle, major national legislation in the 1960s, and progress in many spheres, the separation remains, much reduced in the last thirty years, but still wider than that which separates any other group in American society from the mainstream.

American balkanization remains I believe a chimera. Despite the misguided political efforts that gave legal status to minority groups—affirmative action programmes, the language provisions of the Voting Rights Act, the mandating of bilingual teaching programmes by federal and state legislation and regulations[11]—assimilation does proceed. Asian-Americans, it is now generally recognized, should not be protected by affirmative action: they already equal or surpass other Americans in education and income, despite the fact that their numbers are rapidly increasing because of immigration. Hispanic American groups show a wide variation in education and income, though by such a key index as intermarriage rates, one sees that they are well on the way to assimilation. Native Americans or American Indians, a small group, less than 1 per cent of the population, do remain separate in large measure owing to a very special history as the original inhabitants of the land, who were despoiled of their land, and confined on reservations. But if we consider multiculturalism as a new and unique departure in American education and public life, its explanation and potential seriousness must be traced to the black condition, not to the increasing diversity fostered by the immigration of the past twenty-five years.

It is not easy to conclude what Europe can learn from this experience, aside from the fact that a major fissure in the population, whether based on race, religion, culture, or ethnicity, is always a problem. A regime of formal equality, while necessary—and this prevails in the United States as well as in Europe—is not sufficient to overcome such a fissure. Most Americans believe that multiculturalism in education is not the answer either: perhaps even most African-Americans believe this. They would prefer an effective education, regardless of its multicultural character, and progress in the labour market. But the present trends, in the fields of education as well as within the African-American community, favour multicultural content, sometimes to the extent of introducing fantasy and untruth into the curriculum. Other groups follow in the wake of African-Americans, but without the same degree of commitment, or political weight and effectiveness. So it is Martin Luther King and Malcolm X who have become a presence on the classroom walls of the schools of the inner city, and no other figure from any other group matches them.

IV[12]

When it comes to immigration and citizenship, the lessons one may draw from American distinctiveness, though not without ambiguity, are more positive than those one can draw from the present confused state of the discussion over multiculturalism.

Here two stories are revealing. The first is from Ronald Takaki, a third-generation Japanese-American, a writer of important books on multiculturalism and American ethnic history, and a professor of ethnic studies at the University of California, Berkeley, who tells of a common experience. He describes how he will enter a taxi on his way to a college to give a lecture, and the taxi-driver will ask, 'And when did you come to this country?' Takaki has no accent. He was born in the United States, and his parents were born in the United States. Other Asian-Americans tell the same story. Very possibly the taxi-driver himself is an immigrant. But his assumption is that an

Asian must have just recently come to the United States. The point of the story is, how long does it take a person of who is neither black nor European in appearance to be considered an American, like all other Americans?

The second story is from the African-American economist and writer and professor of economics at Boston University, Glenn Loury.

On a recent visit to Australia [he writes], I spent some time with a group of economists and sociologists at the local Bureau of Immigration and Multicultural Affairs. They were eager to explain to a visiting American how well their country was managing its immigration policy. They stressed two main goals: to encourage newcomers to seek Australian citizenship, and to promote the idea of a multicultural identity, so that these newcomers will not feel it necessary to abandon their cultural heritage as the price of adopting a new nation. What struck me about this policy was its seeming incoherence. In what precisely did these analysts imagine Australian national identity to consist? Why would anyone feel loyalty to a country that required so little of him in order to join it?[13]

The point of the two stories is to indicate a central paradox about American citizenship. On the one hand, it is open to all. We celebrate our multifarious origins in the pronouncements of presidents, the museum of immigration on Ellis Island, the Statue of Liberty. Without making fine comparisons between the United States and other countries, it is clear that the United States celebrates itself as a country of immigration more than European countries do. European countries make it clear, understandably, they are not countries for immigrants, except under very special circumstances. They did not after all enter modern history as unpeopled lands seeking immigrants.

The American welcome is also apparent in the fact that we encourage immigrants to become citizens. Indeed, even when we are preparing to become more restrictive on immigration, and penalize immigrants in our welfare laws— this is the result of the welfare reform which became law in 1996—we call on immigrants to become citizens, and make it easier for them to do so. In 1996, there was a good deal of controversy in the popular press over whether the hurdles to becoming a citizen (one is required to know English and some facts about American history and government) had been lowered too far. Republicans believed that the drive to encourage immigrants to become citizens had been spurred by the Democratic Clinton administration to increase the number of Democratic voters. This dispute did nothing to slow the very rapid rise in the numbers of immigrants seeking to become citizens. The numbers of persons becoming naturalized has reached record levels, a million or more a year.

It is clear we do not call on immigrants to become citizens and ease the path to doing so to increase our military manpower, or to settle uninhabited lands, or to increase our wealth—we do so because we consider it the right thing. Those who live in the United States should join it as full members.

On the other hand, the welcome to all embodied in our current immigration and naturalization laws, which make no distinction on grounds of race or national origin, does not impose itself on the popular consciousness, which considers some Americans more natural or suitable Americans than others, as the Takaki story shows. And, to refer to Glenn Loury's comment, we expect something more from the immigrant than some of our liberal fellow countries of immigration do: we expect a greater degree of loyalty and commitment, which is expressed in our oath of naturalization (in which one gives up all previous loyalties to 'foreign potentates or powers'), as well as in the literature distributed by the Immigration and Naturalization Service to prospective immigrants to prepare them for the required tests on American history and the American Constitution.

Perhaps the paradox is best expressed in the comment often addressed to immigrants, when it turns out the person is not a citizen and doesn't intend to become one. The question of the interlocutor will often be an astonished and not friendly 'why aren't you a citizen?', expressing simultaneously annoyance that this person is not a citizen, but also, if one can ignore the annoyance, a willingness—more than willingness, an insistence—on enrolling this person as a citizen, a new member of the all-embracing commonwealth.

How do Americans reconcile a substantial degree of xenophobia with the demand that the stranger, the foreigner, the immigrant, become a citizen, and thus one of them, part of them? An oddity indeed. Recently we have seen a surge in the number of citizenship applications, in response to legislation that makes it harder for non-citizens to receive certain benefits. Citizenship classes are jammed. One response to this recent surge could have been antagonistic: let's make it harder for all these people to become citizens, why do we need so many more citizens? The official response has been quite the contrary: it has been that we must accommodate all these people who want to become citizens, we must make it easier for them to get through the bureaucratic hoops. Doris Meissner, the Immigration and Naturalization Service Commissioner, advocates an expanded naturalization programme, arguing that as a matter of policy and national interest the INS should encourage eligible legal immigrants to seek citizenship. She proposed a programme that would enlist educational institutions—such as community colleges—to give the face-to-face interviews that immigration officers now conduct with all immigrants applying for US citizenship.

There have been different reasons over time why permanent residents have been pressed to become citizens. In World War I and its aftermath, it was because of fears over loyalty: this is the way one showed one was a good American. In the early days of the Cold War, there was a similar motivation: that was the heyday of the 'I am an American' ceremony to induct new citizens. Today loyalty is a less pressing matter, and the immigrant is urged to become a citizen for reasons that, in the popular mind, are somewhat obscure.

Is it because it will clear up an ambiguous status; because it is better for the immigrant—he won't have to worry about welfare, or health and education benefits? Is it because in the popular mind the refusal to become a citizen while living in the United States casts doubt that America is the best, the ideal, country?

Underlying all the different motivations is one underlying rock-bottom belief, held broadly by Americans, regardless of their political orientation: it is better to be an American, and anyone who legitimately can should become an American citizen. That 'anyone' used to be limited, in law or consciousness, to whites, or Protestants, or Christians. But it now does truly include anyone. There has grown a commitment to the making of Americans, regardless of race or ethnicity or religion, that is now unchallengeable.

So there will be no foreign enclaves in the United States, if the laws and common opinion can help it. All should be Americans. That seems to be the lesson of American immigration and citizenship practices that almost all Americans embrace. Multiculturalism, whatever the degree of its acceptance in one or another formulation, and it is widely accepted in schools and colleges, does not mean the new Americans should be different from the others who preceded them in loyalty, in language, in commitment to the common Constitution and the laws. The requirements for citizenship make all this clear. We are more tolerant in accepting difference than we were thirty years ago. But we do insist on a change of political identity in our naturalization laws —there is nothing multicultural about them yet. Our chief problems of diversity and divisiveness have, as I have argued above, quite another source, a home-grown inability to incorporate black Americans fully into American society and economy. But concerning immigrants, we have no such problem.

V

What can Europe learn from this distinctive American experience? One thing it can learn is that a deep divide in the population, separating a more prosperous and educated majority from a less prosperous and more poorly educated minority, is not a good thing for the country. It is even worse if these two groups are separated by race or religion. It will of course breed hostility and resentment, and in contemporary advanced societies where the education and competence of the population is the greatest resource will hold back the entire society. But this is well known, and while such a danger exists in England, France, and Germany, it cannot I think, because of different histories, take on the scale and seriousness it possesses in the United States. There is no equivalent in Europe to the 200 years of African slavery, the 100 years of state-sponsored discrimination, the continuing complex of attitudes as a result of this history. Nevertheless, there is enough evidence in Europe, even if the evidence is only thirty years old or so, of the likelihood of the establishment of such a divide between upper and lower, marked by differences of religion and to some degree race.

Here perhaps the story of American citizenship does provide a more useful lesson. Of course American citizenship has been so inclusive because of our distinctive history. We had to occupy a new land, needed immigrants. In those circumstances there would be a different attitude to immigrants from what we find in Europe. But this openness to immigration was not inevitable. It was a political choice. It determined that immigration would be less restrictive for example than it was in some other new countries. The process of acquiring citizenship could have been made more exclusive and difficult than it was. In time American citizenship was opened wide to people of every race and continent, and became a guarantee of legal equality. This is a very effective way of giving people a stake in the country, of reducing some bases of division and rancour and conflict.

Common views of human rights serve today to bring Europe into line with the United States in this respect. Paradoxically, it is the poorer and the newer countries who in general are more exclusive in maintaining the line which separates foreign from native, outsider from insider. But this American lesson of an open citizenship is not a simple lesson, nor does it provide simple principles to be applied. There is a good reason in history why the ancient states of Europe cannot so easily see themselves as a mixing bowl or melting pot for all the world. Nevertheless, having allowed so much of the world of different cultures, religions, and races to enter, having adopted and promoted the liberal principles that make state distinction on the basis of race, religion, and culture impermissible, they will have to ponder whether the American style of citizenship, which privileges no race, culture, or religion, may not have to be accepted in the end.

NOTES

1. Richard Bernstein, *The Dictatorship of Virtue: Multiculturalism and the Battle for America's Future* (New York: Knopf, 1994): 4.
2. The term of course is widespread and applied to many apparent differences between the United States and other economically advanced countries. Multiculturalism as an aspect of American exceptionalism however is not discussed in Seymour Martin Lipset's comprehensive *American Exceptionalism: A Double-Edged Sword* (New York: Norton, 1996).
3. 'Mrs Clinton delivers a "thank you" to US peacekeeping forces in Bosnia', *Boston Globe*, 26 March 1996, p. 2.
4. See Nathan Glazer, *We Are All Multiculturalists Now* (Cambridge, Mass.: Harvard University Press, 1997).

5. The origins of affirmative action are discussed in many books, from the relatively early *Affirmative Discrimination: Ethnic Inequality and Public Policy*, by Nathan Glazer (New York: Basic Books, 1975), to the recent authoritative work by John Skrentny, *The Ironies of Affirmative Action* (Chicago: University of Chicago Press, 1996).

6. See Nathan Glazer, *Ethnic Dilemmas, 1965–1982* (Cambridge, Mass.: Harvard University Press, 1982): chs. VI and VII; Glazer, 'Is Assimilation Dead?', *The Annals*, 530 (Nov. 1993): 122–36; Michael R. Olneck, 'Americanization and the Education of Immigrants, 1900–1925: An Analysis of Symbolic Action', *American Journal of Education*, 97 (1989): 398–43; Olneck, 'The Recurring Dream: Symbolism and Ideology in Intercultural and Multicultural Education', *American Journal of Education*, 98 (1990): 147–74; and recent discussions in Todd Gitlin, *The Twilight of Common Dreams: Why America is Wracked by Culture Wars* (New York, Metropolitan Books, 1995): ch. 2; David A. Hollinger, *Postethnic America: Beyond Multiculturalism* (New York: Basic Books, 1995); Nathan Glazer, *We Are All Multiculturalists Now* (Cambridge, Mass.: Harvard University Press, 1997).

7. Mary Waters, *Ethnic Options: Choosing Identities in America* (Berkeley, Calif.: University of California Press, 1990).

8. See e.g. Douglas S. Massey and Nancy A. Denton, *American Apartheid: Segregation and the Making of the Underclass* (Cambridge, Mass.: Harvard University Press, 1993), and for a general discussion of the special degree of separation characterizing African-Americans, see Nathan Glazer, *We Are All Multiculturalists Now*: ch. 7.

9. Stanley Lieberson and Mary C. Waters, *From Many Strands* (New York, Russell Sage Foundation, 1988): 173.

10. For one evidence of increasing difference, see Stanley Lieberson and Kelly S. Mikelson, 'Distinctive African American Names: An Experimental, Historical and Linguistic Analysis of Innovation', *American Sociological Review*, 60 (1995): 928–46. '[A]s we enter the 1960s, the period of intensifying African American nationalism, there was already divergence between the two groups [African-American and whites] in their naming tastes.'

11. In 1998, the people of California, which has by far the largest number of public school children speaking foreign languages at home, voted for a measure that would end bilingual education, which in practice means education in the home language, in favour of greater efforts to teach children English immediately. This may mark a general turn against bilingual education, but there are no major efforts in other states at present to change their practices.

12. This last section draws from a longer paper, 'Reflections on Citizenship and Diversity', in Gary Jeffrey Jacobsohn and Susan Dann (eds.), *Diversity and Citizenship* (Lanham, Maryland: Rowman and Littlefield, 1996).

13. Glenn Loury, *National Review*, 1 May 1995: 80.

10

Minorities and Immigrant Incorporation in France: the State and the Dynamics of Multiculturalism

MARTIN A. SCHAIN

INTRODUCTION

French scholars and politicians have consistently argued that in France political and social institutions have historically transformed immigrants into Frenchmen, while in the United States, similar institutions have legitimated, and even generated, a pattern of ethnic pluralism that has weakened the fabric of the national community. In the context of the French debate on immigration during the past decade, the American 'pluricultural' model has been seen largely in negative terms, a way *not* to deal with immigrant incorporation. At the same time, however, there is a recognition that the traditional 'Jacobin model' of integration is no longer as effective as it was once presumed to have been in the transformation of immigrants into Frenchmen, and that there is growing evidence of the recognition of ethnicity in practice if not in theory.

In this chapter, I argue first that the French Jacobin model should not be seen as a fixed formula or a plan for immigrant incorporation. Instead, it is more useful to view it as the result of both evolving state structure and specific dynamics of the political process. Second, the model has been far more an ideal than an empirical model: what Theodore Lowi has called a 'public philosophy' that colours, shapes, and justifies state formation of public policy, but that is challenged by evolving empirical reality and the very public policies it is supposed to describe. I argue that in France in the 1990s, there has been both a reinforcement of the Jacobin model at the level of rhetoric and perhaps commitment, but that the state—sometimes in contradictory moves—has acted to reinforce multiculturalism, first in an attempt to define the problem of immigration, then in an effort to incorporate immigrant communities, then in an attempt to develop a strategy to maintain social order. I focus on multiculturalism less in terms of group identity formation, than in terms of an aspect of state policy formation. Finally, I argue that Europe—France in particular—can learn a great deal about the complexities of immigrant incorporation from the American experience.

FRANCE AND THE AMERICAN MODEL

In France, the American pattern of incorporation is perceived as public support for collective identities, and a recognition of the widespread phenomenon of ethnic lobbying. This is generally compared with the French pattern of free 'private' expression of collective identities, combined with 'colour-blind' public support and recognition for individual advancement. In France, at least in principle, there has been no public support for collective rights for ethnic minorities or communities, no support for multicultural education, no concessions to customs of ethnic or national groups in the public realm. In fact, the very use of these words has been opposed by French representatives within the institutions of the European Union.[1]

As Dominique Schnapper has argued:

The French political tradition has always refused to recognize the American concept of 'ethnicity'. In the school, the factory, in the union (either in leadership or the pattern of demands), the 'ethnic' dimension has never been taken into account, even if social practices don't always scrupulously follow this principle. It is not an accident that there have never been in France real ghettos of immigrant populations from the same country, on the model of black, Italian or 'Hispanic' neighborhoods in the United States, that in poor areas immigrant populations from different countries mix with French people, apparently in the same social milieus. The promotion of Frenchmen of foreign origin comes about individually, and not collectively through groups organized collectively.[2]

This perspective is widely shared both by policy-makers and by scholars. French scholars have also argued convincingly that there are vast differences between the American experience of ghettos and spacial separation of ethnic groups, and the French experience of the expression of identities within relatively integrated urban neighbourhoods. The end product is generally seen as effective integration, in the sense that, after several generations, national origin has no meaning.[3]

Of course scholars have recognized that this approach to immigrant integration 'was never a concrete, historical reality either in France or in the colonies. It was never completely enacted, never completely successful.' Nevertheless, for many scholars, and for much of the political class, '[i]ts principles continue to inspire government policy towards immigrants.' To alter this approach, moreover, 'would break with a long tradition of national integration in France and weaken (and perhaps even dissolve) the social fabric.'[4]

This reaffirmation of the French Republican model, and its use and interpretation of the American ideal of immigrant incorporation, is problematic in several ways. First, it tends to see the American model in ahistorical terms, with little attention to the process through which it has developed;[5] it also tends to exaggerate the extent of spacial separation of American ethnic neighbourhoods.[6] If the American experience teaches us anything, it is that the tension between the ideal and practice is a dynamic that changes both. Second, this reaffirmation fails to recognize the consequences of this tension in both French rhetoric and practice.

I will first briefly examine the American case in terms of the French critique, and then look at the practice of the French model historically and analytically. Finally, I will examine the possible relationship between the American and French experiences.

THE AMERICAN CASE

The ideal of the United States as a 'nation of nations' is a recent phenomenon, dating more or less from the period around the Second World War. During most of the nineteenth century there seemed to be a sense among social and political leaders of something increasingly American. Basically, this reflected a more widespread attitude about the nature of American homogeneity and the basis of American citizenship that endured until the last decade of the nineteenth century. Immigrant integration, like much else in the United States, was part of the process that Theodore Lowi has called the 'automatic society', a lack of a coherent state approach. Assimilation would flow from the operation of social institutions, what John Higham has called

a confident faith in the natural, easy melting of many peoples into one. When fearful of disruptive influences, the Americans sought to brake the incoming current or to inhibit its political power; otherwise they trusted in the ordinary processes of a free society.[7]

For almost one hundred years the federal government played almost no role in controlling immigration. Insofar as immigration was regulated at all, it was minimally regulated by the individual states through their use of police powers, subject to review of the courts. Throughout the nineteenth century, especially after the beginning of successive waves of immigration beginning in the 1840s, there was a large measure of more or less accepted diversity in the United States, and ethnic settlers established distinctive institutions, from schools and universities, to trade union organizations to urban political machines.[8]

Nevertheless, the ideal of the 'melting pot' dominated the thinking of those who wrote about America during this period. Although the English and their descendants constituted less than half the population of the United States at the time of the Revolution, James Madison wrote nothing about ethnicity in his two Federalist papers that dealt with diversity, and John Jay, who descended from Dutch and French Huguenot ancestors, wrote that 'Providence has been pleased to give this one connected country to one united people —a people descended from the same ancestors.' Two generations later, Ralph Waldo Emerson wrote about the creation of 'a new race' out of 'the energy of Irish Germans, Swedes, Poles and Cossacks, and all the European tribes' (he called this the 'smelting pot'). A hundred years later, a Jewish playwright, Israel Zangwill, wrote a popular play entitled *The Melting Pot*, through which he glorified assimilation and intermarriage. Throughout this entire period, the 'ideal' seems to have been an Anglo-Saxon dominated 'melt', an ideal that seemed to follow naturally from the cultural domination of American political and social life of English values.[9]

Indeed, the literature on the ideal of immigrant integration during the nineteenth century in the United States—whatever the contradictions in reality —seemed destined to play a role in America not unlike that of the French Republican model. It supported intermarriage, the hegemony of English cultural and political values together with English as a common language. The ideal gained increased institutional support at the local level, as education spread after the Civil War, even if ethnicity did in fact form a basis for initial settlements and political organization for collective advancement.[10]

Nevertheless, the American Republican model generally lacked institutional teeth until the decade prior to World War I, not surprisingly at the time when the issue of immigration had been racialized within policy-making institutions, and when there were widespread nativist fears that the ideals of the model could no longer be supported by the automatic society.[11] During the decade before the World War I, numerous states, and then the federal government established structures to aid immigrants and (eventually) to encourage 'Americanization'. By 1920, with the impetus of the war, the combined public/private effort was impressive.[12]

In many ways, this progressive/business approach to Americanization provided a response to the racial pessimism of eugenicists and the restrictionists then in control of the Immigration committees of the Congress, as well as some federal agencies dealing with immigration. However, this approach was also a challenge to the optimism of the automatic society, and gave form to a cultural definition of membership in the national community. It associated survival of the national community with the dominance of Anglo-Saxon culture, with the suppression of ethnic culture and identity, and with the development of certain values and habits. 'To be a good American included adopting everything from the American way to clean your house and brush your teeth to the Protestant values of self-control and self-reliance.'[13]

Federal support for the Americanization effort began to ebb after 1920, but numerous states continued what had become a crusade by passing coercive legislation that ranged from requiring that English be the sole language of instruction in all public and private primary schools in fifteen states, to requiring that non-English-speaking aliens attend English classes in two states, to more draconian measures that were eventually declared unconstitutional.[14] By 1921–2 Americanization programmes were cut back, due to the pressures of economic contraction, but the ideals and values remained dominant until after World War II.

Nevertheless, in reaction to the more coercive aspects of Americanization and the restrictive immigration legislation that was passed in 1924, and in an attempt to sustain group identities that were being diluted, immigrant groups themselves began to organize in the 1920s.[15] Although isolated and relatively powerless through the mid-1920s, they would play an increasingly important political role in American politics during and after the New Deal.[16] In this reactive way, the racialization of the public debate on immigration tended to reinforce ethnicity in the United States by giving it political identity.

The effects of ethnic organization were felt even before World War II. By the late 1930s, American textbook authors were writing about a different kind of America by emphasizing the contribution of immigrants to American life.[17] Nevertheless, the hegemony of Anglo-Saxon cultural ideals remained. It was only during the post-war period that the cultural ideals of a unified America slowly gave way to the multicultural ideals portrayed in the French literature, but the model of the melting pot endured in school textbooks and popular culture well into the 1960s.

This change was a result of ethnic organization, and the recognition of the legitimacy of a multi-ethnic America furthered government propaganda during World War II and the emergence of 'black neo-ethnicity' in the 1960s.[18] Indeed, the ideal of neo-ethnicity, a Nation of Nations, began to emerge at the same time that intermarriage among the children and grandchildren of European immigrants was sharply on the rise, and when important indicators of ethnic 'memberships' were on the decline (organizational membership and language ability above all). Government programmes in the 1960s that effectively 'created' minorities 'by ascribing to them certain characteristics that serve to justify their assignment to particular societal roles', represented an attempt to deal with a racial crisis, not immigration or assertions of multiculturalism, but had unanticipated consequences.[19] Within a decade, the impact of 're-ethnicization' had effectively challenged the melting-pot understanding among policy-making élites, and the breakdown of this understanding became evident in the way that the national community was being portrayed.[20]

America, then, provides us with a complex baseline for an understanding of changes that are taking place in France. The model that has represented the ideal of immigrant incorporation has changed over the years, and this change has been related to the very important actions of the ideal.

FRANCE: INCORPORATING EUROPEAN IMMIGRANTS

In this century, four overlapping waves of immigrants were recruited into France from neighbouring countries. The early part of the century was dominated by Italian and Belgian immigration, followed by a period of Polish immigration (and significant 'internal migration' from Algeria),[21] and then (after World War II) by a wave of immigration from Portugal. Since the mid-1960s a new wave of immigrants has been arriving from the former French colonies of North Africa.

In much of the analysis of the impact of the new immigration during the past decade, high concentrations of immigrants—often referred to as 'ghettos'—have been seen as a new phenomenon. In fact, there is ample evidence that immigrant concentrations were as normal during the period between the wars as they are now. Gérard Noiriel notes that 'all of the statistics at our disposal from the beginning of the nineteenth century refute the commonly held notion that the constitution of immigrant "ghettos" is a recent, post-Second World War phenomenon.'[22] As Noiriel explains: 'Each new wave of immigration was translated into the appearance of new ghettos: in the mines of the Nord and Lorraine, in the Paris region, in the valleys of the Alps and Pyrenees.'[23]

In general, these concentrations can be related to a pattern of state intervention that began before World War I. The loss of manpower during the war accentuated the need for immigrant labour, and both public and private means were set into place to recruit workers and to direct them into specific areas. In 1919 and 1920, the French government concluded bilateral agreements with a number of countries (most notably, Poland, Italy, and Czechoslovakia) for labour recruitment, and in the years that followed, commercial agencies organized by employers were authorized to recruit immigrants directly for particular work sites. Polish workers from the same regions of Poland, for example, were sent to the same areas of France. This way of organizing immigration assured that there would be high concentrations of immigrants with similar backgrounds and collective identities installed throughout the country, in places where labour was in short supply, and in occupations that native French workers were less willing to fill. Moreover, the way that they were recruited tended to maximize the collective identity of these workers once they arrived in France.

But the French experience of European immigration was quite different from the parallel American experience. Although there were some violent incidents directed against immigrant groups (notably Italians), and the French state did treat these groups differently for some purposes, state policy did not define immigrant minorities in racialized terms (that ultimately resulted in the establishment of the quota system in the United States); the development of immigration policy did not involve a broad range of interest groups;

and there was no attempt to promote a broad public debate through the legislative process. By the post-World War II period these workers had been integrated into French political and social life. The question is how closely the process of integration conformed with the Republican model, and what impact it had on the model itself.

One key institutional actor in this process was the French Communist Party—an actor *à vocation universelle*. However, where the party was successful in mobilizing immigrant workers, it tended to incorporate them by emphasizing collective, rather than individual benefits. The PCF mobilized immigrant workers and their families in ways that resemble those of American Democratic machines during roughly the same historical period.

In French industrial areas the party served to integrate large numbers of workers into French political life, but in immigrant areas it also established institutions based on *ethnic* working-class identity. Like the Irish 'take-over' of American urban centres from the WASP establishment through the Democratic Party, the Communist victories in these communities (for the most part after World War II) represented a kind of ethnic vengeance of a newly enfranchised electorate that endured in part because the party and the community had been interpenetrated:

In La Seyne-sur-mer, among others, the Communist deputy elected in 1947 (and re-elected until 1969) is the son of an Italian [immigrant], symbolizing the 'working class revenge of the electorate that is majority Italian'.[24]

Although the efforts of the CGTU (the Communist-dominated trade union confederation between 1922 and 1936) and the party were integrative in the sense that they represented and aggregated the interests of immigrant workers together with those of other workers, they were also supportive of the particular interests of these workers as immigrants, and in this sense contributed to the development of ethnic identity. Both the CGTU and the party re-established separate language groups (such groups had existed before the war), and, at the departmental and national levels, the party put into place immigrant manpower commissions. Finally, the party supported ethnic organizations and demonstrations among immigrant groups that were both particularistic and more universal in nature.[25] The establishment of communism in immigrant communities eventually destabilized older political patterns in these same areas, but at the price of the establishment of local ethnic machines, many of which endured well into the Fifth Republic.[26]

At this level, it is difficult to separate ethnic politics from integration of ethnic solidarities into a larger, more universal political project, but two aspects of this process appear to challenge the conventional wisdom of the Republican model. The Communist Party and the CGTU not only recognized the legitimacy of immigrant collectivities, but also gave benefits to these collectivities at the local level. Even during the 'golden age' of the French melting pot, ethnic dimensions were clearly taken into account, at least by the Communist Party and the trade unions in ways that were comparable to their American counterparts at the time. In both countries the ethnic dimension in public discourse was important before World War II, but historically variable over time.[27]

During the post-war period, Communist Party and local PCF officials have progressively de-emphasized the immigrant basis of these communities, and 'by acting in this way, the party tends to eliminate the reasons on which the confidence of the group in itself are based.'[28] None the less, the process through which this happened does not seem to have been substantially different from some aspects of the parallel process in the United States. Both ethnic awareness and ethnic recognition were part of the process, while the melting-pot ideal of the Republican model remained intact.

THE NEW IMMIGRATION

In many ways, nothing much changed with the wave of Third World immigration after 1960. Studies on the ground provide clear evidence of the recognition of immigrant collectivities by both political parties and public authorities. As during the previous period, this evidence is more obvious at the local than at the national level. Finally, there has been a reaffirmation of the Republican model as the ideal of immigrant integration.

Nevertheless, there are some differences both in practice and in the expression of the ideal. I will first summarize these differences, and then analyse them in some detail. First, there has been far more direct intervention from the central state, both in defining the problem of immigrant ethnic minorities and in elaborating modes of incorporation, and less involvement of intermediary groups *à vocation universelle* than during the earlier period. Second, the state has been less effective in maintaining control over the policy debate than it had been before, and has increasingly turned to the larger political arena and the legislative process.

The pattern of policy-making has been conditioned by what Maxim Silverman has termed the 'racialized' view of the post-1960s wave of non-European immigrants. As in the United States at the turn of the century, this perspective has informed the discussions and actions of trade unions, political parties, the government, and the state; and as in the United States, the emphasis on race has probed the limits of the integrative capacities of the French version of the melting pot.

Within the political dialogue and in the construction of public policy during the past twenty-five years, 'immigrants' have been generally presumed to be people originating in Africa and the Caribbean, regardless of whether such people are in fact citizens (either naturalized or born). The 'problem' of immigrants, for all practical purposes, does not include aliens from Spain, Portugal (still the largest single immigrant group in 1990),[29] or other European countries, and the 'problem' of immigration often seems to be less one of controlling the frontiers than of incorporating non-Europeans who are already in the country.

From the early years of the non-Western wave of immigration, policy-makers presumed that these immigrant workers were different from those who had preceded them, in the sense that they were difficult if not impossible to assimilate into French society. Indeed, as Alec Hargreaves has pointed out, this perspective has been widely shared among politicians of the Right and the Left, as well as among a surprisingly wide range of scholars and a broad range of public opinion.[30]

The first attempts by the French state to define a coherent policy about the new immigration began after the May crisis of 1968, and is summarized in a report written by Correntin Calvez for the Economic and Social Council in 1969. The report recognized the continuing economic need for immigrant labour, but for the first time clearly differentiated European from non-European workers. Europeans were assimilable, and should be encouraged to become French citizens, argued Calvez, while non-European immigrants constituted an 'inassimilable island'.

It seems desirable, therefore, more and more to give to the influx of non-European origin, and principally to the flow from the Mahgreb, the character of temporary immigration for work, organized in the manner of a rapid process of introduction which would be linked as much as possible to the need for labour or the business sectors concerned and in cooperation with the country of origin.[31]

Thus, from the beginning of the process of defining and implementing immigration policy, the idea of difference was asserted, a difference that was frequently posed in racialized terms.[32] During the 1970s, the government struggled to develop a policy based on the main lines of the Calvez Report, but was unsuccessful.

Confronted with mobilized opposition of the Left and negative decisions by the Conseil d'Etat, the government avoided any serious attempt to prevent the unification of families of Third World workers already in the country, a policy that had the contradictory effect of converting a population of immigrant workers into one of resident families. This meant that the policy problem was increasingly less one of immigration (i.e. a frontier problem), and more one of integrating of ethnic communities that at best would be difficult to assimilate.

The Left opposition, therefore, was generally successful in checking and limiting what they sometimes termed the 'racist' labour market policies of the governments of the Right in the 1970s at the national level. At the same time, however, representatives of the Left were defining issues and developing integration policies at the local level on similar racial assumptions. In contrast to 'the tradition of solidarity' that Communist-governed municipalities had developed towards predominantly European immigrants, by the 1970s many of these same local governments began to treat non-European immigrants, as well as non-white French citizens from the overseas departments, as temporary residents who must be encouraged to return home.[33] Thus, as during the earlier period, Communist municipalities tended to treat new immigrant communities as collectivities, but—now—in an exclusionary manner. The use of quotas in housing and schools became a widespread practice in the late 1970s. Although the words 'immigrants' and 'foreigners' were used to describe those against whom such quotas should apply, their clear reference was non-whites. In the name of immigration policy, ethnic policy was being developed at the local level that applied both to aliens and citizens.

This pattern was not, however, unique to towns governed by Communists. Virtually every town in the Lyon region, for example, in collaboration with departmental and state authorities, made the same kinds of decisions during the late 1970s, to limit the availability of housing for immigrant families based on an understood notion of a 'threshold of tolerance'.[34] On the initiative of local governments, the state also collaborated in establishing quotas for immigrant children in primary schools.[35]

By the 1980s the racialization of immigration had taken on positive as well as negative aspects. As Gary Freeman has noted:

In a sense, once the state had committed itself to this racially discriminatory policy, it had more incentive than before to increase the effectiveness and generosity of its social policies towards migrants. The fact that a large part of its immigrant population would be permanent persuaded officials that more needed to be done on their behalf.[36]

After the suspension of immigration in 1974, an increasingly dense network of state institutions and programmes was developed to deal with problems of incorporation and integration. The first initiatives in the 1970s were taken in the areas of education and housing. While the objectives of these programmes were often contradictory, they were all efforts that tended to treat immigrant groups as collectivities rather than individuals.

In the 1970s, when policy-makers assumed that there was a real possibility that North Africans would return home, a policy consensus developed around state aid for programmes that would encourage them (or at least permit them) to do so. The Ministry of National Education, controlled by the Centre-Right government, cooperated with numerous Socialist and Communist local governments in developing Arabic language classes within the normal curriculum and special language and culture classes outside of the normal curriculum. These programmes were established through agreements with the countries of origin, and the teachers were recruited by the countries themselves. Although the government hoped that such programmes (combined with *aide au retour*) would encourage North African immigrants to leave the country, it devoted few resources to the effort, which in any case involved no more than 20 per cent of immigrant children. Nevertheless, these early programmes set a precedent for state action that dealt with immigrants as ethnically differentiated collectivities. Leaders of the Right came to understand this a decade later, when they attacked the very programme that they had initiated as weakening social cohesion in France.[37]

The first Minister of State for Immigrant Workers was appointed in June 1974, just prior to the suspension of non-EC immigration. A year later the second minister, Paul Dijoud, was able to secure a major increase in housing funding to assist immigrants. Twenty per cent of a public housing fund established in 1953 (and paid for by a payroll tax on all companies with more than ten employees) would be earmarked for immigrant housing. The programme would be supervised by a new administrative unit, the National Commission for the Housing of Immigrants (CNLI). Although this programme was quickly undermined by corrupt practices (Hargreaves argues that it moved rapidly from positive to negative discrimination), and was virtually abolished by 1987, it did make limited progress in ameliorating immigrant housing conditions.[38] In the 1970s, these initiatives floundered first because of contradictory government objectives, and second because there was little impetus to expand them. Nevertheless, a pattern of dealing with immigrants in terms of their collective, ethnic identities, and direct state intervention had been established. The political and social environment changed dramatically in 1981.

If the Right developed policies that were often ambivalent and contradictory, the newly elected national government of the Left, at least initially, acted with greater certainty. It took several unprecedented steps that involved central state agencies in ethnic construction, recognition, and mobilization. Exclusion gave way to more positive benefits for immigrant groups, and there was a wide-ranging debate between 1981 and 1986 on the proper model for immigrant incorporation.[39] After 1986 the dialogue moved back towards a reassertion of the traditional Republican model, but the public discourse continued to be contradicted by relatively open and political expressions of ethnic consciousness, as well as public policies that in many ways supported this consciousness. These policies not only tolerated the public expression of ethnic differences, but, as Danièle Lochak points out, also tended to manage and institutionalize them.[40]

The most important initiative was the law of October 1981 that liberated immigrant associations from pre-World War II restrictions, and placed them on the same legal footing as other associations in France. Most significantly, immigrants could now administer their own (and French) associations, and receive public funding. This change in the opportunity structure, in turn, coincided with a reaction among young immigrants against discriminatory practices during the past decade. Roughly speaking, the mobilization of immigrants during the 1980s had many of the same roots as the mobilization of similar associations in the United States in the 1930s.

By the mid-1980s, these associations had become a network of established intermediaries for immigrant populations that negotiated with trade unions, political parties, and the state at the local and national levels. By the end of the decade they numbered between 3,000 and 4,000, ranging from about a thousand Islamic associations to the better-known national groups such as SOS-Racism and France Plus.[41] In contrast to earlier periods of immigration, these associations operated outside the established network of intermediary groups, which were then forced to recognize their independent existence. Even when established and more universal intermediary groups did succeed in incorporating their leadership, such incorporation remained conditional and problematic.[42] It is unclear where the difficulty begins, but some social theorists have focused on changing patterns of class consciousness among immigrant workers:

The progressive fusion of successive immigrant generations with native French people of the same social stratum cannot be seen to the same degree as before. Diverse components of the working class increasingly refer to their national, ethnic or religious origins, and refer and less to the social condition that they share.[43]

Is this lack of class solidarity linked to the declining effectiveness of unions and parties—or, as union representatives have claimed, is it that the new immigrants (compared to the previous waves of European immigrants) are more difficult to organize and integrate?

The literature of the past decade devotes considerable time to comparing the differences between ethnic mobilization in France and in the United States, but the essential point is that political mobilization on the basis of evolving categories of ethnicity, while not new in France, is now taking place in a different context, outside of the organizational framework of established union and party organizations. This phenomenon is similar to the pattern of ethnic organization in the United States. What is also new is the intense involvement of state agencies in France in the development of ethnic organization and ethnic consciousness. Of course it is ironic that this considerable involvement of the state (compared with previous periods) should continued at the very time when such action should be excluded by the reaffirmation of the Republican model.

Such involvement can be understood on one level in terms of the breakdown of traditional agents of immigrant incorporation, and the independent development of ethnic organizations. At the same time, state involvement reflects an attempt to deal with a multitude of urban problems that began to emerge during the period of Socialist government, but that have endured since then. In the early 1980s, the involvement of the central state (now controlled by the Left) increased in part because localities (particularly those controlled by the Left) were no longer able to deal with very real problems of ethnic incorporation, problems of education, and the outbreak of urban violence. In education, problems of rising drop-out rates and student failures among the children of immigrants resulted in the establishment of several programmes, the most important of which was the zones of educational priority (ZEP).[44] The designation of these zones—which meant more money from several ministerial sources, more teachers, and more experimental programmes—relied upon criteria that focused largely on the ethnic composition of an area. The programme has endured several changes of government since its inauguration, and by 1994 somewhat more than 30 per cent of those benefiting from the ZEP programme were immigrant children.[45] Certainly more 'disfavoured' native children than immigrant children have benefited from the programme, but the point is that the designation of ZEPs was strongly linked to areas of immigrant concentration.

Zones of priority, by their global vision of the problem of school failure, indicated that foreign children ought not to be treated 'as different'. However, the first government *circulaire* of July 1981, clumsily fixed a 'quota' of 30 per cent foreign children as one of the determining indicators of such zones.

A follow-up *circulaire* stressed that this should be only one criterion among several, but the notion of 'determining indicator' stuck, and applications tended to focus mostly on the proportion of immigrants as a basis of need.[46]

No doubt the tilt away from a more global perspective was related to the larger problem of the emerging urban crisis. Urban riots in the Lyon region during the summer of 1981 were widely reported and were largely responsible for the establishment of an Interministerial Commission on the Social Development of Neighbourhoods and the Commission of Mayors on Security. The Neighbourhood Commission confirmed the essential problem of ethnic concentration, but also recommended more long-term national support for efforts to deal with security and urban problems at the local level. As periodic urban riots continued through the early 1990s, the involvement of the state grew, and its efforts contributed to the development of ethnic organization as state agencies engaged in a sometimes desperate search for *intérlocateurs valables* among the 'second generation'.[47]

FAS AS A KEY ACTOR

By the early 1980s the *Fonds d'action sociale pour les travailleurs immigrés et leurs familles* (FAS) had become the key institutional actor in the effort by the state to deal with the immigrants. The FAS (sometimes referred to as the 'bank for social action') became the principal agency through which the state funded associations organized within immigrant communities or on behalf of immigrants. It also was responsible for funding a broad range of programmes to aid and service immigrant communities. With a budget of almost 1.2 billion francs in 1994, the FAS had 219 administrators in place throughout the country, who worked directly with representatives of immigrant groups, as well as local institutions and political structures, to develop programmes to deal with integration and urban problems.[48]

During the first three years of Socialist government administrative ascendancy marked its growing political importance. From 1980 to 1986 its budget doubled, and the number of associations that it funded increased four times. Even more important, its importance gained significantly in the autumn of 1983, when the fund was 'regionalized', that is when it was outfitted with its own field-service personnel that related directly to its clientele. Regionalization is described by the former director and by civil servants at the agency as a struggle to establish both independence and democracy. In terms of policy choices, the new structure gave the FAS the muscle, at least for a time, to support less traditional associations against the *avis* of the prefecture. Until 1983, decisions on financing were made centrally, by the Director of Population and Migrations (DPM), and then implemented by the FAS.[49] When the regionalized structure was set into place, the key decisions were made regionally by FAS, and then ratified centrally.

In a process that is reminiscent of the fate of the American OEO in the late 1960s, the financing of immigrant associations was gradually linked to urban policy. As decentralization was implemented during the 1980s, FAS policy was increasingly influenced by the priorities of big-city mayors, and it became increasingly difficult to finance less traditional immigrant associations over the opposition of regional ministerial field services and local elected officials. What is most striking about the period since 1985 has been the consistency of policy among governments of the Right and the Left on the emphasis of the relationship between FAS policy and urban policy. In effect, all governments have focused on a policy of co-optation of immigrant groups, but with respect for and a recognition of (even support for) collective differences.

When the Right returned to power in 1986, FAS director, Michel Yahiel, who had arrived just three days before the elections, was left in place, and the number of associations supported by FAS continued to increase. What changed was in part a result of policy preference, in part a logical result of the new administrative structure. In an attempt to break the link between some immigrant associations and the Left, the Right moved to increase financing of local groups at the expense of the larger, more politicized national immigrant groups, and also to expanded support for local government efforts to deal with urban problems through *accords de la ville*. FAS also increased its funding for job-training, and increasingly focused its funding on specific target areas: sixty cities in 1988, and then 400 sites *pilotes pour l'intégration* within cities between 1990 and 1993. When the Left returned to power in 1988, they retained the decentralized orientation of FAS, and re-emphasized the link with urban policy. Governments spoke less about immigrants as such, and more about *les exclus* and *la population marginalisée*, and since 1984 no government ministry has carried a specific reference to immigrants. Avoiding reference to immigrant ethnic populations, however, could not change the fact that in practice, policy focused almost entirely on these groups.[50]

Clearly, governments of both the Left and the Right have endeavoured to develop instruments through the FAS that would serve the integration of minority communities. At the same time, however, they could not avoid dealing with and even supporting the collective representatives of those communities. In spite of stated government policy since the mid-1980s that it would not support multicultural endeavours, as late as 1993 (after the change in government), the programme of the FAS clearly stated that it would support activities that help immigrants maintain relations with their home countries, that it would aid local immigrant groups in developing local radio stations, and support associations that help understand immigrant cultures and contribute to the utilization of immigrant languages.[51]

By 1994, there was a clear attempt by the Minister of Social Affairs, Simone Veil, to orient the priorities of the FAS more strongly towards goals of integration. The legal touchstone for this reorientation was a ministerial *circulaire* issued in September, 1993,[52] in which the minister directed the regional and departmental prefects, as well as the FAS director to develop policies that would facilitate integration through naturalization. To this end the FAS was instructed to give priority in funding to groups that support three lines of action: the support of family stability; support for the autonomy of women in 'the prevention of practices and behavior that victimize too many immigrant women, and are contrary to our values and often to our laws'; and support for young people, to aid them in succeeding in the education system, and to encourage them to assume French nationality.

In different elaborations of these objectives, ministerial and FAS officials made clear that their objectives were to strengthen integration, if not specifically to weaken traditional ties to ethnic communities.[53] Government statements did acknowledge, however, that these goals contained inherent contradictions. Thus, Mme. Veil acknowledged that the challenge to tradition by immigrant women threatened the stability of the family: 'Often, why hide it, the demands by young women for a western lifestyle are the cause of serious family conflicts.' However, the key goal would have to be integration. 'Perhaps it is because these acts are liberating that female immigrants are the essential actors of integration.'[54]

Nevertheless, if the support for groups applying for funding would be carefully scrutinized in term of integration goals, state support for immigrant organizations was not questioned.

But this duty to adapt, which we have recalled for all parts of the administration that deal with the public to implement, applies most of all to a specialized public agency such as the FAS. Its good working order, its rapidity of reaction, are essential to support and endorse the civic commitment of immigrants through the exercise of their right of association. The maintenance of the FAS budget at a high level in 1994— and this was not easy during this period of budget restrictions—attests . . . to my deep conviction of the role that this institution must continue to play, for which I have concluded that it has the technical means and the familiarity of the terrain necessary for the implementation of the integration policy of the government.[55]

The FAS has never devoted more than a small percentage of its budget to the direct funding of associations, and, indeed, most of the associations funded have not been clearly ethnic or *communautaire* at all.[56] From 1981 through 1993 programme funding roughly doubled, but the number of diverse groups funded (from ethnic associations to schools, housing, and departmental and local governments) increased from about 600 to 4,600.[57] Among these, funding was given to about 3,000 associations (registered with the state as '*associations loi 1901*'), among which 45 per cent are estimated to be ethnic-type organizations. After the change of government in 1993, the actual number of funded associations declined slightly (as did the programme budget), but the proportion of funded ethnic associations remained the same.[58] Nevertheless, every franc that the FAS spends is directed to programmes and institutions that serve immigrants and immigrant communities. Therefore, these efforts directed towards facilitating integration, are complicated by the fact that they are filtered through direct support for ethnic associations and indirect recognition of ethnic identities.

The best Jacobin intentions of French governments are tempered by emerging realities. Given the decline of the historical agents of integration, there seems to be little alternative to dealing directly with organized representatives of the immigrant communities. This is particularly true when the government wishes to coordinate policies against urban violence with policies to facilitate integration.[59]

HAVE INCORPORATION PATTERNS CHANGED?

Two patterns distinguish collective representation of immigrants since the 1980s from the pre-war pattern. The first is the greater recognition of these groups as direct intermediaries, relatively unfiltered through institutions *à vocation universelle* such as unions and political parties. This pattern began in a more or less *ad hoc* manner in the early 1980s, largely as a reaction to urban violence, but was formalized at the same time that the Republican model was being officially reasserted. The second is direct subventions by the state to support and maintain links with ethnic associations.

However, if the practice of incorporation has adjusted to new realities, there is also clear evidence that the ideal of the Republican model has changed as well, despite the pronouncements of governments and scholars since the mid-1980s. Only in the most formal statements issued by the state does the Republican ideal remain the kind of 'programme of action' described by Dominique Schnapper. During the 1980s the effective programme of action of the state, described in the programmes of some state agencies and local governments, has supported a collective approach to immigrant incorporation, and has viewed ethnic identification in positive terms.

Although the state is certainly not consistent in this approach, the inconsistency is in itself an indication of the degree of change that has taken place during the past fifteen years. Patrick Ireland cites the struggle of the Haut Conseil à l'Intégration (HCI) to both promote integration *à la française* and, at the same time, focus on very real problems of urban decay in the 1980s. On one hand the HCI condemned the 'communitarian drift', and on the other decried the lack of reliable Muslim interlocutors. In the end, the HCI 'celebrated voluntary associational life, especially at the local level, as the ideal means for expressing cultural and ethnic diversity, dealing with the problems of daily life and stitching together the "social fabric".'[60]

Even those government representatives most committed to the Jacobin ideal have been drawn to this contradiction. In 1990, in reaction to the Islamic headscarf affair, Socialist Minister of the Interior Pierre Joxe invited representatives of Islamic organizations to form a Deliberative Council on the Future of Islam in France (CORIF), an institution that would be the parallel of comparable organizations of Protestants and Jews. The hope was that such institutionalized consultation would help to undermine the rise of Islamic fundamentalism. In fact, dissention within the CORIF undermined its effectiveness. When the Right returned to power in 1993, the new Minister of the Interior, Charles Pasqua, attempted to work with a new organization dominated by the Algerian-controlled Grande Mosquée de Paris, CRMF, which was challenged in January, 1995 by several other organizations.

This did not deter Pasqua and his successor from pursuing a long-term project, begun under the Socialists, to encourage the development of a French Islam, relatively free from foreign influence. In 1991 and 1993 three training institutes for imams were opened in France, at least one with the blessing of the Balladur government as well as Jacques Chirac, then mayor of Paris. In a speech at the inauguration of a new mosque in Lyon in 1994 Pasqua praised the effort to build a 'moderate' Islam that would be compatible with the French Republican tradition:

We need to treat Islam in France as a French question instead of continuing to see it as a foreign question or as an extension into France of foreign problems. . . . It is no longer enough to talk of Islam in France. There has to be a French Islam. The French Republic is ready for this.

According to Alec Hargreaves 'this is considerably less than the full-blown policy of multiculturalism once apparently favoured by some on the Left, (but) it also falls a long way short of the intolerant mono-culturalism for which right-wing nationalists have traditionally argued.'[61] Governments of both the Right and the Left appear to have accepted that cultural differences can be made compatible with the traditions of French Republicanism and *laïcité*. Moreover, in different ways, governments have taken a proactive role in influencing and encouraging the organization of these differences.

COMPARATIVE DYNAMICS, OR WHAT IS TO BE LEARNED?

The key question raised by the American case is important for France and Europe in the 1990s: why and how do models of incorporation change? Part of the answer seems to lie in the understanding of decision-making élites, since it is their understanding of policy that shapes policy outputs.

Decision-making élites in France and the United States (in two different periods) went through somewhat similar processes. For reasons that had little to do with mass opinion or reaction to immigration, they defined a new wave of immigrants as racially different. The new immigrants were dangerous in the sense that they could not be assimilated into the general cultural framework of the nation, analogous to previous waves of immigrants. This way of defining the problem of immigration generated different policies in both countries, but similar problems and conflicts.

The essential problem for policy-makers was this: if the new immigrants could not be assimilated, policies based upon melting-pot assumptions were no longer workable. Moreover, if the new immigrants could not be expelled —and they could not for a variety of reasons—their racial difference raised significant questions of multiculturalism and ethnicity. The élite debate in each country generated conflicting policies, which in turn opened the possibility for ethnic organization. It also effectively 'created' minorities by ascribing to them certain characteristics, and nurtured ethnicity through policies and practices, both negative and positive.

In both the United States and France continuing urban violence—in the 1960s in United States and the 1980s in France—provoked the state to seek and promote ethnic *interlocateurs valables* at a time when traditional integrative institutions had weakened. In the American case, the focus was more on racially defined groups than on immigrant/ethnic organizations, but the effect was to reinforce the development of both. In the French case, the emphasis has been on support for immigrant intermediaries, but with strong racial overtones.

In France the definition of the immigration problem and the stress on the distinctiveness of the new immigration both contributed to and was magnified by the electoral success of the National Front. This success, while limited in electoral terms, has had a major influence on the agenda formation of all governments since the mid-1980s. The successive cycles of electoral challenges has forced governments to deal with incorporation issues, and the racist rhetoric has had an impact on the public perception of immigrant communities. On the other hand, the pressure created by National Front successes in just those areas where there are concentrated immigrant communities, has provoked reactive expressions of identity and organization among immigrants themselves.[62]

In France, by the 1990s, it is no longer accurate to say that political and policy practice tends to contradict the ideals and objectives of the Republican model. As a programme of action for the state, the Republican model has been severely compromised, and seems to function primarily on the rhetorical level. Insofar as it constrains state action, it appears to do so on the margins.

On the other hand, the French melting pot appears to be working better than anyone had imagined. The most recent study of the integration of immigrants in France, for example, indicates a steady process of quiet integration for Algerians: a high level of intermarriage (50 per cent for men and 24 per cent for women born in France of parents born in Algeria) and a low level of religious practice that equals that of the 'native' French population.[63]

In general, this process is similar to the one in the United States during the post-World War II period. The racialization of American immigration policy, that reached its peak between the wars, strongly encouraged the mobilization of second generation immigrants around ethnic identities. Nevertheless, the melting pot seemed to be progressing well until the urban crisis of the 1960s, which provoked a movement towards neo-ethnic organization at the very time when the 'old' European immigrants were beginning to show high levels of intermarriage. In the United States, as in France, the role of the national and local state in ethnic mobilization and legitimation was of key importance.

There are differences of course. Even if we consider the influence of the American state in the enforcement of affirmative action criteria, the influence and penetration of the state in France in the construction of ethnic organization appears to be substantially more important than in the United States. Several scholars have argued that the French state has intervened in a more positive way than the American state to support and preserve ethnic cultures (the American state has focused on suppressing barriers to the advancement of ethnic minorities, they argue).[64] In addition, the American state no longer professes any coherent 'model' of incorporation; the so-called 'pluralist model' is far more a product of group interaction and intellectual dialogue than of official state pronouncements. I believe that this comparison tends to underestimate the positive role of the American state in support for ethnicity, and overestimate the importance of cultural support for the development of ethnic political influence in France. However, I do agree with the more general analysis of the importance of state intervention in the development of ethnicity in France. It is also important to emphasize that the French state is far more capable than the American state of imposing constraints on expressions of ethnic diversity. The real problem appears to be not some idealized model of society as the basis for public policy, but the dynamics behind the development of public policy.

The dynamics through which the American ideal of the melting pot has changed during the post-war period offers important insights into the process through which these models evolve. The ability of any state to maintain the myth of the melting pot in the late twentieth century is indeed challenged not only by the diversity of the population to which it is applied, but by the complexity of the modern state and the multiplicity of its sometimes conflicting goals.[65] Thus, in both France and the United States, reluctant or enthusiastic state support for ethnic diversity can be seen as emerging from the growing political priority of the maintenance of order, and an attempt to link order to a process of consent.

NOTES

My thanks to Nancy L. Green for her careful, attentive reading of this chapter.
1. Dominique Schnapper, *La France de l'intégration* (Paris, Editions Gallimard, 1991): 81–104. More recently, see Schnapper, 'Immigration and the Crisis of National Identity,' *West European Politics*, 17/2 (1994): 133–5.
2. Schnapper, *La France d'intégration*: 91.
3. National origin, for example, has played a relatively unimportant role in identifying important political leaders. Thus, former prime minister Edouard Balladur was born in Turkey, while his predecessor, Pierre Bérégovoy, though born in France, is from a family that immigrated from Yugoslavia. On the other hand, there are some exceptions. The fact that Léon Blum and Pierre Mendès-France were of Jewish origin was an important element of how they were evaluated in political life.
4. Schnapper, 'Immigration and the Crisis of National Identity': 133–4. Another way that the difference between France and the United States has been portrayed is that 'the French promote the ethnicization of majorities, and Americans that of

minorities.' See Sophie Body-Gendrot, 'Models of Immigrant Integration in France and the US: Signs of Convergence?' in M. P. Smith and I. Fagen (eds.), *The Bubbling Cauldron* (Mineapolis: University of Minnesota Press, 1997).

5. See Nancy Green, 'L'immigration en France et aux Etats-Unis: historiographie comparée', *Vigntième siècle*, 29 (Jan.–March 1991): 67–82.

6. See Loïc J. D. Wacquant, 'Banlieues françaises et ghetto noir américain: de l'amalame à la comparaison', *French Politics and Society*, 10/4 (1992): 81–99; and Henri Rey, *La Peur des banlieues* (Paris: Presses de la FNSP, 1996): 32–40.

7. Theodore Lowi, *The End of Liberalism* (New York: Norton, 1969): ch. 1. Higham, *Strangers in the Land: Patterns of American Nativism 1860–1925* (Forge Village, Mass.: Atheneum, 1963): 234.

8. See some of the vivid descriptions of ethnic institutions established during the 19th century. in Lawrence Fuchs, *The American Kaleidoscope* (Middletown, Conn.: Wesleyan University Press, 1990).

9. The citations are all from Lawrence Fuchs, 'Thinking about Immigration and Ethnicity in the United States', in Donald Horowitz and Gérard Noiriel (eds.), *Immigrants in Two Democracies: French and American Experience* (New York: New York University Press, 1991): 41.

10. See Fuchs *The American Kaleidoscope*: ch. 1; and Amy Bridges, *A City in the Republic*: chs. 3–5.

11. I have analysed the racialization of the immigration issue in the United States, as well as the construction of policy-making institutions based on this racialization in 'The Development of the American State and the Construction of Immigration Policy (1880–1924)', prepared for delivery at the Annual Meetings of the American Political Science Association, New York, New York, 1–4 Sept. 1994.

12. See John F. McClymer, 'The Federal Government and the Americanization Movement, 1915–1924', in *Prologue* (Spring 1978), cited in Noah Pickus, ' "Human Nature Cannot Be Changed Overnight:" Reassessing the Americanization Movement of the 1920s', delivered at the 1993 Annual Meeting of the Southwestern Political Science Association, New Orleans, Louisiana, 17–20 March 1993: 13.

13. See Noah Pickus, 'Human Nature Cannot Be Changed Overnight': 24–6.

14. Higham elaborates these new laws in *Strangers in the Land*: 260.

15. See Higham, *Strangers in the Land*: 254, and Lizabeth Cohen, *Making of the New Deal* (Cambridge: Cambridge University Press, 1990): chs. 2 and 3.

16. See V. O. Key, 'A Theory of Critical Elections', *Journal of Politics*, 17 (Feb. 1975).

17. FitzGerald, *America Revisited*: 79–83.

18. Martin Kilson, 'Blacks and Neo-Ethnicity in America', in Nathan Glazer and Daniel P. Moynihan (eds.), *Ethnicity: Theory and Experience* (Cambridge, Mass.: Harvard University Press, 1975): ch. 8.

19. Nathan Glazer, 'Ethnic Groups in America: From National Culture to Ideology', in Monroe Berger, Theodore Abel, and Charles H. Page (ed.), *Freedom and Control in Modern Society* (New York: Van Nostrand, 1954): 158–73. See Patrick Ireland, *The Policy Challenge of Ethnic Diversity* (Cambridge, Mass.: Harvard University Press, 1994): 10–11.

20. Arthur Schlesinger, Jr. summarizes this process in his book *The Disuniting of America: Reflections on a Multicultural Society* (New York: W. W. Norton, 1992): chs. 1 and 2.

21. By 1931, France had the highest proportion of foreigners in the world. See Gérard Noiriel, *Le creuset français* (Paris: Ed. du Seuil, 1988): 21.

22. Silverman, *Deconstructing the Nation*: ch. 4.

23. Noiriel, *Le creuset français*: 171. His source is George Mauco, *Mémoire sur l'assimilation des étrangers in France* (Paris: Institut international de coopération intellectuelle, 1937) (mimeo).

24. Noiriel, 'Communisme et immigration, éléments pour une recherche', *Communisme*, 15–16 (1987): 95.

25. Wenden, *Les Immigrés et la politique*: 50. Language and 'ethnic' sections endured until the late 1930s, and were important arenas of organization both for the Communist Party and for the CGTU. See Nancy L. Green, *Ready-to-Wear and Ready to Work: A Century of Industry and Immigrants in Paris and New York* (Durham, NC: Duke University Press, 1997): 257–67.

26. I have looked at the relationship between immigrant mobilization and the rise and decline of the PCF in 'The Decline of French Communism: Party Construction and Party Decline', in Anthony Daley (ed.), *The Mitterrand Era: Policy Alternatives and Political Mobilization in France* (New York: New York University Press, 1996).

27. See Nancy L. Green, *Ready to Work*: 290–2.

28. Noiriel, *Longwy: immigrés et prolétaires 1880–1980*: 387. See 371–91 for some challenging ideas on the decline of communism in the region.

29. Africans were still a minority of all resident immigrants in France in 1990. See INSEE, *Les étrangers in France: portrait social* (Paris: 1994).

30. Alec G. Hargreaves, *Immigration, 'Race' and Ethnicity in Contemporary France* (London and New York, Routledge, 1995), p. xv. Hargreaves cites such scholars as Safran, Fitzpatrick and Heisler and Heisler. I should add that while acceptance of this perspective in no way implies approval of government policy based on such assumptions, such acceptance is almost never based on comparative analysis with Europeans who are generally presumed to have been more assimilable, because they have been assimilated. Maxim Silverman, in *Deconstructing the Nation*: 70–94 (see below), analyses the emergence of the consensus.

31. Correntin Calvez, 'Le Problème de travailleurs étrangers', *Journal Officiel de la Republique Française, Avis et Rapports du Conseil Economique et Social*, 27 March 1969: 315.

32. The discussion of 'racialization' of ethnic minorities has been widespread among scholars, and has not been limited to France. The Dutch sociologist Jan Rath has analysed this discussion in some detail. In 'The Ideological Representation of Migrant Workers in Europe: A Matter of Racialization?', in John Wrench and John Solomos, *Racism and Migration in Western Europe* (Providence, RI: Berg, 1993), he differentiates among several processes of 'signification' on the basis of how groups are identified (races with inherent characteristics or ethnic groups with alterable characteristics), and whether these categories are understood in terms of equality or inferiority (p. 222). Also see Marco Martiniello, *Sortir des ghettos culturels* (Paris: Presses de Sciences Po, 1997).

33. Martin A. Schain, 'Immigrants and Politics in France', in John Ambler (ed.), *The French Socialist Experiment* (Philadelphia: ISHI Press, 1985).
34. R. D. Grillo, *Ideologies and Institutions in Urban France* (London: Cambridge University Press, 1985): 125–7. The initiative taken by the prefect of the Rhone to block immigrants from public housing is also referred to by Jacques Barou, *Processus de segregation et ethnicisation de l'espace*, final report to DPM, October 1994: 24.
35. Schain, 'Immigration and Politics in France': 176–81.
36. Freeman, 'Immigrant Labour and Racial Conflict: The Role of the State', in Philip E. Ogden and Paul E. White (eds.), *Migrants in Modern France: Population Mobility in the Later 19th and 20th Centuries* (London: Unwin Hyman, 1989): 169.
37. Hargreaves, *Immigration, 'race' and ethnicity*: 204.
38. Ibid. 198.
39. There is an excellent summary of this period in Patrick Ireland, *The Policy Challenge of Ethnic Diversity*: ch. 2.
40. Cited by Miriam Feldblum, 'Paradoxes of Ethnic Politics: the Case of Franco-Maghrebis in France', *Ethnic and Racial Studies*, 16/1 (1993): 57. This article contains an important and inciteful analysis of the evolution of the association movement among immigrant groups.
41. An analysis of the various kinds of associations that have emerged since 1981 can be found in Catherine Wihtol de Wenden, 'Les associations "beur" et immigrés, leurs leaders, leurs stratégies', in *Regards sur l'actualité*, 178 (Feb. 1992).
42. See Martin A. Schain, 'Ordinary Politics: Immigrants, Direct Action and the Political Process in France', *French Politics and Society*, 2–3 (Spring–Summer 1994).
43. Jacques Barou, *Le Processus de segregation*: 24.
44. Many of these programmes are described by Michel Caron in 'Immigration, intégration et solidarité', *Regards sur l'actualité*, 166 (Dec. 1990).
45. F. Lorcerie, 'Les ZEP 1990–1993 pour mémoire', *Migrants-formation*, 97 (June 1994).
46. See Jacqueline Costa-Lascoux, *De l'immigré au citoyen* (Paris: La Documentation Française, 1989): 93–4.
47. See Sophie Body-Gendrot, *Ville et Violence: l'irruption de nouvaux acteurs* (Paris: PUF, 1993): chs. 5 and 6; and Adil Jazouli, *Les années banlieues* (Paris: Seuil, 1992); Vincent Geisser, *Ethnicité républicaine: Les élites d'origine maghrébine dans le système politique français* (Paris: Presses de Sciences Po, 1997): ch. 11. A similar analysis has been developed for the 'ethnic minorities policy' in the Netherlands in the mid-1970s. See Jan Rath, 'Minorisation in the Netherlands: The Political Pariticipation of Immigrants', a paper presented to the Meeting of the Research Committee on Migration of the International Sociological Association, University of Utrecht, The Netherlands, 30 March–April 1989: 15–16; and Rath, 'The Ideological Representation of Migrant Workers in Europe': 227–8.
48. The budget of the FAS almost doubled between 1981 and 1990; it then began to decline slightly year by year. Compared with 1990, these 1994 figures represent a slight reduction of funding, a reduction of personnel of about 40%, but an increase of groups funded of about 17%. For 1994, see Ministère des

Affaires Sociales, de la Santé et de la Ville, 'De nouvelles mesures en faveur de l'intégration des immigrés', Notes et Documents, 11 (June 1994): 38; for 1990, see Caron, 'Immigration, intégration et solidarité': 6–7. For the budget figures for the FAS for 1981–94, see André Lebon, *Situation de l'immigration et présence étrangère en France 1993–1994* (Paris: La Documentation Française, 1994): 70.

49. Interview with Michel Yahiel, Director of FAS from 1985 to 1990.

50. See Martin Schain, 'Policy-Making and Defining Ethnic Minorities: The Case of Immigration in France', *New Community*, 20/1 (1993).

51. See *Orientations 1992–1994 du FAS: Programme 1993*, Supplément à la lettre du FAS, 35 (Jan.–Feb. 1993): esp. 2. For a deeper analysis of this programme, see John McKesson, 'Concepts and Realities in Multiethnic France', *French Politics and Society*, 12/1 (1994): 28.

52. *Circulaire* DPM No 93/22, 2 Sept. 1993.

53. This was particularly clear in the application forms for funding, which specify: 'The FAS wishes to favour innovations and new experiments dealing with practices favouring integration, especially those linking institutions with governmental and private structures.' See FAS, 'Appel à projets pour l'intégration des personnes issues de l'immigration: circulaire d'information sur la procédure de dépôt des dossiers—campagne 1995', July 1995.

54. Speech by Simone Veil, reprinted in 'De nouvelles mesures en faveur de l'intégration des immigrés': 3.

55. Address to National Council for the Integration of Immigrant Populations (CNIPI), 27 May 1994, repr. in 'De nouvelles mesures en faveur de l'intégration des immigrés', Annexe: 5.

56. FAS statistics do not differentiate between ethnic-based and other associations, nor are such associations defined in any FAS documents. However, there have been several attempts to estimate the number of such associations supported by FAS funding. In one such report to the director the author notes: 'We have selected associations for which the majority of the bureau was composed of immigrant representatives, or which are known for efforts on behalf of one community in particular.' Nourredine Boubaker to François Beaujolin, 'Part du financement des associations communautaires dans les financements du FAS', 14 May 1993: 1.

57. *Dossier d'information sur le FAS*, April 1995: 4.

58. My thanks to Ann Golub, Responsable du département études FAS, and to Laurence Mayeur, Service documentation FAS for supplying me with these estimates, which derive from an internal document entitled: 'Statistiqes GESTDOS sur les associations par nom d'organisme.'

59. The 1995 *Appel à projets* states clearly (p. 3) that 'The FAS is a partner in urban public policy: also, local projects must be related to the logic of territorial integration.'

60. Ireland, *The Policy Challenge of Ethnic Diversity*: 96.

61. See Alec Hargreaves, *Immigration, Race and Ethnicity*: 206–8.

62. See Martin Schain, 'The Immigration Debate, the National Front and Agenda Formation in France', in John T. S. Keeler and Martin A. Schain, *Chirac's Challenge: Liberalization, Europeanization and Malaise in France* (New York: St Martin's Press, 1996).

63. These are results of a study by INED, which were published by Michèle Tribalat, *Faire France: Une enquête sur les immigrés et leurs enfants* (Paris: La Découverte/Essais, 1995): see 76–80 and ch. 4, esp. table 25. Excerpts from this volume were cited in *Le Monde*, 31 March 1995: 8. For additional data, see Michèle Tribalat, *De l'immigration à l'assimilation: enquête sur les populations d'origine étrangère en France* (Paris: Editions la Découverte, 1996).

64. Jocelyne Cesari, citing William Safran, makes this comparison in *Etre musulman en France* (Paris: Karthala-Iremam, 1994): 261–2.

65. For a similar argument that focuses on the role of the state in identity formation, see Riva Kastoryano, *La France, l'Allemagne et leurs immigrés: négocier l'identité* (Paris: Armand Colin, 1996): chs. 5 and 7.

11

'Good To Think': The American Reference in French Discourses of Immigration and Ethnicity

ÉRIC FASSIN

THE GEOGRAPHY OF A QUESTION

What can Europe learn from North America? Perhaps we should start with a caveat. Analysing the French discourse of immigration and ethnicity in the American mirror implies a double limitation: the subject is France—rather than Europe; and the object is the United States—rather than North America. Of course, that the question should thus be doubly circumscribed may have something to do with this particular author's competence (or lack thereof). However, more generally (and more interestingly), it reflects the way in which the question is most often framed in France today: when debating issues of multiculturalism, minorities, and citizenship, the reference to North America is almost always limited to a discussion of the United States. On the one hand, NAFTA notwithstanding, Mexico is still perceived as belonging to a different world. On the other hand, Canada still appears undifferentiated from the United States. Mere ignorance (for example, of Will Kymlicka's work) is not the sole explanation. Significantly, the perspective does not become less narrow even as interest grows in the writings of Charles Taylor: his Canadian specificity is generally overlooked in favour of his Americanness.

The problem is not an excess of knowledge of the United States: ignorance is the rule, rather than the exception. From the viewpoint of Parisian intellectual debates, all Americans look the same, just as all minorities look the same—hyphenated Americans, as well as African-Americans (despite the historical specificity of the black issue in the United States) and Native Americans (despite the political specificity of the Aboriginal issue in Canada). This is why in this text 'America' does not refer to the United States; it should be understood only as a French mythical construct purporting to portray the United States. Following the lead of Jean-Philippe Mathy, we can thus focus on the French 'rhetoric of America', in which America is an imaginary figure, or rather, more precisely, a rhetorical device which serves political purposes for French intellectuals: as Mathy points out, 'judgements passed on the United States *from* France must be read as discourses *about* France.'[1] The American mirror reflects France, much more than it does the United States.

One last preliminary point is in order: obviously, France is not Europe (and vice versa). But from a French viewpoint, it often is, at least when, in the opposition between 'us' and 'them' underlying much of the discussion on multiculturalism, the 'others' are not Europeans. Today, immigrants (and their descendants) are assumed to be non-European, insofar as what is debated is always immigration as a 'problem': in France, it is obvious that the debates never revolve (any longer) around people of Belgian or Italian, Spanish or Portuguese origin. However, if we consider the 'hosts', and not the 'guests', in order to compare models of integration, and not the reality of immigration, oppositions between 'us' and 'them' can separate Europe from America, as well as divide European nations. Indeed, as we shall see, the 'French model' is often defined today in contrast to what is somewhat strangely called the 'Anglo-Saxon' model (in which Britain and Germany are often associated with the United States). The relation between the part (France) and the whole (Europe) is thus quite complex.

THE AMERICAN (COUNTER-) MODEL

With these warnings in mind, we can now return to our original question: 'what can Europe learn from North America?'—and rephrase it in more specific terms: what can *France* learn from *'America'*? In the last ten years, this question has clearly become central in all the French discussions of multiculturalism, concerning both ethnicity and immigration—whether we listen to politicians and journalists or read political scientists and social scientists, in the discourse of academics no less than that of public intellectuals. Indeed, it has become a topos of French rhetoric, and thus, before even trying to answer this question, it can be studied as such, focusing on the construction of this representation, rather than on the social realities it is supposed to represent. These reflections will thus revolve around the American 'detour' in French discussions of immigration and ethnicity, part of a study on the contemporary French rhetoric of America.

The French-American comparison already played a crucial role in 1988, in the now classic book of a social historian, Gérard Noiriel, *Le Creuset français*.[2] This work is the first book-length study of immigration in France,[3] and one of its most interesting features is that the author tries to account for the lack of a French historiography on which to build for his own research. Noiriel's discussion of the French *'non-lieux de mémoire'* on the subject of immigration is based on a contrast with the American experience, in which immigration is very much part of the national definition. This contrast is one between 'amnesia' and 'memory'. However, the contrast is undermined by a deeper identification: if American ethnicity is but a myth, as Stephen Steinberg would have it,[4] then, after all, the reality of integration may not be so different in both cultures: *'En dépit des différences de système politique, l'efficacité du travail collectif d'assimilation est la même, quant au fond, en France et aux États-Unis'* (p. 347). This is why the American 'melting pot' translates well (both linguistically and culturally) into the French *'creuset'*. As a consequence, whereas the French should learn from the lucidity of Americans on immigration, at the same time, they should not imitate their handling of ethnicity, largely an invention of third-generation intellectuals: historically, the *'mythologie des origines'* is not without danger, and sociologically, 'categorization' rimes with 'stigmatization'.[5] The American reference thus functions in the book both as a model and as a countermodel.

Noiriel's argument has political consequences; but it is primarily a scientific one: through the French–American comparison, immigration becomes visible, and can thus be studied. More often than not, however, the use of this comparison is primarily polemical. Another example can illustrate this, borrowed from a very different, if not opposite, intellectual and ideological sphere. In 1989 (in the wake of the infamous 'Scarves' Affair), an article by a public intellectual, Régis Debray, in the somewhat left-wing, somewhat highbrow magazine *Le Nouvel Observateur,* formulated an opposition between two social models defined as two national ideologies, which was to become part and parcel of common intellectual parlance: *'républicains'* and *'démocrates'*. The Republican political model is doubly defined by the citizen as individual, and by the state. By contrast, the democratic polity is understood as a society comprised of communities. *'En République, l'État surplombe la société. En démocratie, la société domine l'État. [. . .] En République, chacun se définit comme citoyen, et tous les citoyens composent "la nation". En démocratie, chacun se définit par sa communauté, et l'ensemble des communautés fait "la société"'* (30 November–6 December 1989, p. 51). The contrast is explicitly between French and American societies—as well as between a good and a bad model, as Debray's identification with the tradition of the Third Republic as truly 'Republican', and thus essentially French, makes clear. His initial question ('Are you a *"démocrate"* or a *"républicain"*?') could therefore be translated as: 'Are you (still) French, or are you (becoming) American?'

What is of particular interest is the double rhetorical strategy developed here. First, when discussing the politics of multiculturalism, 'America' is the Other—a radically different culture of cultural difference; and Debray develops a systematic opposition for each defining characteristic of the two models. At the same time, the Other is a threat: we may not be so different any longer, we are indeed already engaged in a process of Americanization. Hence the prophetic tone: this could happen to us (the French) tomorrow; it may be happening to us today. The comparison has a polemical, as well as descriptive function: 'America' (the menace) is indeed a rhetorical weapon used to denounce French social developments, both real and imaginary.

Both in the historian's book and in the polemicist's article, the approach is ambivalent: 'America' is the Other—but then, maybe not (any longer). On the issue of cultural difference, we may not be so different after all. Or are we (still)? I am not in any way insinuating that Debray and Noiriel belong in the same intellectual category, or share the same political agenda. On the contrary, what I find striking is precisely that both academic and journalistic approaches to the politics of cultural difference have 'naturally', i.e. spontaneously, resorted to the transatlantic comparison, paradoxically defined in both cases simultaneously through opposition and identification. They do not say the same thing; but they use the same cultural 'lexicon'. In fact, the vocabulary of this French discussion is to a large extent a translation of American words, whether we think of 'multiculturalism', 'minorities', 'ethnicity', etc. (whereas some words, interestingly enough, do not even translate well into French, such as 'identity politics', 'affirmative action', not to mention 'political correctness').

THE SOCIAL FUNCTION OF THE CONTRAST

A more recent example of this ambivalence is to be found in an important book by Robert Castel, *Les Métamorphoses de la question sociale*. Castel refuses to use the word *'exclusion'* to characterize what he would rather call *'désaffiliation'*, on the one hand, because he wants to emphasize the process of social marginalization, and not the result, but also, on the other hand, because France is not, as America seems to be, a 'dual' society: there (in the United States), it might make sense to talk of an 'underclass', he suggests; but here (in France), the social context is not the same, it is not as critical and ethnicized—and he adds: *'Nous n'en sommes pas là—ou pas encore—en France. Même le phénomène "beur", en dépit d'une référence à l'ethnicité, ne recouvre pas une culture spécifique.'*[6] The argument is thus twofold: one (reassuring), France is not in an American situation; two (threatening), it may be imminent. However, as the fear of social (and in particular ethnic) Americanization has intensified in journalistic and political discourse over the last few years (as attested by the inflation of terms such as *'communautarisme'* and *'ghettoïsation'*), intellectual discourse has grown more and more wary of identifying French and American experiences, and on the contrary, the emphasis has been much more on the contrast.

The critique developed by Sophie Body-Gendrot and Loïc Wacquant against the use of the word 'ghetto' to describe urban, or rather suburban realities in France is a case in point. First formulated in *Le Monde*,[7] their argument was soon reiterated and reinforced. Body-Gendrot's book on urban violence (*Ville et Violence*) concludes with relative optimism on the persistent contrast between the European and the American contexts: *'la segmentation moins accusée des populations, les transferts opérés par les États en direction des espaces précarisés, et la plus forte intégration historique et idéologique de ces sociétés ne les alignent pas à ce jour sur les schémas américains de violence urbaine.*[8] For her, France is *still ('à ce jour')* a far cry from American society in terms of violence. Wacquant developed his own comparative argument in a series of articles, in which he pointed out transatlantic differences between the *'banlieues'* and the 'inner cities' in intensity (hence his notion of the 'hyperghetto'), in organizing principles (in the United States, race weighs more than class), in political treatment (in France, the state is comparatively present): the *'cité'* is no 'ghetto'. The insistence on the contrast, and the virulence of the tone, may be understood as a reaction against what Wacquant (after Stanley Cohen) calls 'moral panics', in which the confusion of French and American social realities is mainly a way to import the discredit attached in the United States to the 'undeserving poor'. But despite the strong contrast he offers, Wacquant himself concludes with the suggestion that the French use of the term 'ghetto' might contribute to the *'stigmatisation qui tend à faire des "banlieues" autant de ghettos symboliques.'*[9] Castel, Body-Gendrot, and Wacquant, could share the same question: 'Not yet?'

In order to eliminate the anxiety raised by such an interrogation, Emmanuel Todd's much less academic but unfortunately much more influential essay *Le Destin des immigrés* provides the most radical version of the contrast. Todd's comparative analysis is based on what he considers to be anthropological structures: each national culture is defined by its original system of kinship. This sentences the United States to an eternal and essential 'differentialism', not among whites (this he calls 'the multiculturalist illusion'), but between whites and blacks: *'Les citoyens des États-Unis jouissent d'une liberté politique, économique, sociale étonnante. Mais ils ne sont pas libres d'accéder à une conscience égalitaire et universaliste. Ils sont prisonniers d'une détermination anthropologique qui leur échappe.'* Symmetrically, this means that, National Front notwithstanding (not to mention left-wing once-fashionable differentialism), i.e. despite influential differentialist ideologies, France cannot 'convert' to differentialism: the French are bound to their universalist aspirations, and any intellectual discourse that would contradict the anthropological determination of assimilation is but an expression of *'fausse conscience'*.[10] Not only do the French assimilate foreigners, just as Monsieur Jourdain spoke in prose, *'sans le savoir'* (a point with which most social scientists would agree), but for Todd, they even do it *'sans le vouloir'*—or better, even when they don't want to. This somewhat bizarre anthropological determinism allows a perfect (and perfectly reassuring) contrast.

THE AMERICAN VERSION

The contrast has become so obvious, and so necessary, that it appears almost as a cultural nature of the two societies, at least in this last version. This illusion could be reinforced by the fact that the opposition between the lands of

universalism and multiculturalism is not only present in the French context—
it is also to be found in the United States. Despite the odd *'Vive la différence!'*,
France is generally depicted today in the American press as a country that
rejects cultural difference—both regionalism and ethnicity. This can of course
lead to different appreciations. For example, in *The New Republic*, Martin Peretz
could display his irony at the expense of a Parisian conference on racism: to
him, the French were blind to the fact that in population or ideology they
were but the equivalent of the Germans, and thus fundamentally different
from Americans: 'unlike the French or the Germans, we are not an ethnic
nation and our demographic profile has always been changing. There is nothing in the public debate in the United States about immigration that even
faintly resembles the debate in France.' Of course, this was written in 1993
(15 November): since then, immigration has become a polemical issue in
American politics, the United States is no 'exception to the worldwide sweep
of xenophobia, at least as regards immigrants', and in fact some French politicians have displayed a strong desire to learn from the Californian experience
of Proposition 187. On the other hand, the coverage by the *New York Times*
of issues of *'laïcité'* in French schools (in dealing with Islam in particular)
has been much more favourable: maybe Americans could learn something
there, it was suggested. The French reference works both ways.

This contrast extends to academic characterizations of France: it is implicit in Eugen Weber's classic *Peasants into Frenchmen*. The book concludes
with a chapter comparing the French imposition of 'civilization' upon 'cultures' in metropolitan regions and in the colonies of the empire. The Jacobin
logic inherited from the Revolution, in contrast to American pluralism,
has no respect for cultural difference—or so goes the argument.[11] Again, in
the academic as well as in the journalistic versions, the critical viewpoint
finds its counterpoint in a favourable approach. For example, in Herman
Lebovics's *True France*, recently translated into French, the author drily notes
that though he is analysing a reactionary ideology of France, and not 'True
France' itself, the rejection of cultural difference it illustrates is hardly surprising to a student of French culture.[12] On the other hand, Judith Friedlander's recent introduction to a new translation of Alain Finkielkraut's
Defeat of the Mind offers this archetypal *'républicain'* as a model for dealing with American issues of ethnicity.[13] A few exceptions notwithstanding,
such as Martin Schain reflecting on American Jacobinism and French multiculturalism,[14] American intellectuals seem to share the terms of the opposition
with their French counterparts—if and when speaking of France.

HISTORICAL MODELS

In this double context, where French and American representations partake
of the same logic, it may prove difficult to consider the transatlantic contrast

as a 'construction', and it is certainly tempting to find its roots in the societies themselves. Simply put, the idea that France is to the United States as
universalism is to multiculturalism would be 'true', i.e. 'real'—grounded in
the reality of both societies. These shared representations would be no
clichés after all. However, several points should lead us to reconsider, and
may help us shake the spell of this illusion.

First, the diversity of cultures is not unknown to France: it was precisely
one of the accomplishments of Noiriel's early book on immigration that he
revealed the centrality of immigration in French history, not only in terms of
numbers (foreign ancestry in France exceeded American rates in the 1930s),
but also in terms of social logic (how else could we account for the transformation of France into a modern industrial nation without a massive pro-
letarianization of rural France?), and finally in that immigration transformed
the integrating nation, thus redesigning *'le creuset français'* in the process
of assimilation. France is not, contrary to the assumption of Martin Peretz,
an 'ethnic nation'.

But also, again in contradiction with his prenotions, American recognition
of ethnic diversity has a history which is rather recent, as Nathan Glazer and
Daniel P. Moynihan remind us in their introduction to *Ethnicity*:[15] symbolically, one can trace it, for example, as Martin Schain and Sophie Body-Gendrot
suggest, to President Kennedy's speech on a 'nation of nations'. In any case,
it should not be retroprojected into a distant past. Once we realize that both
the French and the American models have a history, we have to bear in mind
that this history is not over: on the contrary, we may be witnessing changes
both in France and in the United States, and the difference between the two
'cultures' may not be as great as it seemed at first. As these authors point out,

the challenge to and the change in the operating model of integration was the result of a political process that has hardly begun in France, but that can be seen in
the present debate over the nature of French nationality. Thus, in the American experience, if there is a lesson to be learned, it is probably the process through which
well-organized immigrant/ethnic groups were able to alter the model of American
national identity. Until now, immigrant pressure groups have not been able to exert
comparable influence on the political process in France.[16]

These 'national models' are subject to change, and we cannot be sure where
either is headed.

AMERICA, 'GOOD TO THINK'

We should once more go back to our original question: what can France learn
from 'America'? And we can now realize why it may be necessary first to
displace it, rather than answer it. In fact, our question thus becomes: why has

it become necessary, when discussing minorities, ethnicity, or multicultural-ism in France, to focus on the comparison with the United States, if the con-trasted nature of both societies cannot fully account for it? If America is neither the model, nor the countermodel it is all too often presented as in French debates, why this obsessive reference? If the explanation is not to be found in the logic of the construction of societies, it may be discovered in the logic of the construction of their representations—which requires an analysis of intellectual rhetoric.

A general answer could be that, today, in France, 'America' is an essen-tial figure in the rhetoric used by intellectuals, academics, and journalists alike; or, shifting to anthropology, one could use a phrase by Claude Lévi-Strauss: America is 'good to think' (*'bonne à penser'*).[17] This means that 'America' is a form which can be used in various contexts, for various purposes—and thus cannot be reduced to a model, multiculturalist, differentialist, or other. It may also enable us to account better, in logical terms, for what I have described, in psychological terms, as 'ambivalence': it does not bear one sin-gle meaning. Finally, this approach of the 'rhetoric of America' may prove a useful strategy in avoiding the essentializing of cultures which is the pit-fall of cultural comparisons.[18]

This is quite visible in a variety of fields. I shall focus here on three examples beyond the issue of 'ethnicity'. The first involves feminism. In the last few years, two French books have attempted to compare French and American feminisms in a historical perspective: Pierre Rosanvallon's *Le Sacre du citoyen* and Mona Ozouf's *Les Mots des femmes*.[19] In the first one, Rosanvallon suggests a new explanation of the late date of female suffrage in France compared not only to the United States, but also to less 'pro-gressive' societies. Of course, this has often been accounted for in classical political terms (in particular, in reference to the rôle of the Church under the Republic in defining female public opinion). But Rosanvallon offers a new hypothesis: this may have to do with the political nature of the social models themselves. In the United States, women in the early twentieth century fought for suffrage in the name of their difference: they could contribute something to American democracy as a group, as women. On the contrary, in France, women had to become fully emancipated individuals, defined not by their specificity but in abstract terms, as citizens undifferentiated from men, before suffrage could be granted to them.

This argument is taken up by Mona Ozouf, who combines it with another, first formulated by Philippe Raynaud in a short article in *Le Débat*:[20] not only is there a difference in political organization, between a society that will recognize communities and one that will acknowledge only the existence of individuals, but also, there is a fundamental difference in cultural organiza-tion, which can be formulated in Tocquevillian terms as an opposition between a democratic society ('America') and a culture in which the Old Regime still partly defines 'civilization' (France). The social interaction between men and women, according to this interpretation, is smoother and more pleasant for both parties precisely because the rules of the social game make it necessary, and ordinary, for men and women to interact: this is a 'defence and illustration' of a French model of *'mixité'*, in which women contribute their civilizing influence. Of course, there is a potential contradiction between the two arguments, as 'difference' can be denounced or vindicated, as 'American' or as French: in the political version, French feminism (and femininity) is vindicated because of its rejection of women's difference; in the cultural version, American feminism (and femininity) is denounced because of its rejection of women's civilizing difference. What matters more for our purpose is that the transatlantic opposition, one way or another, is 'good to think', far beyond the example of ethnicity.

A second example concerns homosexuality. A controversial book recently published in France, *Le Rose et le Noir,* by a young sociologist, Frédéric Martel, combines a history of gay and, to a lesser extent, lesbian movements in France in the last thirty years with a polemical conclusion attacking what he considers to be a dangerous evolution in the direction of American-style *'communautarisme'*, due to AIDS: *'Sans la maladie, il y aurait probablement eu une victoire du modèle français d'assimilation (la société intègre les individus mais ne reconnaît pas les groupes) sur le modèle américain communautaire.'* This *'repli identitaire'* is best illustrated perhaps, according to Martel, by the example of the Gay Pride: *'Comment ne pas percevoir une tentative lente d'"américanisation' de la société française à travers la Gay Pride?'*[21] Martel's denunciation is explicitly linked to Finkielkraut's critique of differentialism, in the homosexual movement as well as in anti-racist groups. The politics of difference is not restricted to 'ethnicity'; therefore, the transatlantic comparison extends beyond the question of ethnic minorities, to include all minorities. But what is remarkable, in both examples, is that the language of ethnicity (from differentialism to *'communautarisme'*) becomes the language used to reflect on a variety of other problems: as we can see here, it provides a lexicon with which to approach both gender and sexuality.

A third and final example concerns 'political correctness', a notion which in many ways encompasses all of the above—and this may explain its extraordinary social success, not only in North America but also in Europe, and more particularly in France. I shall not develop here this example; let it simply suffice to say that the transatlantic paradox I have described elsewhere[22] results from the fact that, whereas in the United States, 'political correctness' may be ascribed a French origin (starting with Allan Bloom, the critique of 'political correctness' has often taken the form of a critique of relativism, perceived as a French import: *'c'est la faute à la pensée 68'*), in France, *'le politiquement correct'* has generally been analysed as quintessentially American. This contrast leads to the ambivalence we have already encountered:

'p.c.' is supposed to be radically alien to French culture; but also, it is feared there may be a threat of contagion. It cannot happen to us—at least, once again, not yet.

Thus, today, in France, for all kinds of purposes, 'America' is 'good to think'—but one may ask: good to think what, i.e. what does it enable French intellectual discourse to think? My examples may indicate that the reference to America is a tool to reflect on *French* exceptionalism: the American exception serves as the foundation of the French one. Let me finally suggest that the revival of an exceptionalist approach to France owes a great deal to the revival of the French *'libéraux'* in the last twenty years, in whose thought 'America' plays a crucial role—first, in the early 1980s, as a model (the good Revolution), second, since the late 1980s, as a countermodel (the egalitarian disease). One could thus (and I have begun to do so elsewhere) retrace the history of this American reference.[23]

FROM GERMANY TO AMERICA

The importance of the American example (either as model or as countermodel) in a variety of contexts means it has largely replaced Germany in the one particular context we are interested in here: Germany was traditionally the Other in the French debate over national culture, as evidenced in the history of the *culture vs. civilisation* debate. Today, it is of course discussed, sometimes in parallel with the American example; and clearly, from Louis Dumont to Alain Finkielkraut, and not forgetting Dominique Schnapper,[24] Germany is not absent from contemporary French debates on 'multiculturalism, minorities, and citizenship'. None the less, whereas it used to be *the* Other of French cultural discourse, Germany is now only the other Other.

Of course, this has to do in part with the fact that the German countermodel was used to reflect on diversity among nations, whereas the United States provides a starting point for an analysis of cultural diversity within the nation—and it is worth noting that there is a potential contradiction between these two definitions of France (as civilization, in opposition to culture, and at the same time as culture, in contrast to cultures). But I also think it has to do, more profoundly (and here we can adapt Claude Digeon's title for our times), with a *'crise américaine de la pensée française'*.[25] To a large extent, 'America' has taken over as a trope in our discussions of multiculturalism.

I may not be able to explain why or even how, as this would entail a broader discussion of both social and intellectual changes in recent France. What I propose to do in this final section is only to provide one context, by analysing the various languages, or at least the most important lexicons used to describe their national societies by social scientists (broadly defined as those whose job it is to interpret society), both in historical fashion and in comparative terms. I shall thus attempt a (cursory, admittedly) transatlantic genealogy of how both societies represent themselves—which is part of their *'outillage mental'*, to borrow a famous phrase from the historian Lucien Febvre, i.e. of the toolbox with which they try to account for their own logic. One should not forget, of course, that we are talking here both about scientific tools and ideological weapons—at the same time.

'NORM' AND 'CLASS' IN THE UNITED STATES AND IN FRANCE

Let us start on the American shores in the 1950s. Whether we think of functionalist sociology, with Parsons and Merton, or of the historians of the consensus, such as Hofstadter, the main language available is that of the norm: the agenda is to demonstrate the organic integration of American society as a whole. Hence the Americanization of Durkheim in sociology. Hence the reflection on American exceptionalism among historians. The dominance of this perspective becomes even more obvious if we consider its contemporary critics: in interactionist sociology, the fascination both for the imposition of the norm (labels and stigmata) and for its subversion (outsiders and deviants) only confirms the pre-eminence of this language in its very critique— although of course the point of interactionists was not to accept the point of view of the mainstream on marginality, but rather to interpret them together. However, functionalist or consensual social science met with at least two problems, i.e. an intellectual difficulty and a political one. The intellectual difficulty is that there is no consensus on the norm—which considerably undermines the strength of the argument. The resulting political problem is that conflict is very much left out of the picture.

If we now compare this context to the French social science scene of the 1950s and 1960s, it is quite obvious that we are entering a different intellectual world. The language of the norm is very much absent, as well as its critique. What we have is of course the language of class. This is true at the time among both sociologists and *Annales* historians. I am not implying by contrast that class did not exist then in the United States, nor even that the language of class was not available—after all, one could study *White-Collar* just as later one could analyse *The Hidden Injuries of Class*. I just want to remind us that, whereas in the United States this language was not readily available, it was in France the obvious reference, including for those who criticized it, such as 'liberal' sociologist Raymond Aron: his very choice of objects is very much determined by the categories he is attacking, whether analysing the ruling classes or industrial society. Just as in the United States, critics of the dominant language had to enter into a dialogue with it. The advantage of this language of class, compared to the language of norm, is that it makes conflict into a central issue, and thus cannot overlook it. The disadvantage is that it cannot account for everything or everyone: whereas the norm may describe even those outside the norm (they are deviants), class was not so convenient when trying to make sense of those who did not identify with a class, despite intellectual acrobatics with the *'an sich'/'für sich'* opposition.

'ETHNICITY' AND 'CULTURE' IN THE UNITED STATES AND IN FRANCE

In the United States, the language of the norm very much collapsed under the weight of the attacks of the 1960s, combining civil rights and student revolt logics, a critique of the social order, and a denunciation of the mainstream. The norm suddenly did not make too much sense anymore. Not coincidentally, this is when the language of ethnicity gained prominence: it offered a new way of thinking about how society works. The language of cultural difference, of course, had something to do with the politics of difference—but it must also be understood as a successor to the previously dominant language of the norm. If we want to see the difference between the new and the old logics, one can look at the simultaneous publication, in 1963, of Howard Becker's *Outsiders*, a critique of the logic of the norm from an interactionist perspective, and of *Beyond the Melting Pot*, by Nathan Glazer and Daniel P. Moynihan, whose importance in the definition of the new paradigm is well known.[26]

In France, the language of class collapsed later, in the late 1970s or early 1980s, under its own weight, but also after the renewed intellectual attacks against Marxism, and as a result of the political success of socialists: the story is well known, and need not be rehearsed. It is remarkable that this is when discussions about 'culture' truly begin in France—culture in a variety of meanings, whether we are talking about national culture (hence the revival of an interest in national historiography, illustrated in Fernand Braudel's last book about *L'Identité de la France* as well as the monumental multi-volume *Lieux de mémoire*), about high culture (although the two may merge, one could list the names of Danièle Sallenave, Alain Finkielkraut, Marc Fumaroli, etc.), and now about 'multiculturalism' (whether we think of critics, in the 'Republican' tradition I have previously discussed, or of more sympathetic observers, such as Michel Wieviorka).[27]

If we compare these two chronologies, it is not surprising that 'America' should function as a reference today in French debates, as the language of 'culture' in France could easily define itself in comparison with, identification to, or more generally rejection of a language previously elaborated in the United States, which thus appeared ahistorically (eternally and essentially) American. This difference in chronology explains in part the transfer and appropriation of language (only in part of course: one should not underestimate the growing intellectual influence of the American reference, especially in academia, due to the financial strength and intellectual attraction of the American universities; the American academic voyage is quite comparable for the French to their German experience a century ago). It is no accident that American and French (more generally, European) intellectuals can converse on these topics in conferences like the one today: the debates may not be the same, here and there, but their terms are often the same, although they take on different meanings as a result of their inscription in different contexts.

This does not mean that norm (in the United States) and class (in France) have become 'unthinkable', but rather that they no longer provide a required vocabulary; on the contrary, using them goes against the grain today. This does not mean either that the language of 'ethnicity' and 'culture' is the only one now available in the United States or in France. In fact, a second language has emerged from the ruins of these two, with comparable transatlantic applications. It is the language of the 'underclass' or of 'exclusion', in the United States and in France—and elsewhere. It could be summarily described, as a combination of the languages of 'norm' and 'class'. I shall not develop this here, because it has been developed by others.[28] But one could find there since the same chronology could be found that I just described for the language of 'ethnicity' and 'culture', with the American formulations preceding the French. Here again, the debate can be transatlantic. And it is not surprising that the same social scientists can resort to both languages, now available in both intellectual cultures.

INTELLECTUAL HYGIENE AS A PRELIMINARY

This presentation focuses on language and rhetoric—and there is a risk, when discussing social phenomena, that discourse could replace empirical work, if not reality. This is all the more a risk when one is producing discourse about discourse: going 'meta' can of course be dismissed, and often rightly so, as a strategy to avoid dealing with 'the real world'. However, insisting on the language that influences us, and the rhetoric with which we influence others, forces us to bear in mind that they find their necessity not always, and not only, in the realities they purport to represent. In the United States, the new discourse on ethnicity may not have unveiled a new reality of ethnicity so much as provided it with new means of expression and recognition. In France, the constant preoccupation with national culture may not indicate a crisis of national identity or a crisis of the national model of integration so much as provide a language with which to express other problems—political, economic, and social. This is why we should not assume an equivalence between the language we use to describe social phenomena and the phenomena themselves. That 'multiculturalism' should be an intellectual issue, here and there, may not imply that it makes sense socially, neither here nor there. It may simply indicate that this is the language we have at our disposition now.

Autonomizing the study of this language thus expresses a dissatisfaction, not simply with one side or the other in these debates, but with the language itself: it does not enable us to describe, let alone account for reality too well. This implies not to identify with one side or the other, with the position of the *'républicains'* or of the *'démocrates'*; with the defence of 'universalism' or 'differentialism': they partake of the same logic, they share the same language. But the critique of our own language as social scientists, and the introduction of a distance in our perspective through the reminder that there is a distance between the vocabulary we use and the realities we try to interpret, between words and things, can serve as a (preliminary) intellectual hygiene.

TWO DIRECTIONS

This preliminary can lead in two different directions—and here we finally come back to our initial question: what can the American reference teach us in Europe? The first direction is more intellectual, the second one is more political—though this opposition may not survive closer scrutiny. In the first case, the comparison between the American experience and the French one is not taken any longer as a starting point, but as the very object of investigation. This academic approach has been recently developed in the study of immigration and ethnicity, following Noiriel's lead. Nancy Green first reformulated and refocused his initial comparison of France and the United States: instead of comparing national models, she argues, we need to define the comparison according to what we are trying to find. For example, 'French Jews may be studied implicitly or explicitly in comparison with: French Catholics or Protestants; Italians or Poles in France; or with American Jews. In each case, the comparative perspective implies a different query, regarding religion, ethnicity, or nationality.' The comparison of social groups thus takes different forms—linear (following immigrants from Naples to New York), convergent (studying both the Irish and Italians in Boston), or divergent (the Diaspora model): as Nancy Green clearly demonstrates, it all depends on the question raised.[29]

This methodological reappraisal of the transatlantic comparison has been further developed in a masterful article published by historian Catherine Collomp. The different status of ethnicity in France and in the United States is here explored historically, through a study of the labour market—instead of national ideologies:

Les plus grands contrastes dans l'insertion des immigrants dans l'un ou l'autre pays ne sont pas de nature idéologique, mais prennent plutôt racine dans des mécanismes différents de régulation économique, en particulier dans l'intervention de l'État (ou sa non-intervention) sur les marchés du travail.

Thus the usual opposition between a French model *('républicain')* and an American model *('démocrate')* becomes that which must be explained, instead of remaining the explanation for everything:

Il n'est qu'apparemment paradoxal de constater que l'immigration collective, organisée en France, et, à l'inverse, politiquement construite comme une démarche individuelle aux États-Unis ait conduit, en France, à ne traiter l'étranger que comme un individu, et aux États-Unis à l'expression collective de l'ethnicité. L'inversion des relations de l'individu à la collectivité s'explique par le vide social dans lequel s'inscrivait l'immigration américaine. C'est dans cet espace que s'insérait l'activité du groupe ethnique médiateur principal entre l'immigrant et la société; en France, en revanche, celui-ci se trouvait sous la tutelle directe des pouvoirs publics.

Not that the state explains it all (that would be another way to return to the very same comparative culturalism): indeed, far from pre-existing, the role of the state in these matters is itself largely a result of the immigration waves from the end of the nineteenth century to the 1920s.[30] This intellectual difference is all the more important, politically, as the historical contexts may change, and thus the conditions which made French and American models possible at a specific moment in French and American history. This kind of work is the first illustration of what the comparison between France and the United States may teach us today about ethnicity in both nations.

The second direction I wish to suggest is of a more openly political nature. In a recent book, Denis Lacorne offers a synthesis on American multiculturalism for French readers, in an attempt to provide accurate historical information for a debate in which such scruples have not prevailed until now.[31] The implicit, and sometimes explicit question is: can anything be learned from the American experience? This theoretical question takes a more precise political meaning when discussing affirmative action: can this notion translate into French? Denis Lacorne's answer is to define the specificity of the American experience, not as the opposite of the so-called French model *('républicain')*, but rather through the tension between the two logics of assimilation and pluralism.[32] The problem with such definitions of national models is twofold: on the one hand, change cannot be accounted for, except as a betrayal of the national tradition; on the other hand, transfers are unthinkable between national models, each trapped in its own culture.

In order to avoid this culturalism when debating multiculturalism, we could start from a different premiss: instead of focusing on multiculturalism, we could address the question of discrimination. This means a change of language: instead of arguing about the representation of cultures, the issue becomes the participation of minorities. 'Multiculturalism' may belong to an American tradition, but discrimination is not specific to any national culture—and the answers may not need to be drawn from a specific national past. Once this shift in language has transformed our political perception, however, the problem is not so much: should we borrow solutions from the American model? but rather: can the American reference help us formulate questions? A positive use of the American mirror thus becomes possible: discrimination, which goes largely undiscussed in French political debates, is at the centre of the American public scene. Is it not worth debating in France, or is the language available today making it difficult to think about discrimination? Reflecting on this transatlantic gap could give another, more useful meaning to the old trope— America, good to think.

NOTES

1. Jean-Philippe Mathy, *Extrême-Occident: French Intellectuals and America*, (Chicago: University of Chicago Press, 1993): 7.
2. Gérard Noiriel, *Le Creuset français. Histoire de l'immigration, XIXe–XXe siècles* (Paris: Le Seuil, 1988; American trans. by Minnesota U. P., 1995).
3. Alongside Yves Lequin's *La Mosaïque France* (Paris, Larousse, 1988).
4. Stephen Steinberg, *The Ethnic Myth: Race, Ethnicity, and Class in America* (New York: Beacon Press, 1981).
5. I discussed this in greater detail in a review article: 'La France des immigrés', *French Politics and Society*, 7/2 (1989): 50–62. The importance of the comparison is made even more apparent by the fact that Noiriel later elaborated again on this topic in a transatlantic book he edited with Donald Horowitz, *Immigrants in Two Democracies: French and American Experience* (New York: New York University Press, 1992).
6. Robert Castel, *Les métamorphoses de la question sociale: une chronique du salariat* (Paris: Fayard, 1995): 15.
7. Loïc Wacquant and Sophie Body-Gendrot, 'Ghetto: un mot de trop?', *Le Monde*, 17 July 1991.
8. Sophie Body-Gendrot, *Ville et violence: l'irruption de nouveaux acteurs* (Paris: PUF, 1993): 244.
9. One version of Loïc Wacquant's argument is to be found in his article: 'Banlieues françaises et ghetto noir américain. Éléments de comparaison sociologique', in the volume *Racisme et modernité*, ed. by Michel Wieviorka (Paris: La Découverte, 1993).
10. Emmanuel Todd, *Le Destin des immigrés. Assimilation et ségrégation dans les démocraties occidentales* (Paris: Le Seuil, 1994): 107 and 373.
11. Eugen Weber, *Peasants into Frenchmen. The Modernization of Rural France, 1870–1914* (Stanford: Stanford University Press, 1976). For a powerful critique, based on a study of regionalism in Third Republic education, see Jean-François Chanet, *L'École républicaine et les petites patries*, preface by Mona Ozouf, Paris: Aubier, 1996).

12. Herman Lebovics, *True France. The Wars over Cultural Identity, 1900–1945* (Ithaca: Cornell University Press, 1992): 200–1 (this passage is left out from the French version: *La 'Vraie France'. Les enjeux de l'identité culturelle, 1900–1945* (Paris: Belin, 1995)).

13. Judith Friedlander, introduction to her translation of Alain Finkielkraut's *The Defeat of the Mind* (New York: Columbia University Press, 1996).

14. Martin Schain, 'Minorities and Immigrant Incorporation in France: The State and the Dynamics of Multiculturalism' (in this volume).

15. Nathan Glazer and Daniel Patrick Moynihan (eds.), *Ethnicity. Theory and Experience* (Cambridge, Mass.: Harvard University Press, 1975).

16. Sophie Body-Gendrot and Martin Schain, 'National and Local Politics and the Development of Immigration Policy in the United States and France: A Comparative Analysis', in Donald L. Horowitz and Gérard Noiriel (eds.), *Immigrants in Two Democracies*: 435.

17. Claude Lévi-Strauss, *Le totémisme aujourd'hui* (Paris: PUF, 1962): 132.

18. I tried to develop this argument in 'Fearful Symmetry: Culturalism and Cultural Comparison', *French Historical Studies*, 19/2 (1995): 451–60.

19. Pierre Rosanvallon, *Le Sacre du citoyen. Histoire du suffrage universel en France* (Paris, Gallimard, 1992), pt. I, ch. 2 *('l'individu autonome')*, and pt. III, ch. 3 *('le travail de l'universalisation')*. His argument is to be found, in a shorter version, in *Femmes et histoire,* Georges Duby and Michelle Perrot (eds.) (Paris: Plon, 1993), *'L'histoire du vote des femmes, réflexion sur la spécificité française'*. Mona Ozouf, *Les Mots des femmes, essai sur la singularité française* (Paris: Fayard, 1995).

20. Philippe Raynaud, 'Les femmes et la civilité: aristocratie et passions révolutionnaires', *Le Débat* (Paris: Gallimard, Nov.–Dec. 1989): 57.

21. Frédéric Martel, *Le Rose et le Noir, les homosexuels en France depuis 1968* (Paris: Seuil, 1996): 404–6.

22. Éric Fassin, 'Political correctness en version originale et en version française. Un malentendu révélateur', *Vingtième siècle, revue d'histoire*, 43 (July–Sept. 1994): 30–42.

23. I have attempted to explore this rhetoric, and this ideology, starting from Mona Ozouf's book, in 'The Purloined Gender: American Feminism in the French Mirror', French Historical Studies, 22/1 (1999), 113–38.

24. Louis Dumont, *L'Idéologie allemande, France-Allemagne et retour* (Paris: Gallimard, 1991). Alain Finkielkraut, *La Défaite de la pensée* (Paris: Gallimard, 1987). Dominique Schnapper, *La France de l'intégration. Sociologie de la nation en 1990* (Paris: Gallimard, 1991). For a discussion of this comparison, see Rogers Brubaker, *Citizenship and Nationhood in France and Germany* (Cambridge, Mass.: Harvard University Press, 1992).

25. See his classic book, Claude Digeon, *La Crise allemande de la pensée française, 1870–1914* (Paris: PUF, 1959).

26. Howard Becker, *Outsiders. Studies in the Sociology of Deviance* (New York: Free Press, 1963). Nathan Glazer and Daniel P. Moynihan, *Beyond the Melting Pot* (Cambridge, Mass.: MIT, 1963).

27. I have tried to account for the battles around the term 'culture' in Éric Fassin, 'Two Cultures? French Intellectuals and the Politics of Culture in the 1980s', *French Politics and Society*, 14/2 (1996): 9–16.

28. Didier Fassin, 'Exclusion, Underclass, Marginalidad. Figures contemporaines de la pauvreté urbaine en France, aux États-Unis et en Amérique latine', *Revue française de sociologie*, 37 (1996): 37–75.
29. Nancy Green, 'The Comparative Method and Poststructural Structuralism—New Perspectives for Migration Studies', *Journal of American Ethnic Studies* (Summer 1994): 3–22 (quotation p. 6). See also her articles in French, Nancy Green, 'L'histoire comparative et le champ des études migratoires', *Annales ESC*, 6 (Nov.–Dec. 1990): 1335–50, and 'L'immigration en France et aux États-Unis: historiographie comparée', *Vingtième siècle, revue d'histoire*, 29 (Jan.–Mar. 1991): 67–82.
30. Catherine Collomp, 'Regard sur les politiques de l'immigration. Le marché du travail en France et aux États-Unis (1880–1930)', *Annales HSS* 5 (Sept.–Oct. 1996): 1107–135, quotations 1110 and 1133–4.
31. Denis Lacorne, *La Crise de l'identité américaine. Du melting-pot au multiculturalisme* (Paris: Fayard, 1997). See my discussion, 'Du multiculturalisme à la discrimination', *Le Débat* 97 (Nov.–Dec. 1997): 131–36.
32. *La Crise de l'identité américaine*: 37.

12

Comments on Glazer, Schain, and Fassin: How can We be European?

ADRIAN FAVELL

Pour voir et sentir l'Amérique, il faut au moins un instant avoir senti dans la jungle d'un downtown, dans le Painted Desert ou dans la courbe d'un freeway, que l'Europe avait disparu. Il faut au moins un instant s'être demandé: 'Comment peut-on être Européen?'

Jean Baudrillard, *L'Amérique*

Nearly all Europeans have a problem with the idea of North America (North America here equated with a certain conception of the USA, and Canada little more than a rather lifeless version of the 'real thing'). In Jean Baudrillard's *fin de millenium* fantasy voyage through the strange New World of contemporary America, he offers a brilliant articulation of the contradictory sensation of fascination and horror that most European thought about North America displays (Baudrillard, 1986). Post-war Europe has been obsessed with consuming American culture, and with the Americanization of industry, technology, and the economy: the USA as the liberal democratic model. Yet equally, the label of Americanization is used to deplore the destruction of national European political cultures, of community, or of welfare solidarity: the USA as nightmare scenario. We deplore American superficiality, ignorance, or craziness, while scrambling for green cards and transatlantic conference tickets. Talk of North American multiculturalism, and a whole series of vivid images are conjured up as the possible end-point of Europe's own multicultural questions: racial gangs, ghettos, and cartoon urban violence; loony campus ethnic boycotts and political correctness; the politics of identity and sectarian grievance out of control. Yet even behind all this, there is the suspicion that the USA is still the open, multicultural ideal made real, with something to teach the rest of the world; a self-conception, as Nathan Glazer here points out, still believed by most Americans, especially those of 'ethnic' origin.

One of the contributors to this volume, Eric Fassin, has pinpointed the source of these distortions in a series of penetrating analyses of the French complex about the USA (France undoubtedly being the West European country with the most overt psychological problem about the idea of America) (Fassin (1993*a*, 1994, 1996); see also Wacquant (1992); Granjon (1994); and Lacorne (1997)). French intellectuals, he argues, are able to seize American examples as rhetorical weapons in their local political or intellectual debates because of the unequal power relations between the continents. We feel we 'know' all about America without ever having to 'know' it in a scientific sense: caricatural examples of North American multiculturalism work so well because each is assumed unproblematically to capture the 'essence' of North American society and politics. American media, Hollywood, and cultural exports seem only to confirm our simplest ideas. We are therefore trapped in the distorting-mirror effects of the ubiquitous American reference in European self-conceptions and European reformulations of 'classic' American political and social ideas.

It follows that the question posed in Part IV of this book is inherently problematic. Transatlantic multicultural answers to the question are inevitably coloured and warped by the unequal power relationship of the two continents. Indeed, as I will suggest, any case-study-based approach to this question puts into doubt the very validity of asking general and abstract transatlantic multicultural questions of the kind posed in the earlier parts of the book. Do the philosophical questions 'does multiculturalism threaten citizenship?' or 'do minorities require group rights?' really mean the same things on both sides of the Atlantic (let alone in France, Germany, or Britain)? In my comment on the three responses to the fourth multicultural question, then, I hope to do two things. I aim to situate these contributions—which are based on context-specific national case studies and comparisons—in relation to the abstract philosophical discussions earlier in the book; and second, I suggest that the three contributions point towards a rather different angle from which the question 'what can Europe learn from North America?' might be asked.

MULTICULTURAL CITIZENSHIP: A TRANSATLANTIC AGENDA?

In recent years, there has been a spectacular proliferation of philosophical discussions of multiculturalism. What should be noted immediately is that practically all the most well-known discussions have a North American origin. Among these, there are essentially two main currents. The first current follows the all-pervasive influence of John Rawls, whose later work in particular has set down the dominant axes of recent philosophical enquiry: centred around the reconciliation of liberalism with communitarianism, universalism with the value of ethnic and cultural belonging, or equality with membership in a specific national society (Gutmann, 1985, 1993; Taylor and

Gutmann, 1992; Rawls, 1993; Spinner, 1994; Kymlicka, 1995). It is no co-incidence that some of the most pertinent applied discussions have come from Canadian (and Quebecois) writers, where these questions are felt even more acutely than in the USA (see Kaplan, 1993). The second current reflects the expansion of feminism and minority studies, and the more 'liberational' drive of multicultural identity politics: attacking the ethnocentrism of Western liberal values and promoting forms of cross-cultural dialogue (Said, 1978; Young, 1991; Benhabib, 1992; Mouffe, 1992). While the theoretical inspiration for much of this philosophical movement is conspicuously European (figures such as Derrida, Foucault, and Habermas loom large), the context of its success—and the frequent mistranslation of French social theory into 'post-modernism' (on this see Calhoun, 1996)—has been very North American: savage campus politics and the power struggle for access to the dominantly New York centred public intellectual spotlight (Fassin, 1993*b*). What is perhaps most curious in recent North American multiculturalism is how distant it all is from the primary origins of multiculturalism as a political movement: Third World anticolonialism, and the attempt by UNESCO and other agencies to protect world cultures and diversity along lines identified by post-war anthropologists such as Claude Lévi-Strauss (Fanon, 1961; Lévi-Strauss, 1983).

In a transatlantic perspective, what is not obvious from even the best of North American reflections on multiculturalism—such as Taylor, Gutmann, Kymlicka, or Spinner—is how far any of their general philosophical positions help elucidate the issues and forms that multiculturalism takes in different European nation-states. The obvious asymmetry of transatlantic comparisons quickly reveals just how much local national institutional contexts and political histories matter, and how multicultural questions in, say, France, Germany and Britain, take on very different contours and substance in each case (Joppke, 1996). The French are obsessed with the dilemmas multicultural *différence* poses to the ideal of the universal *République*; Germans with the difference multiculturalism might make to its primordial *völkisch* national identity; and the British with perfecting the multicultural colonial management techniques developed under the sovereign power of a 'Union' of four 'nations'. Immigrants are not viewed in the same way in these countries; the word 'minority' has very different connotations; and it is unclear, in at least one of these national cases, whether anybody—let alone distinct ethnic groups —has fundamental rights! The lesson from this should be that there is no 'essence' of multiculturalism in theory or in practice. There is at best an uneven 'family resemblance' across different institutional contexts. Philosophers, therefore, cannot hope to formulate empirically useful contributions unless they incorporate a good deal of 'local knowledge' in their reflections. Important national distinctions are often smothered by the general philosophical frameworks and arguments, despite the fact that the North American multiculturalists are used as the main conceptual framework in theoretical and empirical discussions by European and North Americans alike.

One well-worn 'example' from philosophy seminars discussing the liberal-communitarian debate should be taken as a warning: the '*affaire du foulard*', in which three Muslim girls were banned from school in the northern banlieue of Paris for refusing to remove their traditional head-scarves in class. As a philosophical dilemma, this would seem to be a perfect example for discussing the question: 'what are the limits of toleration?' or 'should there be a group right to wear religious symbols?' These philosophical formulations were indeed present in the public debate—in the shape of the philosophical republican hard-line on *laïcité* in the public sphere on the one hand and *droit à la différence* type rhetoric on the other—but there was a great deal more at stake than abstract philosophical principles. It was firstly a case which at its most substantive raised questions about who in a centralized state such as France should have the institutional power to decide and which rationale it should use (should it be the politicians, or the media, or the supreme *Conseil d'État* fixing the principles in advance; or should it be devolved to a local level case by case pragmatism)? Secondly, it questioned who the girls in fact were for the purposes of political decision-making and the wider goals of *intégration* (were they culturally embedded Muslims, *défavorisés* immigrants, oppressed women, or potentially autonomous future *citoyens*, etc?). And thirdly, with intellectuals playing such an important role in the public debate, it asked which type of theories was most important in answering the questions it raised (should philosophical, political, sociological, or anthropological arguments count most in deciding?) (See Gaspard and Khosrokhvar, 1995). In short, the case should not be reconstructed as a one-paragraph 'hard case' that can be reduced to quick 'moral' judgement. As philosophers attempt to push their reflection in an applied, empirically connected direction, they may well be forced to recognize that there are even good theoretical reasons why such abstract formulation of multicultural questions might be philosophically wrong: the practice of addressing 'ethnic dilemmas', unlike its justice-based theoretical formulation, entails more pragmatist considerations about how desirable ends can be achieved, as well as a recognition of the epistemological issues raised by the conceptualization of public problems.

All that said, there is one sense in which philosophers discussing the question of multiculturalism have indeed helped establish a common transatlantic agenda which resonates in the political sphere beyond the intellectual world. This is an agenda that has emerged broadly speaking under the banner of 'the return of the citizen' (Habermas, 1992; Kymlicka and Norman, 1994; Beiner, 1995). Both North American and European political thinking has, in recent years, returned to the discussion of citizenship as a practical way out of the multicultural dilemmas posed by the identity (national/political) versus difference (ethnic/cultural) problematic. Among philosophers, what is perhaps most noticeable in the very large literature that has emerged, is the apparent convergence of the two dominant political philosophical paradigms of the last two decades: the Rawlsian and the Habermasian (Habermas, 1994; Rawls, 1995). Beyond this, the philosophical discussions have been echoed widely in high-level official reflections on citizenship in France and Britain; in changes to the multicultural politics of countries such as Sweden and the Netherlands; and in the marked rise of a European constitutional politics along the lines pioneered in the USA and Canada. Clearly, here, the philosophers seem to be tapping in to a genuinely central political zeitgeist.

A number of reasons for the resonance of this new transatlantic agenda can be suggested. New international migrations, the end of the Cold War, and the increasing freedom of movement of people and capital throughout Europe and across the Atlantic, have each raised the question of the relationship between citizenship and nationality as forms of membership, in both formal legal terms and more fluid cultural and symbolic ones. At the same time, the 'rediscovery' of Islam in Western Europe—and the stark cultural differences it underlines between Western and 'other' practices—has provoked a search for inclusive citizenship-based solutions, which can integrate the religion within secular institutions that separate public and private spheres. In response to these two political problems, a whole new wave of North American studies of immigration and citizenship has opened up transatlantic and cross-national comparisons in an area previously left to very inward-looking nation-based studies (Brubaker, 1992; Cornelius *et al.*, 1994; Soysal, 1994; Baldwin-Edwards and Schain, 1994; Joppke, 1998). A mark of the perceived importance of the subject is the unprecedented amount of money that has been put forward by organizations such as the Marshall Fund, the Ford Foundation, and the Carnegie Endowment to further the transatlantic study of migration, citizenship, and immigration control. At the same time, US State Department officials have started looking beyond American exceptionalism to common transatlantic problems in this area with their EU counterparts.

Despite the obvious attraction of forging a common agenda on questions of multiculturalism and citizenship, or immigration and minorities, it is however far from clear that the two continents are facing the same kinds of problems. Are American concerns with new Mexican or Asian immigrants really the same as European ones (in distinct national contexts) about post-colonial immigrants, guest workers, or third country nationals from Eastern Europe? It seems extraordinary that North Americans today are apparently looking to Europe for enlightenment over their own immigration, multicultural and citizenship dilemmas. In the past, America has almost always aggressively exported its own experience of diversity, pluralism, and minority rights in a developmentalist attitude to the rest of the world, looking down on a Europe divided by 'archaic' national cultural divisions (it is this attitude which still characterizes the rush of interest in East European political problems). In a curious reversal of the distorted optic in which Europe builds its 'nightmare' vision of American ethnic fragmentation, North American political thinkers have recently begun to vaunt the model of European civic political cultures as the exemplar of traditional American virtues of civility, participation and community, now seen as starkly missing in the contemporary USA (Schlesinger, 1992; Barber, 1995; Sandel, 1995; see Favell, 1998*a*). The philosophically virtuous 'civic republicanism' of France and parts of Italy have in particular aroused a great deal of interest (Brubaker, 1992; Putnam, 1993; Hollifield, 1994): this, despite the ease with which these proud national 'traditions' can be dismantled as recent ideological reconstructions of the past, or—as Martin Schain's contribution to this volume underlines—rhetorical 'models' which no longer accurately reflect ground-level policy and political practice (see also Tarrow, 1996).

It is likely therefore that the kinds of 'common' concerns that have typically emerged from the 'return of the citizen' agenda, create as many cross-purposes in transatlantic discussions about multiculturalism as opportunities for advancing a common understanding. 'Citizenship' for sure is an attractive overall frame for this body of work; but we should perhaps be suspicious of the way the 'self-evident' desirability of the normative enlightenment values the frame embodies causes citizenship-oriented writers to blur the descriptive and the prescriptive in their analysis of contemporary events. In short, it is the predominance given to a 'political philosophical' way of reading the politics of multiculturalism that is most problematic. The citizenship optic imposes on our reflections a set of broadly common normative features that can be found in philosophical and empirical studies alike: an accent on constitutitutionalism and rights in a bounded political community; an accent on 'bringing the State back in' as the universal frame of the polity; an idea of the public sphere in which public virtues are distinguished from private interests; a search for shared foundational principles that all, including culturally diverse minorities, can give their conscious consent to; a plea for more active citizens' participation, competence, and transparency. However desirable these features are, it is not clear if they accurately reflect the way in which contemporary liberal democracies actually solve their multicultural questions; nor, as a result, is it likely that invoking these kinds of features is a realistic guide to what can and should be done to improve the treatment of these questions in the future (Favell, 1997*a*).

The three contributions to Part IV each, in their own way, offer reasons for why we should be sceptical about a common transatlantic agenda of multicultural questions. Each is certainly very sensitive to the difficulties of establishing a comparative viewpoint that might bring together North American and European experiences. However, beyond this, they do all point to a rather different way in which we might learn from transatlantic comparisons.

It is this, developing some of the thoughts mentioned above, that I will concentrate on in my (admittedly) rather selective readings of the texts.

THREE VIEWS THROUGH THE LOOKING GLASS

The work of Nathan Glazer has, perhaps more than that of any other writer, helped establish the predominant terms and references of European scholars' understanding of US racial politics and ethnicity 'beyond the melting pot' (Glazer, 1970, 1976). In many other works, he has also sought to bring the American experience into comparative focus with European developments (Glazer, 1983, 1986). Here, however, he offers a series of valuable reminders of why many of the issues turning around multiculturalism and citizenship in the USA cannot be assimilated directly to European debates, as well as a broad overview of the current US scene.

Multiculturalism in the USA is for minorities; and minorities are distinguished primarily by having suffered past prejudice at the hands of the white majority. The question of multiculturalism in practice, therefore, is only incidentally related to immigration, which is the dominant source of multiculturalism in Europe: most recent and traditional immigrant groups in the USA fall outside of its scope. Among the recognized minorities, American Indians and African-Americans are 'native'; while Latinos have always had a close and special relationship to North America. Only Asian-Americans might be seen as a minority requiring multicultural protection of the kind sought for minorities in Europe; and with their startlingly successful assimilation in the USA, they are unlikely to remain a minority long. The question of citizenship in the USA, meanwhile, is not directly concerned with answering multicultural questions. Here the issue is the historical necessity of naturalization, and the conscious affirmation of loyalty and commitment to their new American identity, that is demanded of new immigrants. America is an immigration continent, and it is difficult to transpose the force of this ideology onto the European situation where immigration has not really been a central part of national identity building (with the arguable exception of France, if we are to believe recent French historians of immigration such as Noiriel (1988); Horowitz and Noiriel (1992)). Citizenship and immigration is big news in the USA because of recent cutting of social rights and benefits to resident aliens. Although there are comparisons to be drawn with Europe, there is good reason, argues Glazer, to regard much of what happens in the USA as underlining American exceptionalism.

Where the USA is clearly different, is where it encounters its biggest and most irresolvable 'ethnic dilemma': the place of black African-Americans, the classic 'American dilemma' (Myrdal, 1944). Again, this is not really a multicultural question; nor is it a question of citizenship. The historical segregation, disadvantage, and prejudice against blacks belies much of what multi-ethnic America has achieved elsewhere in the name of multicultural assimilation. Glazer argues that the racial question of black Americans has to be distinguished from the multicultural issues connected to other immigrant or minority groups. The 'rainbow coalition' is often a campus-based illusion, which works to the detriment of the specificity of African-American problems. While Glazer is undoutedly right about this, he perhaps does not go far enough in distinguishing the persisting causes of the black 'American dilemma'. Although racial in origin, it can be argued that the effect of racial disadvantage is declining; many middle-class African-Africans have succeeded as a result in changes in social attitudes after the 1960s civil rights movement, and often with the help of affirmative action. However, because of geographical and social class-based reasons, a portion of the black population remains enmired in an impossible, disadvantaged position to the rest of American society, which the state appears powerless to change (Wilson, 1987; Massey and Denton, 1993). Poverty which appears to be racially or culturally explicable may, more essentially, be structural and socio-economic in root. It is here that Europe might have something to learn. Look again at our 'ghettos'. Are these essentially caused by cultural or racial differences, or are they socio-economic in root? All the talk about multiculturalism, for and against, might actually be missing the point. Questions which should be framed in simple socio-economic terms, have been increasingly overlaid with all kinds of cultural and moral questions, related to the 'multicultural citizenship' optic. Indeed, the emphasis on raising such multicultural questions in political debates ('the problem of immigration for national identity', etc.), might actually be a diversionary tactic by representatives of the state: masking the fact that its interventory powers over social policy—as in the USA—are in decline. It is in this sense that the 'American dilemma' might in the coming years become the 'European dilemma' too.

Martin Schain's contribution attempts to see what can be learned from the comparison of the USA with one of the central European national cases: France. In a series of significant contributions to the field, Schain has developed a reading of social, racial, and multicultural politics and policy in France which offers an authoritative counterpoint to French scholars' self-understanding of the same questions (Schain, 1988, 1993, 1995). Here, he attacks what is perhaps the most sacred assumption by many French observers: that there is no multiculturalism in France. Many of the facts about social policy and associational politics which Schain relates to are well known by French scholars. However, the admission of multiculturalism in practice is still seen to be scandalous by many, an attack on the continued viability of the republican 'model' of *intégration* that in recent years has been reaffirmed by notable intellectuals and official government policy statements alike (see the polemics over the recent collection by Wieviorka, 1996).

Schain's central line is to consider the complex and shifting relation between the 'ideal' model and the evolving state practices for dealing with immigrant groups at the local level. He offers an important antidote to the excessive tendency in the first wave of comparative citizenship and immigration studies to compare European and North American cases on a typological national-model-based way (Brubaker, 1989; Cornelius *et al.*, 1994; Baldwin-Edwards and Schain, 1994). Schain goes beyond this by showing how the ideal model is, first and foremost, deceptive, and the source of a serious *décalage* between ideological theory and pragmatic, adaptive local state practice. Ever since the 1960s and 1970s—regardless of whether the right or left were in power—the French state, and its agencies, have sought to deal with the problem of immigration by seeking racially and culturally distinguished interlocuters at the local level to smooth the path towards social integration. 'Ethnic' immigrant organizations have been able to gain representation and funding through the opening up of associational laws: this is 'multiculturalism' by any other name, even if the theory of republican *intégration* does not call it so. Schain's argument might be taken to be in line with the typical view of American political economists studying French policy in another domain. While French politicians and economists proclaim French *résistance* to 'anglo-saxon' *libéralisme sauvage*, French business is busily being reorganized along decentralized, privatized lines. The distance between political rhetoric and economic reality, however, can be seen to have had seriously damaging effects on the French political and economic system (Schmidt, 1996). Schain, ultimately, appears to be arguing something else: that the rhetorical *décalage* is, in fact, perfectly functional and not in the end contradictory. The ideal model of the state, he argues, has subtly changed now to be able to say that cultural and racial differences are not incompatible with the republican ideal; and, as recent studies led by Michèle Tribalat and others underline, the French melting pot in fact appears to be working far better than anybody imagined (Tribalat, 1995).

Schain is clearly right to go behind the apparent contradictions in state rhetoric, and seek out the complex dynamics behind the development of actual state policy and practice. His no-nonsense, empiricist approach to comparative public policy underlines how distant much theoretical reflection on multicultural questions is to case-study-based findings. Moreover, the Anglo-American concreteness of his viewpoint ought to be required reading for French students still brought up on the ideological mystifications established by some of the major French commentators, such as Dominique Schnapper, Emmanuel Todd, or Pierre-André Taguieff (Schnapper, 1989; Todd, 1994; Taguieff, 1996). However, a public policy study such as this—which characteristically distinguishes between policy formulation, implementation, and adaptation, with the emphasis on the latter stages—does leave some questions unanswered. From a normative point of view, it is surely a problem for democracy in France that the dominant language and justification of public policy is so thoroughly disconnected from actual state practice. Schain raises the question of public consent towards the end of his piece. Clearly, however, on his account, the French democratic public voice would appear to play no part in the process of formulating or legitimating policy practices, since the language that is spoken in its name is said to be predominantly an ideological rhetoric. State actors would appear to be deliberately lying and manipulating the public by constantly invoking a public philosophy that they know is no longer representative of what the state does at the local level. It is hard to believe this is the case.

What Schain perhaps misrepresents in his distinctly Anglo-American point of view, is the degree to which French politics is inherently idealist in nature: in the philosophical sense of the word. When either Jacques Chirac or a left-wing ethnic leader invoke and contest the idea of *citoyenneté* or *intégration*, this language works as both a justification and a representation of French political reality as democratic will (the famous French *volonté générale*). The two levels cannot be seen as distinct and separate, without assuming—as French political discourse or policy formulation never does—that there is a social and political reality outside of the political language used to talk about it. This might sound like meaningless philosophical gibberish to observers brought up on Anglo-American materialism and empiricism. But can we seriously hope to understand the legacy of *la Révolution*, *la République*, or *L'État* in France—three forms of political idealism very much at stake in current French debates on citizenship—without understanding *les acquis* of a French philosophical tradition running back through Durkheim to Rousseau? Strange as this must sound to comparative political scientists, but Anglo-American political differences with France might actually be philosophical in nature (Favell, 1998*a*). When French state actors assert the reality of the republican model in France, it is democracy that is at stake in their representations being believed and consented to. From a French philosophical perspective, what is problematic with the currently dominant French self-representations is, therefore, not that they deliberately misrepresent empirical 'reality' as such. Rather it is that the 'reality' that they speak of is no longer something that can be seen as constructed exclusively by the democratic will of a coherent, self-sufficient philosophical and political collective: *la République*. Europeanization, regionalisation, and the decline of centralized state powers have all taken their toll. If democracy is identified with a president and government ruling in the name of the nation-state—as it typically is by the French—democracy is failing insofar as the nation-state no longer encompasses this political process.

Seen in these terms, the *décalage* identified by Martin Schain's central question—the gap between model and practice—is very far from being a functional thing that can be discounted in the name of Tribalat's overly optimistic picture of classic assimilatory business-as-usual. It is rather a huge problem of democracy; one of the essential roots of the deep malaise that has seen France wracked with political tension over immigration and integration questions for so long now. It has, for example, been the perfect fuel for Le Pen's *Front national* to challenge the Parisian elites and mainstream parties in the name of a French 'people' that he claims is no longer democratically represented at the centre. To really understand the malaise, we have to go back and ask how and why the French political elites in the 1980s reached out for the very philosophical neo-republican idiom, in order to justify and represent policies towards immigrants which had hitherto been defined in a different pragmatic language based on narrower socio-economic and welfare criteria.

It is here that Eric Fassin's contribution to this volume can help further our understanding of the French case, and the central place of North American references in French political discussions. Fassin, in his work, emphasizes that the debates and preoccupations of French intellectuals—like anywhere —take place at some remove, and with a certain degree of autonomy, from other political and social currents. As the work of Pierre Bourdieu underlines, the production of intellectuals depends for its authority and wider social power on its establishing of its own distinct form of symbolic capital in distinction to the public political sphere (see Bourdieu, 1979, 1984; Bourdieu and Wacquant, 1992). However, during the course of the 1980s, a new younger generation of social and political philosophers found they could short-circuit the academic hierarchy by taking their arguments over into the media and public political spheres. As their target, they took their 'anti-humanist' intellectual forefathers: the *soixante-huitard* post-structuralist thinkers, in particular Lévi-Strauss, and all those seen to still be working in a Marxist tradition. They declared 'the return of the subject': the renewal of a classic French political philosophy of republicanism; the rediscovery of individualism and human rights; and they criticized the 'barbarity' of ideas of '*différence*' and the 'nihilist' destruction of the universalist ideal at the heart of French civilization (Ferry and Renaut, 1985*a* 1985*b*; Finkielkraut, 1987; Debray, 1989; Furet *et al.*, 1989; Todorov, 1989; Taguieff, 1988; Schnapper, 1989, 1994). The rising saliance of the problem of immigration and integration, and a political scene increasingly dominated by concerns about racism and the rediscovery of Islam in France, provided the perfect 'applied' background for their arguments. The media feted them; the socialist administration rewarded them with prominent places on national political commissions and *conseils*; the *bicentenaire* crowned their achievement. By 1990, the new republicanism had become the unquestionable language of mainstream politics and policy-makers on all sides of the political spectrum seeking to justify and bolster the shaky French policies of immigration and integration.

Eric Fassin's account centres on the American reference in this new republican philosophical movement. For reasons mentioned at the outset, the

USA has always been a reference '*bonne à penser*' in French political discussions. The 'nightmare scenario' of US ethnic fragmentation, differentialism, and *communautarism* thus became the perfect counterpoint to the exceptional virtues of the universalist, individual rights-based French republican model, seen as the only salvation for a France being drowned by internationalism, Europeanization and Americanization; and a France in which the rhetoric of national identity had been so successfully seized by the cultural exclusionism and racist arguments of the extreme Right. Fassin's account thus helps explain why the new republican idiom is so strong in current French politics; and also why its persistence is having such negative effects on the inertia of French political thought about multiculturalism, for all the local adaptations and innovations identified by Schain. Again, borrowing from Bourdieu, the triumph of an academic language of 'political philosophy' that imposes its form of capital in the political sphere has to be read as a dubious and potentially negative thing (Bourdieu, 1994). This is because it is a form of 'heteronomous' intervention. Policy practices in spheres as distinct as social policy, law, or education would not ordinarily be conceived or described in such an artificial theoretical language: they are denatured by being framed in this way. However, as politicians have certainly found out, a high-flown 'philosophical' argument works very well as rhetoric, even if it contradicts the wisdom of practioners in different spheres of society. Again, the outcome is a situation where the democratic representation of practice and circumstance is distorted, and where the political stakes rising on the question of immigration, integration, and citizenship are inflated into impossibly high symbolic visions of French national integrity and destiny (Favell, 1998*a*).

CONCLUSION: WHAT CAN EUROPE LEARN?

Taken together, these three articles would certainly provide a basis for a thorough rereading of the French case; moreover, they provide more general indications of the kinds of issues that any comparison of multicultural questions in Europe and North America should consider. From Glazer, there is the emphasis on looking behind multiculturalism to more fundamental socio-economic divisions in society; from Schain, the need to look at the transformations of the state and state practices, their relation to ideological justification, and the problem of democracy this raises; from Fassin, a sense of how and when ideas and the language of intellectuals affect social and political spheres, and the consequences this may have. It would be possible to imagine similar studies of other European national cases in terms of a comparison with the USA, or of the role of the North American reference in political discussions.

However, what none of our authors asks is the question that ought to be uppermost in any current comparison of Europe with the USA. Our political context has changed, and we finally have—or seem to be getting—a political entity that can be viably compared with the USA, without the habitual ideological power distortions: the European Union. One of the unfortunate consequences of the multicultural citizenship agenda has been to limit our references to nominalist nation-by-nation studies. This is because the liberal-communitarian debate—when thought of as a problem of citizenship—is generally focused on reconciling distinct ethnic and cultural identities within the traditional liberal-democractic nation-state (see for example Kymlicka, 1995). Nobody, except the most hardened Eurosceptic, seriously believes the EU is going to become a unified state polity in this sense.

Multicultural questions in this context should be lifted to a political sphere beyond traditional citizenship and the nation-state (see Soysal, 1994): a Europe in which the various arms of the state have been disaggregated into distinct legal, bureaucratic, and legislative arenas and separated into various federal and regional levels. It is possible to think of a multicultural, multi-national Union, in which universal citizenship rights based on personhood are combined with a political system based on multilevelled governance and representation; and in which the problems of balancing socio-economic liberalism and technocracy with the decline of the welfare state and the 'rump' of particularist national and cultural ideas in the various states, would certainly be central (see Marks *et al.*, 1996). On all these questions, the constitutional, federal, and social politics of the USA in recent years provide much food for thought in the European case (see Majone, 1996; Bellamy, 1996). These are questions that deserve to be raised in empirical and normative studies alike. It is in this sense, then, that I suggest the question 'how can we be European?' can and should be asked.

REFERENCES

Baldwin-Edwards, Martin, and Schain, Martin (eds.) (1994), *The Politics of Immigration in Western Europe* (London: Sage).
Barber, Benjamin (1996), *Jihad versus McWorld* (New York: Ballantine Books).
Baudrillard, Jean (1986), *L'Amériqué* (Paris: Grasset).
Beiner, Ronald (ed.) (1995), *Theorizing Citizenship* (Albany: SUNY Press).
Bellamy, Richard (ed.) (1996), *Constitutionalism, Democracy and Sovereignty: American and European Perspectives* (Aldershot: Avebury).
Benhabib, Seyla (1992), *Situating the Self: Gender, Community and Postmodernism in Contemporary Ethics* (Cambridge: Polity).
Bourdieu, Pierre (1979), *La distinction* (Paris: Les éditions du minuit).
—— (1984), *Homo Academicus* (Paris: Les éditions du minuit).
—— (1994), *Raisons Pratiques* (Paris: Seuil).
—— and Wacquant, Loïc (1992), *An Invitation to Reflexive Sociology* (Cambridge: Polity).

Brubaker, Rogers (ed.) (1989), *Immigration and the Politics of Citizenship in Western Europe* (New York: University Press of America).

—— (1992), *Citizenship and Nationhood in France and Germany* (Cambridge, Mass.: Harvard University Press).

Calhoun, Craig (1996), *Critical Social Theory: Culture, History and the Challenge of Difference* (Oxford: Blackwell).

Cornelius, Wayne, Martin, Philip, and Hollifield, James (eds.) (1994), *Controlling Immigration* (Stanford: Stanford University Press).

Debray, Régis (1989), *Que vive la République* (Paris).

Fanon, Frantz (1961), *Les damnés de la terre* (Paris: Gallimard).

Fassin, Éric (1993*a*), 'Dans des genres différents: le feminisme au miroir trans-atlantique', *Esprit*, Nov.

—— (1993*b*), 'La chaire et le canon: les intellectuels, la polititique et l'université aux États-Unis', *Annales ESC*, 2 (Mar.–Apr.).

—— (1994), ' "Political correctness" en version originale et version française', *Vingtième Siecle*, 43 (July–Sept.).

—— (1996), 'Two cultures? French intellectuals and the politics of culture in the 1980s', *French Politics and Society*, 14/2.

Favell, Adrian (1997*a*), 'Citizenship and immigration: pathologies of a progressive philosophy', *New Community*, 23/2.

—— (1998*a*), *Philosophies of Integration: Immigration and the Idea of Citizenship in France and Britain* (London: Macmillan; New York: St Martin's Press).

—— (1998*b*), 'A politics that is shared, bounded and rooted? Rediscovering civic political culture in Western Europe', *Theory and Society*, 27: 209–36.

Ferry, Luc, and Renaut, Alain (1985), *Des droits de l'homme à l'idée républicaine* (Paris: Presses universitaires de France).

—— —— (1985), *La pensée 68: essai sur l'anti-humanisme contemporain* (Paris: Gallimard).

Finkielkraut, Alain (1987), *La défaite de la pensée* (Paris: Gallimard).

Furet, François, Juillard, Jacques, and Rosanvallon, Pierre (1989), *La République du centre* (Paris: Calmann-Lévy).

Gaspard, Françoise, and Khosrokhavar, Farhad (1995), *Le foulard et la République* (Paris: La Découverte).

Glazer, Nathan (ed.) (1976), *Ethnicity: Theory and Experience* (Cambridge, Mass.: Bellinger).

—— (1983), *Ethnic Dilemmas 1964–1982* (Cambridge, Mass.: Harvard University Press).

—— and Daniel Moynihan (1970), *Beyond the Melting Pot* (Cambridge, Mass.: MIT Press).

—— and Young, Ken (eds.) (1986), *Ethnic Pluralism and Public Policy: Achieving Equality in the US and Great Britain* (London: Gower).

Granjon, Marie-Christine (1994), 'Le regard en biais: attitudes françaises et multi-culturalisme américaine', *Vingtième Siecle*, 43 (July–Sept.).

Gutmann, Amy (1985), 'Communitarian critics of liberalism', *Philosophy and Public Affairs*, 14.

—— (1993), 'The challenge of multiculturalism in political ethics', *Philosophy and Public Affairs*, 22/3.

Habermas, Jürgen (1992), 'Citizenship and national identity: some reflections on the future of Europe', *Praxis International*, 12/1.

—— (1994), 'Struggles for recognition in the democratic constitutional state', in Amy Gutmann (ed.) *Examining the Politics of Recognition* (Princeton: Princeton University Press).

Hollifield, James (1994), 'Immigration and republicanism in France: The hidden consensus', in Cornelius *et al.* (1994).

Horowitz, Donald, and Noiriel, Gérard (eds.) (1992), *Immigrants in Two Democracies: French and American Experiences* (New York: New York University Press).

Joppke, Christian (1996), 'Multiculturalism and immigration: a comparison of the United States, Germany and Great Britain', *Theory and Society*, 24/4.

—— (ed.) (1998), *Challenge to the Nation-State: Immigration in Western Europe and the United States* (Oxford: Oxford University Press).

Kaplan, William (ed.) (1993), *Belonging: The Meaning and Future of Canadian Citizenship* (Montréal and Kingston: McGill-Queens University Press).

Kymlicka, Will. (1995), *Multicultural Citizenship* (Oxford: Oxford University Press).

—— and Norman, Wayne (1994), 'Return of the Citizen: A survey of recent work on citizenship theory', *Ethics*, 104 (Jan).

Lacorne, Denis (1997), *La crise de l'identité américaine: du melting pot au multiculturalisme* (Paris: Fayard).

Lévi-Strauss, Claude (1983), *Le regard éloigné* (Paris: Plon).

Majone, Giandomenico (1996), *Regulating Europe* (London: Routledge).

Marks, Gary, Scharpf, Fritz, Schmitter, Philippe, and Streeck, Wolfgang (eds.) (1996), *Governance in the European Union* (London: Sage).

Massey, Donald, and Denton, Nancy (1993), *American Apartheid: Segregation and the Making of the Underclass* (Cambridge, Mass.: Harvard University Press).

Mouffe, Chantal (ed.) (1992), *Dimensions of Radical Democracy: Pluralism, Citizenship, Community* (London: Verso).

Myrdal, Gunnar (1944), *An American Dilemma: The Negro Problem and Modern Democracy* (New York: Doubleday).

Noiriel, Gérard (1988), *Le creuset français: histoire de l'immigration XIXe–XXe siècle* (Paris: Seuil).

Putnam, Robert (1993), *Making Democracy Work: Civic Traditions in Modern Italy* (Princeton: Princeton University Press).

Rawls, John (1993), *Political Liberalism* (Princeton: Princeton University Press).

—— (1995), 'Reply to Habermas', *Journal of Philosophy*, 132.

Said, Edward (1978), *Orientalism* (London: Routledge).

Sandel, Michael (1995), *Democracy's Discontent: America in Search of a Public Philosophy* (Cambridge, Mass.: Harvard University Press).

Schain, Martin (1988), 'Immigration and changes in the French party system', *European Journal of Political Research*, 16.

—— (1993), 'Policy making and defining ethnic minorities: the case of immigration in France', *New Community*, 20/1.

Schain, Martin (1995), 'Policy and policy making in France and the US: Models of incorporation and the dynamics of change', *Modern and Contemporary France*, 3/4.

Schlesinger, Arthur D. (1992), *The Disuniting of America: Reflections on a Multicultural Society* (New York: Norton).

Schmidt, Vivien (1996), 'The decline of traditional state dirigisme in France: the transformation of political economic policies and policymaking processes', *Governance*, 9 (1996).

Schnapper, Dominique (1991), *La France de l'intégration* (Paris: Gallimard).

—— (1994), *La communauté des citoyens: sur l'idée moderne de nation* (Paris: Gallimard).

Soysal, Yasemin Nuhoglu (1994), *Limits of Citizenship. Migrants and Postnational Membership in Europe* (Chicago: University of Chicago Press).

Spinner, Jeff (1994), *The Boundaries of Citizenship: Race, Ethnicity and Culture in the Liberal State* (Baltimore: Johns Hopkins University Press).

Taguieff, Pierre-André (1988), *La force du préjugé: essai sur le racisme et ses doubles* (Paris: La Découverte).

—— (1996), *La République menacée* (Paris: Textuel).

Tarrow, Sidney (1996), 'Making social science work across space and time: a critical reflection on Robert Putnam's *Making Democracy Work*', *American Political Science Review*, 90/2.

Taylor, Charles, and Gutmann, Amy (ed.) (1992), *Multiculturalism and the 'Politics of Recognition'* (Princeton: University of Princeton Press).

Todd, Emmanuel (1994), *Le destin des immigrés: assimilation et ségrégation dans les démocraties occidentales* (Paris: Seuil).

Todorov, Tzvetan (1989), *Nous et les autres: la réflexion française sur la diversité humaine* (Paris: Seuil).

Tribalat, Michèle (1995), *Faire France: une enquête sur les immigrés et leurs enfants* (Paris: La découverte).

Wacquant, Loïc (1992), 'Banlieues françaises et ghetto noir américain: de l'amalgame à la comparaison', *French Politics and Society*, 10/4.

Wieviorka, Michel (ed.) (1996), *Une société fragmentée? le multi-culturalisme en débat* (Paris: La découverte).

Wilson, William Julius (1987), *The Truly Disadvantaged: The Inner City, the Underclass and Public Policy* (Chicago: University of Chicago Press).

Young, Iris Marion (1991), *Justice and the Politics of Difference* (Princeton: University of Princeton Press).

INDEX

DATE DUE

APR 0 1 2008		
FEB 2 0 2007		
MAR 1 2 2007		
		Printed in USA